THE TROUSER

D0406410

'[A] remarkably good-humoured book. [...] correspondent memoirs where you sus[...] done in the bar of some Intercontinental H[...] where you simply don't know who may come at you out of the shrubbery, how heavily armed he will be, how fearful of foreigners, and indeed how stoned on whatever local intoxicant is most plentiful.' *Sunday Telegraph*

'It is good to be able to pay Andrew Marshall's book a fulsome Burmese compliment – his writing is nicely rounded.' *The Times*

'A witty account of life in today's diverse and suppressed Burma. Casually weaving relevant political and cultural history into his wry note-taking on what he sees in this largely inaccessible country, Marshall gives us a rare glimpse into the jukes and jibes – both on the pitch and off – of Burma's mysterious balance of power.' *Time*

'An evocative travel book and an adventure story . . . Marshall is a gifted writer.' *New York Times*

'The Trouser People towers above all other contemporary books on Burma, whether they be travelogues, biographies, or scholarly texts trying to explain the complexities of the country's tangled politics. Marshall's book is personal without being egocentric, beautifully written, and tells us more about Burma's past and present troubles than most academic writings.' Bertil Lintner, author of *Burma in Revolt* and *Outrage*

'Marshall emerges from these pages as an extraordinarily intrepid traveller and trustworthy narrator whose account will make readers want to hop on the next plane to Rangoon to help overthrow the general's corrupt, narcodollar-fed regime. Excellent from first word to last.' *Kirkus Reviews*

'Outstanding . . . Marshall provides a vivid firsthand account of conditions in contemporary Burma. Pretending to be a tourist, he travelled throughout much of the country seeking to retrace the steps of the Victorian adventurer Sir George Scott. Marshall suggests that life today in Burma may be no better than it was 100 years ago.' *Foreign Affairs*

'Andrew Marshall's physical objective, in this lively book about Burma, is to reach a small lake in the jungle highlands of the Wa country; the lake is a magical one, the people of its shores were until recently headhunters, the garrison which patrols that mountainous border of Burma with China are involved in opium wars . . . Marshall describes the country vividly and succeeds in making his misty little lake sufficiently magical for the journey to have been worthwhile.' *Spectator*

'Hilarious. Few books I have read have contained so many fascinating stories.' *Asian Review of Books*

The Trouser People
Burma in the Shadows of the Empire

Andrew Marshall

RIVER

BOOKS

For my mother

Revised and updated edition published and
distributed in 2012 by River Books
396 Maharaj Road, Tatien, Bangkok 10200
Tel. 66 2 222-1290, 225-0139, 224-6686
Fax. 66 2 225-3861
E-mail: order@riverbooksbk.com
www.riverbooksbk.com

First published by Viking 2002
Published in Penguin Books 2003

Publisher: Narisa Chakrabongse
Editor: Stephen A. Murphy
Production supervision: Paisarn Piemmattawat
Design: Reutairat Nanta

ISBN 978 616 7339 18 4

Front cover: Mount Popa 1997 © Philip Blenkinsop.

Frontispiece: George Scott with fellow football players in Rangoon in 1879.
          Reproduced by permission of the Syndics of Cambridge
          University Library.

Cover design: Pascal Rüegg.

Printed and bound in Thailand
by Sirivatana Interprint Public Co., Ltd.

Contents

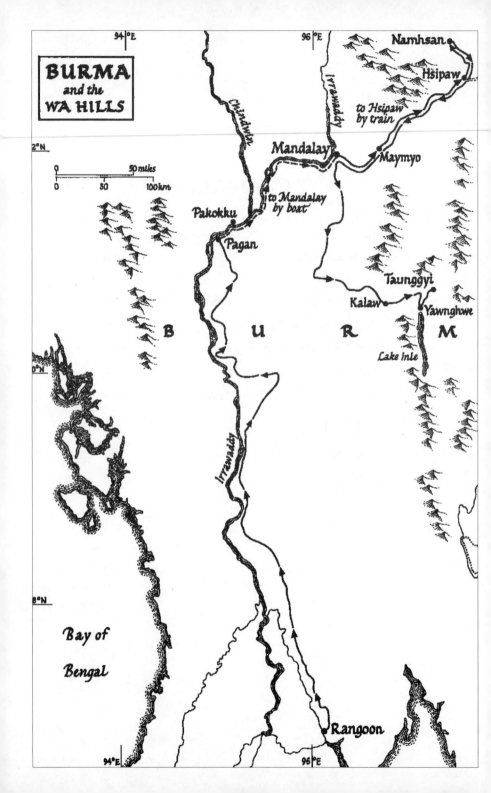

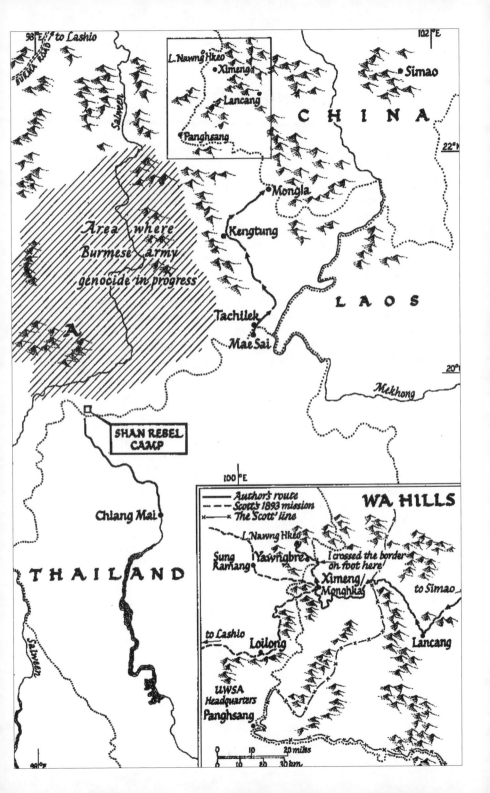

98° E   to Lashio
102° E

L. Nawng Hkeo
• Ximeng

Lancang

Panghsang

• Simao

C H I N A

22° N

Salween

BURMA ROAD

Area where
Burmese army
genocide in progress

• Mongla

• Kengtung

L A O S

A

Tachilek

Mae Sai

20°

Mekhong

SHAN REBEL
CAMP

100° E

——— Author's route
– – – Scott's 1893 mission
×—×—× The 'Scott' line

WA HILLS

Chiang Mai •

L. Nawng Hkeo

Sung
Ramang

Yawngbre

I crossed the border
on foot here!

Ximeng/
Monghlia

to Simao

THAILAND

to Lashio

Loilong

× ×

Lancang

Salween

UWSA
Headquarters

Panghsang

0   10   20 miles
0   10   20   30 km

Author's Note

Burma is changing. A rigged election in 2010 installed a nominally civilian government which, to everyone's surprise, launched a series of dramatic reforms. Aung San Suu Kyi and other political prisoners were freed, media controls relaxed and ceasefires struck with ethnic rebel groups. Western countries began lifting economic sanctions. For the first time in generations, many people in Burma had cause to hope.

This book is a journey through a darker but still very recent era in Burma's turbulent history. It is the result of perhaps a dozen trips to the country over as many years. It is a reminder of what Burma has endured during half a century of isolation and misrule, and of the challenges its people now face as they build their nation anew.

The identities of some people in this book have been changed to protect them.

Prologue

The Thai-Burma border

Philip the Miracle Monk rummaged at length in the mysterious folds of his orange robes and retrieved a trilling mobile phone.

'Excuse me for a second,' he apologised, but I was getting used to it. Philip's robes had been ringing all morning.

Hairless, podgy and swaddled in robes, Philip reminded me at times of a very large, very bright baby. I had met him in Chiang Mai, in northern Thailand, soon after dawn, and it was immediately obvious that he was a highly unusual monk. For a start, most monks were not fanatical fans of the heavy-metal group The Scorpions – at least not as far as I knew. Monks weren't usually called Philip either. His Buddhist holy name was as long as his arm, and was a bit of a mouthful for foreigners, so he had chosen an English name inspired by an electrical appliance. 'I liked the sound of it,' he told me. 'It sounded very *modern*.' Nor are monks supposed to know as much about troop movements as Philip seemed to: the Shan State Army, he whispered, had just dispatched 2,000 fighters to positions in north-east Burma. Not long ago, it was rumoured, Philip had returned from Thailand's frontier with Cambodia, where he had negotiated the release of a clandestine arms shipment from some overzealous border police. His heavenly powers of persuasion in such dealings had earned him the nickname 'Miracle Monk'. Sometimes he was also called the Combat Buddha. Later on, in the jungle, I spotted him sitting with sculpted calm, his robes wrapped tightly around him, reading *Guns & Ammo* magazine.

The miracle expected of Philip today was a relatively minor one. It was his task to spirit a small group of journalists and aid workers over the Thai border to the jungle stronghold of the Shan State Army, an insurgent group fighting against the Burmese military junta. We were going there to witness the celebrations for Shan New Year, and to meet the reclusive commander of the Shan rebels. The unfathomable depths of Philip's robes would prove invaluable for smuggling film past the Thai border guards, none of whom would dare frisk a monk – not even a highly unusual monk called Philip.

I left Chiang Mai in the back of a speeding Toyota pick-up truck crammed with sombre Shan men wearing military fatigues. A warm drizzle pelted my face. The road meandered through fields of dead paddy, then climbed in steep, switch-back curves beneath rain-drooped bamboo and watchful pines silhouetted by mist. We rose high enough to glimpse a long, deep valley boiling with clouds and, massed along the far horizon, the dark ramparts of the mountains bordering Burma's Shan State – our destination. Then the road cork-screwed down into the gloom again. A few hours later we hit a Thai military checkpoint, and it was time for Philip's miracle.

Soothingly, he told the Thai soldiers we were not journalists but 'friends of the Shan people' who had been invited to celebrate New Year with the rebels. The Thai soldiers decided to believe him. They confiscated the cameras we hadn't hidden, then took a group photo of us all for their intelligence files. For a moment the whole process took on the air of a jolly Sunday outing.

Beyond the checkpoint, our truck swept through another curtain of mist and emerged in a landscape of mythic beauty. The road was now a dusty red channel winding between immense towers of craggy limestone, part of an army of stacks that marched down the Thai-Burma border to the oblivious beach resorts of the far south. These stacks were in turn encircled and dwarfed by an arena of cloud-shrouded peaks of a deep, aching blue. We were now inside the fortress of mountains I had seen from afar. It felt like an undiscovered place. Thick mist crept through the rolling forest in hot pursuit and swallowed the road behind us.

'Yup,' drawled the Associated Press photographer, an American ex-military type with a talent for mood-wrecking one-liners, 'this is just about as far out into the boondocks as you can get.'

It got dark. The road shrank to little more than a mud-filled groove through thick jungle. The Toyota's engine screamed blue murder as it propelled the truck up improbably steep hills. We stopped to give a ride to two bleary Shan villagers, their breath reeking sweetly of rice wine. The road ended abruptly in a small hillside clearing. I jumped out, massaged my legs back to life, and by torchlight followed the others along a narrow path winding up into the jungle. More torches approached us, and there was the smell of cheroot smoke and the squawk of walkie-talkies. Unseen hands reached through the darkness and wordlessly relieved us of our bags. I trudged on, following the circle of my Maglite, and soon I heard the deep boom of a Shan long-drum carrying far through the damp night air, and saw through the trees a few smudges of light.

Philip's voice rang through the darkness. 'Welcome to Shan State, everyone,' he announced. 'No visa required.'

The rebel camp was scattered along a narrow, sloping ridge. At the top was a parade ground of packed mud dominated by an enormous flag featuring the crossed sword and rifle of the Shan State Army. At the lower end were rough bamboo stalls selling dry goods and illuminated by candles, or by lamps fashioned from dead beer cans. Wood smoke bathed the scene and turned torch beams into light-sabres. A small crowd of mostly women and children waited by a makeshift stage where giant moths battered themselves to death on the fluorescent strip lights.

Most SSA soldiers I saw were very young. They wore yellow neckerchiefs fastened with woggles, and carried Vietnam War-era M-16 assault rifles – weapons older than they were. They looked like heavily armed Boy Scouts. There were a few older soldiers, their dark skins etched still darker with magical Shan tattoos believed to deflect bullets and keep out the cold. The SSA had a few thousand troops. It was massively outnumbered by the 400,000-strong Burmese army, whose nearest camp was, unnervingly, only on the next hill-top. 'We flash our torches at them,' a rebel told me cheerfully, 'and they always flash back.'

The SSA men cleared a circle in the crowd for the musicians. I had arrived just in time to see the ka-toe, a traditional Shan dance featuring a pantomime long-horned deer, which shambled in after the musicians. Everything about this grossly elongated invention was ridiculous. The costume was made of green and red felt, and the yellow, papier-maché head was too small. Instead of hooves the deer had muddy jungle boots, which belonged to the two Shan soldiers inside. They were evidently making final adjustments, for just before the show began a disembodied arm extended comically from a hole beneath the deer's tail to pass a torch to a nearby soldier.

But then the music began, and it was as if a powerful electrical current now coursed beneath the skin. The deer leaped with astonishing speed around the circle, sending spectators scurrying backwards. It would suddenly freeze, then slowly rotate its head to scan the crowd, its mechanical ears twitching with irritation. Or it would crouch and shudder its spine as if preparing to pounce. This was no longer a bumbling pantomime animal, but a creature with all the menacing agility of a Chinese festival dragon. The boom of the long-drum, the drone of gongs, the dark, infinite jungle all around – the whole performance was mesmeric.

Just before midnight, the young SSA soldiers fell in before a bamboo flagpole. The camp's civilians formed ragged columns behind them. The SSA was one of the few rebel armies still fighting the Burmese junta; nearly every other ethnic insurgent group had signed ceasefire agreements with the generals. What I was seeing here were the last free Shan in Shan State. A few monks appeared, among them a grave-looking Philip. The Shan flag was raised and saluted, and the Shan national anthem was sung. Then Philip and the other monks chanted a blessing. It was a solemn occasion, a mourning rite for a people without a nation.

The celebrations started up again. The deer reappeared, wilder this time, twitching, pouncing, pestered into a whirling frenzy by boy soldiers. A monster cheroot was put in my mouth and lit, and in the fragrant burst of light-headedness that followed I found myself dancing around the deer too.

On the stage, a couple in Shan national dress began to dance, and the bamboo floor trampolined gently beneath them. They were accompanied by traditional Shan music, pre-recorded and played back through a scratchy sound system at a volume that made my internal organs vibrate. I was shown to a raised bamboo sleeping area reserved for honoured guests – right next to the loudspeakers. The Associated Press photographer lay beside me and groaned.

'It sounds like a poor defenceless animal being slammed over and over and over in a car door,' he said. Then he wrapped a blanket around his head and, to my great envy, fell fast asleep.

It was the diaries that had brought me here.

Only a few months before, but a world away, I had sat in the pin-drop silence of the British Library in London poring over a collection of nineteenth-century notebooks. Only a handful of determined scholars had ever dusted them off before me, and I could understand why. Blotched with jungle mould, and unimproved by later decades in a damp Sussex attic, the diaries were virtually illegible. But I read them with growing excitement.

They had belonged to Sir George Scott, an unsung Victorian adventurer, war correspondent, photographer and sportsman with a fondness for gargantuan pith helmets and a bluffness of expression that bordered on the Pythonesque. 'Stepped on something soft and wobbly,' he recorded in his diary one dark night. 'Struck a match, found it was a dead Chinaman'. Born in 1851, the year of the Great Exhibition, George Scott was a natural imperialist who was instrumental in imposing British colonial rule in Upper Burma. Armed with nothing more than the moral force of the Raj, this diminutive preacher's son from Fife hacked, bullied and charmed his way through the uncharted Burmese highlands. The diaries noted jungle firefights with angry natives, bullets flying everywhere, and as Scott strode unarmed into a hail of spears and buckshot there were manly exchanges like this:

'Have a revolver if you are going on,' called out the Colonel.

'Send me a box of matches, my pipe's out,' returned Scott.

Part of Scott's job was to map the lawless frontiers of this 'geographical nowhere' with China, and for years the Indian Empire's easternmost land border was marked by something called the 'Scott Line'. But he also widened the imperial goalposts in another way: he introduced football to Burma, where today it is the national sport. The boisterous Burmese loved the game, Scott noted, 'because it's just like fighting'.

Reading the diaries, I formed an impression of Scott as bluff, mouthy and artless – a kind of Victorian-era New Lad larging it through the imperial hinterlands. But that was only half the story. Scott was also a pioneering photographer, as well as a gifted and prolific writer. His masterpiece, *The Burman* (1882), still in print today, was an unrivalled authority on everything Burmese, from ear-boring and exorcism to monastery construction and the funeral requirements of sacred white elephants. Two genres he spectacularly failed to master were adventure yarns – he penned strikingly bad novels – and Foreign Office dispatches. 'Truly Indian in its prolixity,' remarked a shattered British official who read one of his epic reports.

Scott spent most of his working life in the mountains that now brooded massively in the darkness all around me. Ancient migration routes between India, China, Tibet and Assam had seeded this wilderness with a baffling array of ethnic groups, each evolving outlandish customs quite distinct from those of the majority Burman people who populated the lowlands. Some tribes ruled mountain fiefdoms half the size of England; others occupied a single, remote hilltop and spoke a language unintelligible to their neighbours in the valley below. Scott plunged into this great unknown to record tribal customs and photograph a way of life that had remained unchanged for centuries. One of these tribes was the ferocious Wild Wa – headhunters with betel-blackened teeth who lived in skull-ringed mud fortresses and, rather incongruously considering their savage reputation, claimed to be descended from tadpoles. Negotiating jungle paths strewn with decapitated corpses, Scott became the first European to study them in depth. Cunningly, he once disarmed a party of headhunters by telling a joke so funny that it survived being translated through four separate tribal languages before reaching the Wa tongue. Though unbelievably dirty and permanently drunk, the Wa made a favourable impression on Scott. 'They are an exceedingly well-behaved, industrious, and estimable race,' he concluded, 'were it not for the one foible of cutting strangers' heads off and neglecting ever to wash themselves.'

Fast-forward a hundred years. Burma was no longer a British colony, but a military dictatorship – one of the world's most brutal and enduring. Scott's tribal stamping grounds had been ravaged by the Burmese army, and the country whose borders he helped to map was now delineated by misery. Any memory of Scott himself was buried deep beneath the rubble of Burma's turbulent post-war history – its coups and massacres, its endless civil war.

After months spent deciphering Scott's diaries, I found myself embarking on an oddly obsessive quest to rescue this singular Scotsman from obscurity. How could someone who had once been a living legend in Burma be so little known today? The answer was obvious: Scott had been forgotten because Burma had been forgotten. Isolated and impoverished, Burma was trapped in a time warp. Few big countries were so little known.

Scott knew all too well that British rule was slowly eroding native traditions. The invasion of the 'Trouser People' – as white colonialists were known by the country's sarong-wearing civilians – wrought immense change, and doubled Scott's resolve to record Burma's dazzling ethnic diversity before it was lost forever. Now, as the Burmese military finished with chilling thoroughness what the British had begun, I wanted to discover whether the traditions that Scott had meticulously documented had survived. Did the witch doctors of the Pa-O still recommend tying a lock of your grandmother's hair around your neck as a cure for insanity? Were young girls of the Padaung tribe still wearing the brass neck rings that earned their mothers the nickname 'giraffe women'? Did Palaung women still don the complex tribal dress which commemorated their mythical descent from a lovesick she-dragon? I was also intrigued by romantic accounts of the saophas, or 'lords of the sky' – Shan princes who took countless wives, sent their children to English public schools, and ruled their mountain fiefdoms during Scott's time with an opulence which recalled the maharajas of India. What memories of them persisted?

The only way to find out, of course, was to go. As a journalist based in Thailand for four years, I had already made several trips to Burma, posing as a tourist. While certain areas were now open to foreign visitors, war, drug lords, government restrictions and bad roads meant that much of Burma remained as remote and dangerous as it had been a century before.

I began to plan a series of journeys, starting in the Burman-dominated plains and travelling up into the troubled heartland of tribal Burma, into the wilderness where Scott had his greatest adventures and closest shaves. One of those journeys would be a clandestine cross-border foray over the 'Scott Line' and into the opium-rich badlands of the Wa. The Wa were no longer headhunters, or so they claimed. Nowadays they were heavily armed drug traffickers, and responsible for much of the heroin sold on the global market. But in some ways it sounded as if nothing had changed. 'It's like the Stone Age there,' an American missionary told me, 'except they all carry AK-47s.'

Along the way I would realise that my obsession with a long-dead Victorian explorer had a curious modern resonance. Scott was a child of the Empire, and embodied many of its ambiguities; I could imagine him agreeing with Charles Napier, the conqueror of Sindh and a fellow Scot, who defined empire building as 'a good thrashing first and great kindness afterwards'. I knew Burmese people who looked back on British rule with nostalgia – a nostalgia they might not have felt had their present government treated them better. As for the Burmese government, it despised all things British. The 1962 military coup had ushered in a rabidly xenophobic regime bent on eradicating all Western cultural influences in the country. Foreign books were censored into extinction, Christian missionaries expelled, beauty contests outlawed; one female singer was even banned for five years for performing in hot pants. To neutralise any colonial associations in the word 'Burma', the country was renamed 'Myanmar'.

Burma had won its independence in 1948 – that is, over fifty years ago – but its generals behaved as if the Brits had left only last Tuesday. The military's disastrous rule had led a prosperous, fledgling democracy into misery and ruin. Yet, according to their bilious propaganda, all the nation's modern woes – poverty, Aids, the booming narcotics trade – were 'pernicious legacies' of the Empire that Scott had helped to build. Aung San Suu Kyi, the courageous leader of Burma's embattled democracy movement, was branded 'a satan of destruction sent by the Western colonialists'. Similarly, spurious conspiracies involving shadowy foreign agents were invented, all for the same purpose: to legitimise the junta's tyrannies against its own people and justify Burma's crippling isolation from the rest of the world.

There was a bitter irony in all this. While the regime's propaganda machine railed against Western imperialists, its soldiers subdued the population with much the same terror tactics used by the British a century before: arbitrary arrests, village burning, summary executions, exemplary beheadings. Burma's generals were the new colonialists – the new Trouser People. It was no coincidence that Aung San Suu Kyi had described the democracy movement as 'the second struggle for independence'.

This struggle had many front lines – military, political, cultural, personal – and I was sleeping on one of them. Or trying to. The celebrations at the rebel camp went on all night. At around three a.m. a Shan maiden took to the bamboo stage and sang a lament urging all young men to fight for the cause. It was very loud. My only solace, as I lay there listening to her keening voice, was knowing that the Burmese soldiers on the next hill could hear her too.

In the morning we hung about, waiting to meet the Colonel. The camp was a desolate place by daylight. Refuse clung to the parade ground and cascaded down both sides of the ridge. Beyond the trees the land was cancelled out by clouds, which cocooned the camp and lent it an entirely false sense of security. Hard-bitten peasant women with groggy-looking children shivered over the embers of last night's fires; their menfolk squatted nearby and spat between their sandals. These people were not just Shan, but Lahu, Akha and Muso hill tribes with strong, dark, secret faces raked by the elements. All were products of a ferocious counter-insurgency campaign by the Burmese army in Shan State. Thousands of refugees had spilled into northern Thailand to work for low pay at lychee farms or construction sites until the Thai police or army, in the latest caprice that passed for policy, herded them up and dumped them back on the border again. Hundreds more scratched out a semi-nomadic existence in the Burmese jungle, or arrived in silent, exhausted groups at Shan rebel camps like this one, hoping for food and protection.

With Philip's help, I asked some refugees to tell me their stories. For a while nobody said anything. Then a young mother stepped forward, carrying a toddler in a faded Disneyland baseball cap. Her name was Nang Seng Tong.

'They gave us one day,' she said flatly. 'They came in the morning and said that anyone who was still there in the evening would be shot.' Burmese soldiers had heard gunfire in Nang Seng Tong's settlement, part of a vast shanty town of internal refugees who had been relocated by the military; they assumed that the community was harbouring Shan rebels. At dusk the soldiers returned, and the shooting began. Nine people were killed. 'The old people and the children moved too slowly, and some were burned to death in their houses,' said Nang Seng Tong. Her sickly grandfather died in a bonfire of his meagre possessions. Her uncle was shot dead.

The others fled with what they could carry. Burmese soldiers butchered the livestock, and shot any villagers who crept back to salvage crops or possessions. Nang Seng Tong and her daughter trekked through the jungle for the Thai border. She now lived in a hut nearby, and moved on whenever there was fighting. 'I do not feel safe here,' she said quietly. Why would she? She lived in a war zone. The day before I arrived a ten-year-old Shan boy had had his foot blown off by a Burmese landmine at a nearby spring.

A little girl wearing only one wellington boot was pushed forward. She had also been trapped in the fire at Nang Seng Tong's settlement. The girl sat down in front of me and tugged off her wellington. Her leg ended in a stump. At first I thought that she had also stepped on a mine, but in fact her foot had been crushed and bent forward, and the fire had fused it to her shin. The girl put both arms round the wellington boot and hugged it.

A posse of Shan rebels arrived to take us to the Colonel. The ruler of this bleak, apocalyptic place was not, as I had idly imagined, an unhinged recluse who stroked his bald head and growled, 'The horror, the horror . . .' Colonel Yawd Serk was a plain, businesslike man in pressed khakis, with a farmer's haircut and spectacles the size of Game Boy screens. The meeting took place on a nearby hilltop beneath a thatched canopy. The journalists and aid workers sat on benches of twine-lashed bamboo. Small men with big guns crouched in the bushes all around.

We asked about troop strengths and rebel strategy and dry-season offensives. The Colonel answered methodically in Shan, and someone translated. He talked to us as he might to his soldiers; his quiet resolve and optimism were meant to inspire us. But this was the Burmese border, a region of the world where politics was so muddied by decades of ethnic war, and people so compromised by the lucrative trade in narcotics, that it was hard to tell who the good guys were any more. Nobody in our party seemed ready to trust him.

But I had a sneaking admiration for the man. There was a kind of formulaic outrage in writing about Burma that turned its people into little more than featureless victims. The Colonel's rebel army was tiny; his war against the Burmese military juggernaut was unwinnable. But he was not a victim. He continued to insist that the destiny of his people would not be decided by the generals in Rangoon. In Burma – a country once described as a prison with 50 million inmates – I would meet many more like him. For, despite the best efforts of the military dictatorship, the peoples of Burma were cultured, deeply eccentric and justly proud of their vibrant traditions. It was this courage and individualism that I hoped to seek out and celebrate as I set out in Sir George Scott's footsteps.

The Colonel spoke earnestly and at some length, mostly about the future. As he spoke, I watched a leech wriggle slowly across the table in front of him, climb on to a tape recorder lying there, and arch itself into a dot-less question mark.

PART ONE
INTO THE HILLS

1

In the dead hours of a tropical night, a television set in a Rangoon electrical shop switched itself on and began showing a football match live from the World Cup finals in France – the USA-Iran game, by my calculation. It was the summer of 1998, a Sunday. Ten minutes later the television exploded. Blood gushed from its shattered screen. There were screams, and cups and glasses spinning through the air, and light bulbs popping like Chinese firecrackers. Afterwards, when everything was a bit calmer, sobbing could be heard in the darkness.

Or so went the electric rumours that crackled across the city's synapses at daybreak. Were they true? It didn't really matter. By mid-morning a crowd was gathering outside the shop, which was called Golden Land. One man, who was almost certainly from Military Intelligence, tried to photograph the shop front, but an unseen force wrenched the camera from his hands and smashed it on the ground. The same force knocked off a policeman's hat, much to the delight of the onlookers.

The monks were summoned. They said mantras and sprinkled holy water on the televisions, but the water sprang back in their faces. They dabbed their chins with a dry corner of their robes and declared that the spirits were not Buddhist, they were Muslim. But an imam's prayers had no effect either. That night, strange markings appeared on the walls of a nearby tea shop, and some people said they heard the unmistakable noise of thousands of marching feet.

These spirits would not easily be appeased. They were unimpressed by the usual rituals. Everyone in the swelling crowd knew why.

Ten years before, to the very day, thousands of students had been marching into downtown Rangoon to join a pro-democracy demonstration. They had got as far as Myenigone market, just opposite the Golden Land shop, when armed police and military units attacked. An army truck pulled up, crushing two schoolchildren beneath its wheels, and soldiers opened fire. Students scattered into the alleys around the market. A pitched battle began. The soldiers fought with Bren guns and assault rifles, the students with bricks and stones, or with sharpened bicycle spokes flighted with chicken feathers and fired from home-made catapults. Over eighty protesters died in Rangoon that day, the bloody culmination of a week of angry demonstrations against military rule. No last rites were held for the dead. The bodies were loaded on to army trucks, the weight of the dead finishing off the still living, and driven off to be burnt like old rubbish.

That was ten years ago. As every Burmese who recalled the massacre understood, the restless spirits of 1988 had returned.

The haunting was never mentioned in the state-run media, but the news spread anyway. It was whispered in the mouldering teak mansions of Golden Valley, and in the candlelit shacks along Pazundaung Creek. By now over a thousand people had assembled outside the Golden Land shop. The road was blocked with cars as motorists slowed down to stare. Such a crowd was a rare sight in Burma: street gatherings of even a handful of people were illegal. It was curiosity that had drawn many onlookers to Golden Land. But now the crowd was something else. It had become a demonstration by default, a defiant act of remembrance for the thousands who had perished in the summer of 1988.

The soldiers came a few days later, with assault rifles and water cannon. They meant business. The great crowd quickly evaporated in the gathering heat. The people who refused to move – many were relatives of the dead students – were arrested. So was the unfortunate owner of Golden Land. Then, as with the students' corpses, except with more care, the soldiers loaded the unbroken televisions on to their trucks and drove them away, and that was that.

Soon a rumour began circulating that the military was 'testing' them at an army laboratory. But everyone knew that a few colonels would now be watching the World Cup on a new television.

While all this was going on I was two miles across town, perched on my friend the diplomat's antique sofa, watching beads of sweat drip from my forehead on to his finely polished parquet floor. It was dusk, and the power was down – again.

The diplomat's bungalow – I was staying there while he was on leave – was dim and stifling. The electric ceiling fan had spun to a standstill, and mosquitoes were nibbling experimentally at my ankles. The dead air was thick with jasmine and frangipani. It was too dark to read; soon it would be too hot to think. I was about to make what would feel at the time like an important decision: I would drink all the beer in the fridge before it got warm.

I had been in Rangoon for a week already, but had yet to hear an adequate explanation for the nation's catastrophic power shortages. Different reasons were given depending on who was speaking to whom. The generals lied to the diplomats that energy was being diverted to drive Burma's spectacular industrial progress. The bureaucrats assured the businessmen that the cause was only a temporary lack of spare parts for the British-built hydroelectric dams. Everyone else in Rangoon told each other various things while believing none of them. A drought had brought the dams to a standstill. (Drought? It was the monsoon season, and immense curtains of rain swept operatically across the city every afternoon.) Or else ethnic insurgents had felled the electricity pylons with high explosives. Or whatever.

The government didn't acknowledge the national energy crisis, so officially there wasn't one. Burmese who could afford it bought Japanese-made generators. The rest of us simply noted when the lights usually went out each day, tried our best to deduce a pattern (in Rangoon, about eight hours of electricity every day; in Mandalay, about eight hours every three days), and rearranged our lives and businesses accordingly. It was like some massive, nationwide initiative test.

I cracked open a beer, feeling as if I'd passed.

On the George Scott front, however, I was having less success. I had come to Rangoon to see if I could find out anything about his early days in the city. This was proving harder than I'd thought. I wandered the hot, claustrophobic streets of old Rangoon, where only the faintest breeze from the river penetrated the lofty colonial tenements, hoping to find some physical trace of his life here – a forgotten back alley once named in his honour, or a dead-eyed bust in a grimy niche of a public building. I consulted two distinguished Burmese historians, who smiled blankly when I mentioned Scott's name and referred me to a distinguished librarian, who referred me to books I had already read in London or Bangkok.

It was (I was slow to realise) a bad time for a single white European to be wandering around Rangoon asking questions – any questions, even harmless ones about dead Scotsmen. The tenth anniversary of the great pro-democracy uprising of 1988 was approaching. Burmese exiles and foreign activists had been predicting that people would again take to the streets, and the atmosphere in Rangoon was tense. Tanks had been spotted entering the city by night. The intersections were clogged with teenage soldiers cradling assault rifles with fixed bayonets; whenever I caught their eye they would grip their weapons a little tighter and stare back with blank hostility. Students had briefly clashed with police outside Aung San Suu Kyi's house, while her supporters were being swept into unmarked vans in pre-dawn raids and jailed until they recanted their allegiance. Rumours sprouted in the darkness and ran rampant in the tropical heat. Superstition was rife. When an earthquake occurred on the Thai-Burma border, some people said it was a portent of the regime's imminent collapse. (Tellingly, the state-run media did not report it.) It was as if the country was slipping into a darker age, an impression the power blackouts only reinforced.

A rumour spread that Ne Win was on his deathbed. General Ne Win, the grisly old tyrant himself, the architect of the 1962 military coup – dying at long last! This kind of rumour needed no encouragement; the whole of Burma wanted to believe it.

Ne Win was a man so superstitious, so addicted to power, that he once married a woman called Daw Kyar San – meaning 'The One Who Would Stay in Power Longer'. Recently, it was said, he had summoned nine monks to his heavily guarded lakeside compound to pray for his health; nine was his lucky number. BBC radio reported the rumour as fact, and, if the BBC said Ne Win was dying, then nothing could persuade the Burmese people otherwise – not even the truth, which was that he was tucked up in bed with a cup of cocoa and the latest copy of *Octogenarian Despot Monthly*.

By day, Rangoon did a good impression of normality. It was my second time here, and I had spent a leisurely few days getting to know the place again. The downtown area was the same mixture of bustle and sloth. The young men idled at street-corner tea shops, smoking, blethering and nibbling greasy samosas. Shrugging off Indian money-changers, who cruised the streets with bricks of Burmese currency tucked beneath their armpits, I negotiated crumbling pavements crowded with stalls. Many sold only a single product: toothpicks, perhaps, or posters of Leonardo Di Caprio, or an ingenious new method for choosing a more propitious name. On Mahabandoola Street I would sit in a tea house and watch the traffic cops wheedling bribes from blameless motorists, admiring the way they palmed the notes as adroitly as tableside magicians. As dusk approached I left the frenetic city centre and strolled home through the old colonial quarters, where dark, dilapidated mansions with baroque spires hibernated amid rioting tropical vegetation, and where fresh flowers on a spirit shrine outside were the only indication of life within. Near the diplomat's house I stopped to say good evening to an elderly Burmese man walking his pet goat on a leash.

I had spent most of my twenties in Asia, first as an editor in Tokyo, then as a feature writer roving the Far East, but Burma had always fascinated me. One reason was purely professional. Very few journalists went there, and when they did they rarely left Rangoon. Once their articles had been published they were blacklisted by the

Burmese government and refused re-entry; their first story about Burma was usually their last. I had long been eager to explore the country in more depth. I was also fascinated by the Burmese Conundrum – the contradiction between the 'land of fear' I had read about in press reports and the surface normality of places like Rangoon. To the thousands of tourists who visited Rangoon every year, I reflected, the city must seem like simply a nice place with lots of soldiers. Its colonial architecture wept with neglect, but there were no slums. Its leafy university campuses were oases of tranquility. The traffic on its roads was blessedly light compared to that of Bangkok or Jakarta, and a disproportionate number of cars were Mercedes. Not many capitals in Southeast Asia (or in Europe, for that matter) could boast the same.

But, you know, it's an odd thing. Mature totalitarianism is invisible to outsiders; only its absences betray it. Rangoon had no slum-dwellers because they had been moved at gunpoint to a swamp across the river. The universities were tranquil because most had been closed since 1988 to prevent further protests erupting on campus. The comparative lack of traffic indicated how far Burma's isolated economy had stagnated while the rest of Southeast Asia had boomed. And the Mercedes – well, they all belonged to the generals.

Frustrated by my lack of progress on Scott, I went to see the Doctor. A medical man by training, now retired, the Doctor was an amateur historian, a passionate Burmese democrat and, as I'd found after meeting him through a mutual friend on my previous trip, an ornate but reliable barometer of the political atmosphere. He lived in a wooden house which, like the good doctor himself, was in an advanced state of dishevelment.

'Lies,' growled the Doctor. 'Lies, lies, lies.'

We were sitting in his study, with the comforting smell of mouldering literature emanating from a large, murky store-room nearby, which was liberally sprinkled with mouse droppings. I had just asked him about a recent government pledge to reopen the universities. 'Lies!' he exclaimed, his unshaven jaw rigid with indignation. 'The government is determined to keep all the students off the campus. They want to keep the people ignorant, you see? It suits their purposes.'

My conversations with the Doctor were always a bit disjointed. As we talked, he would be reminded of some book or document and dart into the storeroom to rummage for it. Whatever he emerged with ten minutes later usually bore no relation to our topic of conversation. I suspected the Doctor didn't know much about Scott either, but he was an expert at fudging things he didn't know much about – a talent which, as a journalist, I could only respect.

'That book of Scott's, *The Burman*, it has many mistakes in it, you know,' he said. Mistakes? 'Oh yes. Particularly the chapter about sacred white elephants.' Then he plunged once more into his back room, crashed around for a while, and emerged five minutes later with a painting of a rare medicinal flower.

The Doctor clearly had other things on his mind. He expected violent demonstrations during the anniversary period, and was secretly stockpiling medicines to treat injured protesters. There was trouble ahead, he believed, and the death of Ne Win would be the catalyst.

'But is the old man really dying?'

'Oh yes!' cried the Doctor. 'I can even tell you when.' A solar eclipse was due to occur the following month, he had calculated, and, when the shadow passed over the sun and the birds fell strangely silent, Ne Win would clutch at his heart and fall strangely silent too, because in Burmese *ne win* means 'brilliant like the sun' – a dictator eclipsed.

'What a coincidence,' I marvelled.

The Doctor narrowed his eyes and said, 'There are many such coincidences in Burma' – meaning, of course, that there were none at all.

Rangoon had always been a city bubbling with events and portents. When Scott arrived here in the 1870s it was on its way to becoming the busiest rice port in the world. The harbour was packed with country boats ferrying the paddy downriver to be processed at smoke-belching mills and loaded on to European steamships or 'ditchers', named after their homeward route through the Suez Canal. On the bustling wharf, past the timber yards where elephants dragged immense logs of valuable teak, a row of monumental colonial buildings rose above the treeline. Beyond them, hovering ethereally in the heat haze, was the magnificent gold *chedi* of the Shwedagon Pagoda, the most venerated Buddhist temple in all Burma. 'It is a revelation,' observed Scott over the well-oiled tips of his magnificent moustache. 'Majestic, impregnated with the worship of countless centuries, the great golden stupa rises high into the serene and thrilling blue with an infinite grandeur impossible to put into words.'

Scott was a handsome man, a bit on the short side (he was not much more than five feet tall), but with a street fighter's build and brown, borehole eyes – a small but perfectly formed Victorian. 'He was always in good condition, for he was sparing in what he ate, and continually exercising,' wrote his third wife and hagiographer, Geraldine Mitton. 'He could ride, wrestle, shoot, play football and cricket, row and swim. His bright brown eyes went questing everywhere. Never was a man more alive. No department of human life but was interesting to him. His broad nostrils, firm chin and high forehead showed his quality both in intellect and pugnacity. He was ever a fighter.'

Scott would have been well aware that Rangoon was still trying to shake off an unwholesome reputation. For, while its commercial significance was growing fast, as a place to live the city stank, and not just because the task of refuse collection fell largely to an imported army of highly temperamental Madrasi street sweepers. Rangoon was a notorious sinkhole for criminals from other parts of the Empire, yet had only 300 miserably paid policemen for a population of over 100,000. There were lugubrious opium dens and rowdy bars, and a burgeoning community of Eurasian children to testify to the popularity of the brothels. Built on a swamp, the town was hot and humid the year round, and visited by all the nastier tropical diseases. Cholera epidemics were annual events: Scott would describe how the Burmese would shout and beat their roofs with sticks to frighten away the malignant demon that caused them. 'The Government officials are helpless against the superstition,' he noted, 'and English police-inspectors have simply to stand by foolishly with their hands to their ears till the clatter and clamour dies down.' Rabid dogs with a taste for English ankles patrolled the streets ('all eastern dogs have a maniacal hatred of white men'), and in the dry season whole neighbourhoods were devoured by fires, one of them caused by an amateur alchemist spilling mercury in his crucible. 'For greater secrecy, and because his horoscope said it was a favourable time, he was working at three in the morning,' recalled Scott. 'When day dawned the whole of Edward Street – one of the wealthiest inhabited by Burmans – was a heap of smouldering ashes.'

Arriving at Rangoon harbour, Scott might have reflected on an already peripatetic life that had begun at another port over a decade before. At the age of thirteen he stood on a wind-swept pier in Fife with his elder brother, Forsyth, waiting to board a steamer for the Continent. Scott had grown up in the small weaving community of Dairsie in Fife, where his father was the Presbyterian minister. The Revd Scott died when George was nine, and his mother decided that her boys would be educated in Stuttgart, for reasons that would always mystify them. ('I don't know where my mother heard of the place,' wrote Scott.) They were schooled in German, and by the time war between Austria and Prussia forced the Scott clan back to England, in 1866, George spoke the language fluently – one of seventeen foreign languages he would master.

Mrs Scott's German gamble paid off. Forsyth was accepted at Cambridge (he would become the university's vice-chancellor), while George won a place at Oxford. But then, disastrously – fatefully – Mrs Scott went broke. A close relative squandered the family's moderate wealth on a mining scheme in Scotland, an ill-conceived venture that Scott would sum up with the dry observation 'Uncle Robert had great ideas of coal-getting' And so – Bob's your uncle – George was forced to abandon his studies to find work to support his mother and brother. He would characterise this setback as an early example of the 'cursed bad luck' which he was convinced dogged his entire life – an odd obsession for a man rescued from certain death in the Burmese jungle on more than one occasion by sheer good fortune. And perhaps it was no setback at all. For this was the high noon of the British Empire, when no adventurous young man was wholly without prospects, particularly one born in the year of the Great Exhibition. And by this time, we learn, George Scott had heard 'the call of the East'.

Scott's first taste of Asia came as a war correspondent for the London *Standard*. In 1875 he joined a British punitive expedition to the Malay state of Perak, where the resident had been slaughtered by the sultan's henchmen. It was 'a most desperately jungly country, full of cane-brake and wait-a-bit thorns and creepers', wrote Scott. 'Everything, too, seemed festooned with leeches suffering from abnormal thirst, and with the expanding capacity of a toy balloon.' The young Scotsman's buccaneering disregard for personal danger made him popular among the troops. But theirs was an inglorious campaign – a 'butcher and bolt', in British army parlance – with the soldiers shooting wildly into the jungle. Nobody knew how many of the sultan's rebels had been hit, if any. Nevertheless, the expedition commander 'gave a most flamboyant account of the affair', wrote Scott, 'and explained all the operations so admirably that none of the force recognised [it]'. Scott's similarly flamboyant account for the *Standard* launched his journalistic career.

When Scott arrived in Rangoon he took a job as a teacher at a missionary school, St John's College, to supplement his journalistic income. He immersed himself in Burmese culture. A natural linguist, he soon spoke Burmese fluently. Unlike less adventurous colonials, he ate the oily and pungent local food with his hands, just as the natives did, and often wore a Burmese longyi or sarong. His early years in the city were eventful. One day Scott felt the streets shudder with a powerful earthquake; on another occasion a disoriented tiger swam the Rangoon River and briefly terrorised the population until a police chief shot him. There was even a famous haunting. Hundreds of people flocked to a house on 21st Street, supposedly built on a pagoda destroyed by the British, where poltergeists were throwing stones, setting clothes on fire, and pinching onlookers so hard that many fled with ripening bruises on their arms.

As colonial postings went, however, Rangoon had few social diversions. There was the stifling decorum of the Gymkhana Club, a laughably ill-stocked museum that nobody visited, and, if you were lucky, a military band in Fytche Square on a Sunday. The only other option was to go stark raving mad – and, judging by the number of colonial records marked 'Lunacy' which I later unearthed, many people took it. A gregarious man and an all-round athlete, Scott set about organising more vigorous outdoor entertainments. Boat races had been banned for encouraging gambling until Scott organised, and rowed in, a regatta on Rangoon's Royal Lakes in 1881. Over 10,000 people came – possibly the biggest gathering since the 'Rangoon Pet' had wrestled the 'Moulmein Slasher' in a bout at the Shwedagon Pagoda five years before. Scott also attended Rangoon's biannual horse races, which attracted champion jockeys from Bengal, fleet-footed ponies from the Shan states, and every high-rolling gambler for 100 miles or more.

But it was a sport still not widely played among even his own compatriots which Scott would introduce to Burma with the most astonishing success. Even before the Football Association was established in England in 1863, wherever the Brits went in the world the beautiful game went with them. British railway engineers took the sport to Argentina; Scottish textile workers taught the Swedes; the Russians learned it from English cotton-mill managers. And one day in 1878 George Scott strode on to the bumpy games field next to St John's College with his curious students, punted a football through a blue afternoon sky, and the Burmese game was born.

The first organised football match ever played in Burma took place at St John's College around 1879. Scott captained the St John's team, whose opponents were a scratch eleven from the southern port town of Moulmein. The game began inauspiciously, reported the *Singapore Free Press*:

In the punt-about just before the match the ball collapsed, and Scott and the present writer got into a gharry and tore all about the town to raise a bladder, even should it extend to the purchase and immediate slaughter of an animal. How Scott did bang the back of that gharry-wallah with that bust football to urge him to greater speed...A bladder was got from some fisherman or other at last, and the historical game played.

Matches were soon drawing large crowds, not only in Rangoon but across British-occupied Lower Burma. There was some concern at the passion the game aroused among the natives, but also relief that Association rules had been adopted.

'To think of hot-headed Burmans engaged in the rough-and-tumble of Rugby excites lurid imaginings,' shuddered one colonial official. For the British, football was a way of communicating ideas of fair play and respect for authority. For the Burmese it was something else: a rare opportunity to thrash their colonial masters at their own game.

The Burmese were no slouches with their feet. They had grown up with *chinlon*, a kind of volleyball played only with the feet and head, and using a rock-hard rattan ball which could split a man's eyebrow clean open if headed wrongly.

Hard-fought contests between British and Burmese footballers became regular affairs during the cool season. The Burmese team was called The Putsoes, a *putso* being a longyi that has been tucked neatly up around the thighs like a large, decorative nappy. The British team was called The Trousers. Scott recalled a memorable three-match tournament played between the two teams. 'In the first, the Burmans got well drubbed,' he reported, although the second match ended in disaster for the British. Jerry Morrison, considered the finest goalkeeper in British Burma, was (rather suspiciously) felled by food poisoning before the match. His replacement was a bit hazy about Association rules. The Burmese had scored twice before the British discovered that their goalkeeper attempted to save only shots which were heading *over* the crossbar, and ignored everything that went under it. At the other end of the pitch the agile Burman keeper, Harry Hpo Min, saved all but one European shot at goal. The final score: Putsoes 2, Trousers 1.

'The result produced a scene of the wildest excitement,' reported Scott. 'The Europeans took care to arrange for the third match when Jerry hadn't a tummy-ache, and they won by two goals to nil.'

*

I knew St John's College was still standing. One afternoon, in an airless hiatus between monsoon showers, I set off to investigate. As my taxi sped past the south gate of the Shwedagon Pagoda, I caught a glimpse of worshippers removing their shoes in the shadow of giant, snarling leogryphs. Above them the pagoda's great golden belly glowed magically against the rain-blackened sky.

At a nearby roundabout a group of soldiers were standing around a huge fibreglass statue of a traditional Burmese doll. This was the official mascot of Burma's tourist campaign. Identical statues bestrode intersections and other strategic locations around town. Plump and evil-looking, the mascot bore an unfortunate likeness to Chucky, the killer doll from the cult horror movie *Child's Play*, who dispatches his victims in creatively gruesome ways then chortles satanically, 'Don't fuck with the Chuck.' The Burmese army hated the statues because they were hollow. I saw one soldier open a trapdoor in one of the chubby legs and rootle around inside, obviously looking for bombs. Everyone else hated them because, well, Chuckies gave you the willies. I heard of a Rangoon expatriate who said that the mascot gave her children nightmares.

St John's College was a low-slung, red-brick building not dissimilar to an open prison, overlooking a shaggy lawn monitored by hundreds of dragonflies. It wasn't called St John's College any more, but No. 1 Basic Education High School, although I found the old name on a small plaque outside, which also bore the date 1864 and the school motto, *'Animos Illumina'* – 'Enlighten Our Minds'. I walked through the gates with some reservations. Snooping around schools wasn't a great idea. Students, including schoolchildren, fought and died in the 1988 uprising, and the regime had spies on every campus. To my relief, however, I was welcomed by one of the masters, U Thein Htike, who wore a teacher's green longyi and spectacles with Coke-bottle lenses which made his eyes bulge alarmingly. He had an enormous small-toothed smile, which I saw a lot of since he was delighted to find someone interested in the school's past.

Over two bottles of sweet orange pop, U Thein Htike confessed that the school had been entirely rebuilt in the 1920s; the original teak structure that Scott would have known, and which I had seen in old photos, was long gone. There were now three houses, all named after former teachers. 'Unfortunately there is no Mr Scott house,' U Thein Htike apologised. 'He wasn't here very long – just three years.' Until recently, St John's was considered the best school in the country, famous for past graduates like James Hla Kyaw, pioneer of the modern Burmese novel, and Sir Sao Hke, the first Shan chieftain to dine with Queen Victoria. Another old boy, added U Thein Htike proudly, went to work for NASA.

U Thein Htike had no records or documents from Scott's time, and only one ragged yearbook from the pre-war period. Everything else disappeared when the school was nationalized in 1964, he said. The nationalisation programme that followed the 1962 coup was Burma's Cultural Revolution: much was lost during the state's mass grab of private property – 'lost' being a common euphemism for 'destroyed' or 'stolen'. Today the pupils of St John's had no reason to know about Scott. 'But I tell them that Mr George Scott was a teacher here,' smiled U Thein Htike, 'and that he was the man who introduced football in Burma.'

We walked out along hushed, dusty corridors to look at the football pitch – *the* football pitch, where Burma's first matches had been played. It was a patch of mud marked out with grassy touchlines, with time-tilted goalposts and puddles for six-yard boxes. Looming above the far goal was a mammoth structure of damp red brick – formerly Dufferin Hospital – and behind that was the Gymkhana Club, one of Scott's old haunts, now an inaccessible government building.

'This was once the best football pitch in Rangoon,' said U Thein Htike dreamily. It began to drizzle.

I had half-hoped to find a statue of Scott at St John's College, the kind you nod to on Founder's Day and use for target practice the rest of the year. But he had left no trace here either. I exchanged warm goodbyes with U Thein Htike and walked into town. On the way it struck me that, in one sense, Scott's legacy in Rangoon was all around me.

The city was racked with World Cup fever. Every conquerable inch of the downtown streets was a makeshift football pitch with tiffin-box goalposts. Kids were making smudged photostats of that night's fixtures to sell on the ancient, snub-nosed Chevrolet buses – Rangoon's equivalent to the London Routemasters – or on the battered commuter ferries crisscrossing the river. The value of Burma's fragile currency, the kyat, was plummeting thanks to an increased demand for US dollars to use in gambling. There were rumours of truckloads of pay-off cash being ferried between the rich Chinese community and high-ranking military men. The World Cup coincided not only with the anniversary of the 1988 democracy uprising, but also with Buddhist Lent, a time when many young men enter the monastery to gain spiritual merit. Rangoon was overflowing with newly inducted monks. They swaggered through the streets with close-shaven heads and robes the colour of dried blood, resembling soccer hooligans draped in team colours.

The World Cup was a blessing even for the rare Burmese who didn't like football. Fans in neighbouring Bangladesh had gone on the rampage the previous Saturday night when their country's overloaded national power grid had shut down.

Burma's generals were clearly not prepared to risk similar unrest here – not with the anniversary of 1988 approaching. All matches were shown live on state television. And, almost unfailingly, as the teams began warming up in French stadiums 6,000 miles away, Burma's electricity snapped back on.

'Don't believe what you hear about Ne Win,' a source at the embassy warned me. 'The general's not dead at all. We believe the regime is deliberately spreading rumours to distract attention from something else.'

Something else? What, exactly?

'I don't know,' said the embassy source sharply – meaning that she did, and just wasn't telling.

I soon realised that she was talking about the Golden Land ghosts. News that pro-democracy poltergeists had returned to haunt the site of an old massacre took a shamefully long time to reach my ears. 'You haven't heard?' asked Mary, the diplomat's Burmese housekeeper, as she served me dinner by obligatory candlelight. Mary, who knew I was a journalist, suggested we visit the area together. Her friend Ba Maw would drive us.

I was very excited. The Golden Land poltergeists seemed proof of an embryonic theory of mine: that the Burmese, a profoundly superstitious people, summoned agents from the supernatural world to vent the anger and frustration they felt, but could not safely express. I had already read of one extraordinary example. After the generals placed Aung San Suu Kyi under house arrest in 1989 and nullified the election results that would have swept her party into power, there were reports that Buddha statues in temples and homes across the country were growing breasts. There was a rational explanation for this: when Burmese worshippers apply gold leaf to Buddha statues they often place it over the heart – hence the bulging chest. But the population was in no mood for rational explanations. The phenomenon was interpreted as a spiritual sign of one woman's rightful position as the nation's democratically elected leader. At the time, the regime was so worried that some temples were cordoned off by troops.

The Golden Land haunting seemed another clear indication of the nation's mood. Even the shop's name was deeply significant: 'Golden Land', or 'Shwe Pyidaw', was an old name for Burma.

The shop stood on an unnaturally quiet corner of an otherwise busy intersection not far from the Shwedagon. Ba Maw parked his car nearby while I got out to investigate. There wasn't much to see. The shop's shutters were down, and it was guarded by a handful of soldiers. Loitering about were a few men in civilian clothes, whom I didn't really register. By the time I got back to the car they had already questioned Mary and Ba Maw.

'They wanted to know where you come from,' said Mary as Ba Maw started the engine. 'I said I didn't know. I said we came here to buy fruit at the market.' We drove off, and I saw many soldiers lurking behind the bushes around the intersection. I know that Mary saw them too, although she was looking straight ahead. 'Many children died here,' she said quietly. Ba Maw headed for home.

We were driving along a lakeside road when Ba Maw began slowing down. The car started to shudder; Ba Maw was clearly in too high a gear. Then I realised he wasn't concentrating on his driving any more. His eyes were fixed on the rear-view mirror. I glanced over my shoulder to see what he was seeing. It was a white Japanese sedan, and it was slowing down too. We were being followed.

My stomach churned. It suddenly occurred to me that I had no idea what to do. My first thought, which seems stupid now, was to stop the car. Stop the car and talk to them. Give an innocent explanation of why we had parked next to the Golden Land shop. *We only went there to buy fruit.*

But Ba Maw had other ideas. Ignoring the turn-off to the diplomat's house, he swung sharply into an ill-lit backstreet and accelerated rapidly. I looked back. There was a pause of a few seconds, then I saw the Japanese sedan turn too. I knew it was the same sedan because the otherwise nondescript car had one distinguishing feature: it had a faulty headlight. Ba Maw turned hard again, almost running over a startled dog, then gunned the engine. I counted to three and looked through the back window. And there, with the surreal persistence of a bad dream, was the white car with the mismatched headlights again.

Ba Maw knew Rangoon's murky backstreets well, and he drove fast but steadily. For the next ten minutes, as the Japanese sedan pursued us through winding, deserted lanes, he was as cool as a croupier. It was almost as if he'd done this before. When the chance came, he seized it. He spun out of a narrow side street just as another car pulled in, and while our pursuer's path was momentarily blocked he sped along a main road and ducked into another side street. I looked back. The mismatched headlamps were gone. We had lost them.

I felt sick with relief. I knew there was a high chance that our pursuers had noted Ba Maw's licence plate and could use it to track us down. The worst that could happen to me was a swift deportation, but my Burmese companions could be interrogated, imprisoned and tortured. But they smiled and told me not to worry. Belatedly, I realised what Ba Maw and Mary had risked to take me to the shop, and even as I marveled at their bravery I cursed myself for letting them.

My brush with Military Intelligence had a sobering effect. Until the car chase, I had been lost in misty-eyed reflections about George Scott and Burma's colonial past. Now I had been given an unsettling glimpse of the machinery of a modern dictatorship at work.

Mary and Ba Maw saw it all the time, of course, but, like most Burmese, they shielded foreigners from the ugly reality. Vast, omniscient and inhuman, the machinery was never at rest, but always watching, always alert, always primed and programmed to control all aspects of everyday life in Burma. And, once glimpsed, it was never forgotten. The desire to find out how it worked would become part of what drew me back to Burma again and again.

By the time we returned to the diplomat's house that night the electricity was on again. I stayed up to watch the England-Argentina match in the company of a large lizard, which wedged itself behind the bookshelf above my head and chuckled maniacally when England lost the penalty shoot-out. Then the power shut off again, plunging the house, the neighbourhood and the city into blackness – as if somebody somewhere had decided that we'd all had enough for one day, and had thrown an almighty switch.

2

I boarded the ship before dawn, picking my way carefully along the litter-strewn riverbank and up the slippery gang-plank. The night sky was brilliant with stars, the Irrawaddy so placid that the larger constellations were reflected perfectly in its depths. Shooting stars streaked across the heavens, pursued by their mirror images. It was still dark when the gangplank was pulled aboard and, with a rev of distant engines, the ship began a lazy pirouette through the sandbanks into deeper water.

Shadows moved among the cargo: the other passengers were waking up. Wrapped in blankets, entire Burmese families emerged from the cramped spaces between the sacks of charcoal, rice and onions piled up on both decks. The women now combed and plaited their long black hair, then mixed thanaka bark on heart-shaped slates and applied the astringent paste to their cheeks in bold stripes. Their children stared groggily at me. Breakfast passed in a cacophony of rattling tiffin-box lids and mewling infants, and afterwards the women opened their sacks of soya patties or dried fish and set up shop. The menfolk lit the day's first cheroot and considered the sunrise. It was brief and spectacular. It set the palm trees along the banks ablaze, then shot a bolt of fire across the unruffled water to illuminate our ship's peeling flanks. As the sun burned its outline through a curtain of mist, a flock of stately herons crossed its circumference in dramatic silhouette – right on cue.

A pot-bellied crew member ran a greasy cloth over a wobbly table and laid out a few packets of instant noodles and – hurrah – the restaurant was open. I bought coffee, and curled up in a wicker armchair on the chilly upper deck. I had now spent a week travelling up the Irrawaddy from Rangoon, at first following the river's course by bus, then boarding a ship at the town of Pakokku bound for the fabled destination of Mandalay. Apart from traditional rowing boats, with their carved prows curling up like Victorian banister ends, I had seen little traffic on the water. Roads had long since usurped the Irrawaddy's ancient role as Burma's central artery, and the sleepy riverside towns I passed through seemed marooned in the past. Giant fruit bats chattered in immense rain trees planted during colonial times to provide shade for pasty district superintendents; dilapidated gharries plied the torpid streets. The rest houses I stayed in all blurred into one: the same artful splashes of betel juice behind the bed; the same rat poison in the corners; and, in the morning, as the streets slowly resurfaced through a dense blanket of wood smoke, the same washing facilities – a communal trough of ice-cold Irrawaddy in the backyard.

Today the great river was as calm as a lake, and the sound of clothes being slapped clean on rocks travelled easily from the faraway shores. Brahminy geese, said to mate for life, paired off and canoodled in the sparkling shallows. The banks beyond were rolling dunes of yellow sand – a barren, almost Arabian, scene – but the subsoil was rich in nutrients, and the banks were often planted with beans or rice or tobacco. The soil was also rich in gold: both river banks were pimpled with piles of earth which had been sifted by small-time prospectors.

A woman sat next to me between two sacks of dried fish. She had seen the dollar bill I was using as a bookmark, and asked to look at it. I passed it to her and it circulated among her friends, and soon a little George Washington appreciation society had formed. The woman then opened one of her sacks and weighed out some dried fish on hand-held scales, using five dud Chinese batteries as counterweights. Each battery represented five ticals – or, to give its dull imperial equivalent, about two and a half ounces. She held up two bags of fish in one hand, and the dollar in the other: I was being offered a deal. I thanked her, took the pungent bags, and shoved them deep into my backpack. I was more than happy to exchange one dollar for twenty-five ticals of dried fish. Tickled, in fact.

At noon Mandalay Hill loomed through the haze – a faraway smudge of grey speckled white with temples – then disappeared beneath the treeline. I went ashore briefly at Sagaing, our penultimate stop. Standing on a spur of sand, where a man was lovingly washing his bicycle, I got my first real view of the ship. It was not a pretty sight. It was a Japanese vessel with an English engine, flat-bellied, snub-nosed and weeping with rust. I'd seen better-looking boats 120 feet beneath the ocean with an air canister on my back.

Still, it was exciting to think that the ship that first brought George Scott up the Irrawaddy would not have been dissimilar, although in those days it would have been steam-driven. Scott docked at Mandalay in 1880 amid chaotic scenes. The steep, muddy banks seethed with desperate families clamouring to board the steamer on its six-day return voyage downriver to Rangoon. Thousands more had already fled on dangerously overloaded vessels. An unprecedented exodus from Mandalay was under way, and Scott, then special correspondent for the London *Daily News*, had been dispatched to Burma's royal capital to find out why.

Mandalay in 1880 was not a safe place for a white man. Apart from a handful of people sheltering in the poorly fortified British residency, only three Europeans dared to wander the streets: a fiery Baptist missionary, a retired major 'of weak intellect', and Scott. But the young journalist was hoping to blend with the crowd in his sarong and sandals, and his upper arm now bore a traditional Burmese tattoo said to protect the wearer from all harm. Scott – a vain man with one eye always fixed on posterity – would bequeath the tattoo to the Royal College of Surgeons, 'to be removed when I am dead and kept as a sample'.

Thus attired, he set out to record his first impressions. 'Mandalay presented a series of violent contrasts,' he reported, 'with jewel-studded temples and gilded monasteries standing side by side with wattled hovels penetrated by every wind that blew.' Dominating the city was the palace, a fairy-tale collection of exquisitely carved teak pavilions with tiered golden roofs, protected by a thick red-brick wall and a moat as wide as a football pitch. On a gem-encrusted throne within sat His Most Glorious, Excellent Majesty, Ruler of the Sea and the Land, Lord of the Rising Sun, King of the Umbrella-Bearing Chiefs, Sovereign of Life and Death, and Arbiter of Existence: King Thibaw – 'the most inhuman of a long line of savage despots', wrote Scott.

Thibaw had ascended the throne two years earlier, at the tender age of nineteen. His reign had begun with a time-honoured Burmese tradition: the extermination of all potential rivals to the throne. Over eighty royals, including eight of his brothers, were tied up in large velvet bags and clubbed to death in the palace grounds while a court orchestra played to drown their screams. The corpses were trampled into enormous trenches by elephants. Despite this messy precaution, bad omens circled the palace like vultures. Thibaw's infant son had died during a recent plague of smallpox, and a fist-sized ruby considered emblematic of the king's rule had mysteriously vanished from the crown jewels. Then his pet tiger had burst from its bamboo cage, mauled its keeper to death, and terrorised the ladies-in-waiting. This, explained Scott, was 'a most ominous circumstance, not only for the poor wretch whom the tiger killed and half ate, but for the city and the entire kingdom. The appearance of wild animals in a town is a sign that it will speedily turn into a wilderness.'

Scott had arrived in time to witness an ancient royal dynasty in its death throes. Thibaw was descended from the bellicose and bloodthirsty King Alaungpaya, who in the eighteenth century initiated a series of campaigns in Thailand so brutal that many Thais still despise the Burmese for them today. But the warrior blood of Alaungpaya ran thin in young Thibaw's veins, where it was

Thibaw with his queen Supayalat, nicknamed 'Soup-plate' by the British.

King Thibaw's ragtag army depicted in *The Graphic*,
4 October 1879. Soldiers wear sarongs or trousers – or both.

also diluted with gin, of which it was said the young king had grown overly fond. Effete, decadent and fatally introspective, Thibaw would rule only long enough to set his fragile hermit kingdom on a collision course with the mighty British Empire.

But this was not why Thibaw's subjects were fleeing – the royal soothsayers were to blame for that. When Mandalay had been founded, fifty-two people had been buried alive beneath its walls in the belief that their ghosts would guard the city against evil. Now the soothsayers declared there was only one sure way to propitiate the spirits and end King Thibaw's run of terrible luck: the ritual slaughter of another 600 men, women and children, including 100 Europeans. 'This the king agreed to,' wrote Scott, 'and arrests forthwith commenced. A frightful panic spread in Mandalay after the first day. Every steamer leaving the capital was crowded to suffocation, boats went down the river in dozens, and there seemed every possibility that Mandalay would be deserted.'

During the following year a quarter of a million Burmese would leave the kingdom for British-ruled Lower Burma. Those who remained lived in a city of increasing lawlessness, with gangs of armed robbers roaming its suburbs. The king's soldiers had little motivation to restore order in the city or to fight the sabre-rattling Shan chiefs in the hills beyond. Their wages had already been spent on fine French jewellery by Thibaw's vain and ruthless queen, Supayalat – later rechristened 'Soup Plate' by British troops. Queen Supayalat and her mother had masterminded the palace massacre, and any courtier who dared challenge them soon found himself 'spread-eagled in the court of the palace with a vertical sun beating down upon him and huge stones piled on his chest and stomach', said Scott. Death by lingering torture also befell women who copied Supayalat's hairstyle, which she had patented, and the queen had once ordered some errant maids to be raped to death by Burmese pony stallions. 'Thibaw could not be otherwise than miserable,' Scott concluded. 'The harridan queen kept him in most humble subjection.' The king and queen quarrelled with such ferocity that the palace gates were closed to prevent the rows causing unrest in the city.

Misruled by a feeble, gin-soaked tyrant and his evil queen, the kingdom slid towards anarchy. In a last-ditch attempt to refill the royal coffers, Thibaw's ministers seized upon the idea of public lotteries. Tickets could soon be bought at booths on every street corner, although many people were bullied into buying them by roving thugs employed by lottery managers. Honest trade all but ceased. 'The town is in a state of perpetual excitement,' Scott reported. 'Everyone hovers around the lottery offices and longs for the draw.' Lending the manic atmosphere a truly surreal edge were the pigs – the streets of Mandalay were clogged with them. Thibaw's late father, King Mindon, had fed 1,000 pigs every day to gain religious merit, and when he died the swine were released. They now truffled happily through the city's refuse with the impunity of holy Hindu cows.

Quite how Scott managed to blend in as he explored the rest of Mandalay was a mystery to me. How *do* you remain inconspicuous with a white face and a moustache long enough to ripen bananas on? But in fact our *Daily News* correspondent might have strolled unremarked through a city already swarming with human diversity. Scott would observe:

> the Chinaman, smooth-shaven and prosperous as always, smoking his opium pipe with supreme composure; the bearded Surati with solemn face; the Palaung come down from the north with his bamboo rafts laden with pickled tea; the stalwart Shan with baggy blue trousers and tattoo marks down to his ankles; the heavy, easy-going Karen; the lithe, treacherous Kachin, spying out villages easy to raid in a night attack; all these, and a host of others, might be seen any day in the Royal City of Gems.

One day Scott's wanderings led him into Mandalay's silk bazaar, where he took to admiring some 'very pretty' Burmese women at a stall. At that moment two men grabbed him violently from behind and dragged him behind a row of stalls. Each man was naked to the waist, and bore a dragon tattoo on the nape of his neck – the distinctive sign of a palace soldier.

Scott might have feared that he had become one of the 100 Europeans whom the king's soothsayers sought for human sacrifice. That was not the case, although his actual predicament was just as dangerous. The soldiers were moonlighting as lottery thugs, and wanted Scott to buy some tickets – or else, they said, 'we'll denounce you as a spy of Prince Nyoung-Oke and you'll be crucified down by the bund'. Prince Nyoung-Oke had escaped the royal massacre to stage an abortive uprising against the king. 'Thibaw had got it into his head that the British were in some way responsible, and quite a number of men in Upper Burma had been seized and executed on the ground that they were British spies,' wrote Scott. 'My position was somewhat ticklish.' He agreed to accompany the men to a nearby lottery office.

On the way they passed a toddy shop, and Scott suggested they all stop for refreshments. He ordered Chinese *samshu* rice spirit and Eagle brandy, 'the latter as fiery as a blast-furnace', and urged the soldiers to drink. 'One of the two filled a tumbler with brandy and samshu, drank half of it, declared that he had never tasted anything so good before, and subsided on to the floor. The other confined himself to brandy, and grew talkative.' Scott refilled his captor's glass and listened.

Life in Thibaw's army was tough, the soldier explained. When the king reviewed the troops from his elephant, the men had to prostrate themselves in the dirt. And the latest indignity? The troops had been ordered to wear trousers, a newfangled garment they regarded with 'very grave suspicions'. They soon reverted to wearing their sarongs, although the trousers, neatly folded, were carried in one hand to show high status.

For a small man, Scott had a Tardis-like capacity for alcohol, a capacity developed with no small help from his father, who would reward young George with drafts of ginger wine for reciting Bible passages from memory. That afternoon in Mandalay, Scott drank and drank until the second soldier slumped among the empty brandy bottles. 'Shortly afterwards he fell asleep,' Scott recalled, 'and I deposited him after dark in a convenient back garden, and put his friend in another some way off. The royal lotteries lost some money that day; but I did not hang about the Mandalay silk bazaar any more after that experience.'

My ship reached Mandalay in the late afternoon. There was no dock to speak of, just a stretch of packed earth crowded with listing barges that a well-aimed bucket of water could scupper. A conveyor belt of labourers, whippet-thin and stripped to the waist, heaved sacks of rice up to vehicles waiting in the shade of antique trees. A solitary pony and trap provided a period touch, and the whole scene was washed in the warm sepia light of old photographs. A young woman in an azure sarong stood hip-deep in the shallows, massaging shampoo into her long black hair – oblivious, it seemed, to the ship's massive bulk bearing down upon her. When it was less than ten yards away, she shot us a wicked look through a turban of shampoo foam, then waded with unhurried elegance to a spot further along the bank. There was a blast on the ship's horn, and even before the gangplanks thudded down porters had leaped aboard over four feet of oily water to tout for business. The ship was tied not to a bollard (there wasn't one) but to a sturdy wooden spike which was tossed ashore and pounded into the hard Irrawaddy mud with an enormous mallet.

I rattled into town in the back of a pick-up truck, pursued by a faint odour of dried fish.

Mandalay. What single, sonorous word better captured the romance, the adventure, the sheer exotic otherness of the Orient? Who could forget the immortal lines of Rudyard Kipling's popular ballad?

For the wind is in the palm trees, and the temple bells they say,
Come you back, you British soldier, come you back to Mandalay!

Kipling – who, let it be known, never visited Mandalay – had a lot to answer for. There was no wind in the palm trees, or anywhere else for that matter. In fact there weren't any palm trees. Modern Mandalay was a hot, dusty, featureless grid of concrete shop-houses, its beautiful teak dwellings devoured in 1984 by a fire started in a cobbler's shop.

I had visited Mandalay before, and had found it a hard place to like. Built by the devout King Mindon to fulfill ancient prophecy, it was a city of monasteries, some of them quite beautiful – and, like the Incomparable Monastery, beautifully named too. It had more monks per square inch than any other place in Burma. Traditionally, it was a cradle of art and culture, and its genteel inhabitants were said to speak the most refined form of Burmese. All this had changed in recent years. Mandalay had become a boom town, fuelled by the mercantile spirit of hundreds of thousands of immigrants from China – almost half the city's million or so inhabitants were now Chinese – and by a massive influx of drug money from wealthy Wa and Kokang heroin traffickers. I checked into a Chinese hotel with the usual collection of carved wooden furniture squatting monstrously in the lobby. Outside, the Burmese rickshaw-wallahs lounged redundantly in the shade, watching the city's new bustle as if from another world.

One thing hadn't changed since Thibaw's day: the popularity of lotteries. Strolling the baking backstreets, I was passed by curious hand-pushed barrows garlanded with tickets for the state draw. These contraptions pumped out music at a brain-wrecking volume, rivalled only by the amplified mantras from the city's myriad temples. The main thoroughfares were dominated by convoys of trucks. These bore Burmese licence plates, but betrayed their origin and ownership by the classical Chinese scenes painted on their sides. China was only a day's drive away along the famous Burma Road. Built in the late 1930s, this had been a vital supply route for Chinese Nationalist forces battling against the Japanese

Imperial Army. Today it was the lifeline for an otherwise isolated Burmese regime. Trucks loaded with Burmese gems, jade, teak and food poured across the border into China; so did Burmese heroin and Burmese methamphetamine, bound eventually for the streets of America and Europe. In the opposite direction came trucks carrying Chinese spoons, bowls, pans, beer, clothes, autoparts, electrical goods, fuel . . . pretty much everything. As even this partial shopping list suggested, Burma didn't really *make* anything. It was utterly dependent on its powerful neighbour for even the most basic products. 'When China spits,' a local saying goes, 'Burma swims.'

The Burma Road also brought people. A lucrative racket had sprung up to provide Chinese immigrants with identification cards, which were bought from the families of dead Burmese. Their arrival had driven up house prices and forced impoverished Mandalay families to sell their homes in the city centre to developers and move to grim suburban estates, which as often as not were built on Chinese-owned land. I wondered – as I paid my hotel receptionist six dollars just to receive a fax – what level of resentment all this was creating among ordinary Burmese. In 1967 scores of Chinese had been killed in communal riots in Rangoon. Mandalay's Chinese population seemed to be taking no chances. Their shop-houses were like mini-fortresses, each one equipped with ramps so that the family van could be driven inside and secured behind an impregnable iron grille.

My main business transactions in Mandalay consisted of marathon haggling sessions with the city's taxi drivers. They drove not cars, but disintegrating Mazda tuk-tuks dating back to the very dawn of the Japanese automotive industry. One day, after negotiating a fare only three times the going rate, I wedged myself into the back of one of these clapped-out three-wheeled fart-buggies and headed for Mandalay Palace. Soon we were going flat out along a moat-side road, the engine rattling like a washing machine full of aircraft wreckage, when a man on a bicycle drew alongside, nodded politely, and leisurely overtook us.

All that remained of King Thibaw's spectacular palace was its austere ochre walls. The rest had been destroyed on a single day in March 1945 by low-flying British bombers trying to flush out Japanese soldiers. The pavilions which stood there now were replicas. In the early 1990s the junta decided to rebuild part of the palace to 'uplift national prestige'. Slave labour was used to dredge and widen the moat, and a new road was built. To accommodate this, many moat-side buildings were destroyed by the military.

Others were simply sliced in half and some of these architectural oddities still stand along the southern wall. Crossing a bridge over the moat, I stopped to watch a cormorant cruise low over the water.

I paid a five-dollar entrance fee and entered through a mammoth old gateway flanked by modern sentry boxes. In Thibaw's time European visitors were admitted through a cripplingly low gateway which obliged them to bend double, a cunning device to make the presumptuous barbarian bow before the Burmese throne. Now the ramparts were hung with a huge banner proclaiming, in English only, 'TATMADAW AND THE PEOPLE COOPERATE AND CRUSH ALL ENEMIES OF THE STATE' – the Tatmadaw being the Burmese military.

The replica palace occupied only a small part of the huge grounds. The rest was an army barracks, and there were signs everywhere warning non-military personnel to keep out. A disused railway, built by the British, entered through a gate in the southern wall, and somewhere within the walls, I was told, was Mandalay's most prestigious golf course. I wandered around the Hall of Audience, with its impressive roof of diminishing golden tiers, where King Thibaw's throne had once sat. In Burmese cosmology, this throne was regarded as the centre of the universe – a universe which, strictly speaking, would for a while pivot around the Calcutta museum where the plundering British took the throne to be displayed.

Afterwards I climbed the spiral staircase of the watchtower. Queen Supayalat had stood on the original watchtower and gazed out in horror at British warships sailing up the Irrawaddy. Now the river was lost in the dusty horizon. Down below, the sun-baked grounds were deserted apart from a few couples smooching on the shaded steps of a lesser queen's chambers. The rest of the palace was still very much a work in progress. Painters on gantries swung from the curling oriental eaves, slapping yellow paint on wooden pillars whose prototypes would have been thickly papered in gold leaf.

The palace was said to be a faithful reproduction, right down to the small huts perched on the roofs around the Hall of Audience. These had been occupied by royal archers, whose task it was to shoot down crows, vultures and other unpropitious birds that flew over the palace. Sadly, however, there was no replica of the luxurious pavilion which housed Thibaw's white elephant. This sacred beast was a living symbol of royal legitimacy and power. An earlier Burmese king sent his army to vanquish the Siamese capital when he heard that its court had four white elephants.

The most venerated examples were immense creatures with nine extremities touching the ground: four feet, two tusks, trunk, tail and penis. Scott described Thibaw's sacred elephant as more of a 'dingy, smoke-smirched cream colour' than actual white. 'His tusks, however, were magnificent – white, smooth, and curving forward in front of his trunk so that they almost met.' The elephant's pavilion was decorated with the seven-tiered spire of royalty, and when he was young dozens of Burmese women waited outside for the honour of suckling him. His immense pale flanks were bathed in water scented with sandalwood; he ate from vessels of hand-beaten gold. He was lulled to sleep by palace musicians, who took pains to avoid those great tusks, which had already killed once. 'His lordship was very bad-tempered,' Scott explained.

In the end, this elevated beast died of the lowliest disease: colic. Later I consulted my prized copy of *The Care and Management of Elephants in Burma* by A. J. Ferrier (1947), a forgotten classic I had bought in Rangoon, and found the following treatment for colic: 'Give copious enemas of soap and warm water, and after a good evacuation has been effected give 4 drachm [half an ounce] doses of opium or ganja every two or three hours until the pain has subsided.' No wonder the elephant died. Considering his evil temper and proven homicidal tendencies, I could imagine the palace cry of 'Whose turn is it to give His Lordship a soapy enema?' being met by resounding silence.

The sad demise of Thibaw's white elephant had a bizarre postscript. In his twilight years the poet William McGonagall was approached by emissaries of 'King Theebaw of Burmah and the Andaman Islands', who conferred upon him a title for his services to poetry. Poor McGonagall never discovered that the Burmese royal emissaries were actually pranksters from Edinburgh University, and until his dying day he proudly used the title they had given him: Sir William Topaz McGonagall, Knight of the White Elephant.

I didn't much enjoy my tour of the new Mandalay Palace. Everything seemed sterile and lifeless, and hardly rivaled the palace I had already reconstructed in my imagination. However, at the entrance to a long pavilion called the Hall of Victory, I did find a cheering piece of pure Disney: a life-size model of King Thibaw reclining on a golden couch next to a sign warning 'DO NOT TOUCH'. (I touched.)

It was Scott's main aim while in Mandalay to secure an interview with Thibaw. This would be difficult – more difficult, he wagered, than meeting even the Grand Lama, or the Sharif ül-Islam of Mecca, for Thibaw had sworn by the sacred hairs of Gautama never to look at an English barbarian again. There is still some doubt whether Scott succeeded, although this did not stop him writing a vivid first-hand account of bribing one of Thibaw's grinning ministers and joining a party of foreigners for a private audience in a mirrored pavilion at the palace.

Thibaw entered the chamber briskly, trailed by a pageboy carrying a box of cheroots, and threw himself impatiently on a raised golden couch. While a herald began the laborious ritual of chanting the visitors' names, Scott reflected on how gin had taken its toll on the king. 'When he acceded to the throne, he was very handsome; the handsomest Burman in the country, it used to be said. Now his face is puffed out and bloated, his eyes sunken and dead, his whole appearance unwholesome and repulsive.' By this account, Thibaw also bore an angry red scratch on his cheek, and Scott wondered idly 'whether the queen had done it'. The formalities over, Scott found to his frustration that his party could address the king only through a royal interpreter of staggering verbosity:

> Thibaw asks if we are well. We announce that we are, and the interpreter, who sees fit to translate bald monosyllables into grovelling periods, says that by his majesty's merciful permission we are in the enjoyment of perfect health. Thibaw then demands our business. The interpreter replies that we have come to view the glories of his majesty's mighty kingdom, and to lay our heads under his golden feet . . .

And so it went on. To enliven the meeting with controversy, Scott's party ventured that lotteries were considered 'a very bad thing' in Europe. 'The interpreter gazes for three-quarters of a second reproachfully at us,' wrote Scott, 'and then says that we are lost in wonder at the wisdom which has fallen upon such a method of increasing the revenue, which had never occurred to the unilluminated minds of barbarian financiers.' Then the young king, clearly as bored by such exchanges as his visitors, got up and left the room. Scott's party was afterwards served with teacups which turned out to contain brandy.

Scott did not return to Mandalay for six years. During that time he roved across Asia. At one time we find him stranded in a Bombay hotel room, racked with fever and on dwindling expenses, praying through his increasing delirium for Gladstone not to stop the Afghan War – his next assignment. Then we find him beneath the walls of the Forbidden City in Beijing, buying the funeral pall of the teenage emperor T'ung Chih out of a basket lowered from the ramparts by a corrupt eunuch. He reappears as a *Standard* reporter covering the French army's conquest of Tongking, before being invalided back to London to study law and to pen a scholarly book on France's colonial aspirations in Indo-China. He was a leading light at the Savage Club in the Mall, and scored 'three hundred goals in first-class football' for his team, London Scottish.

The year 1882 saw the publication of *The Burman: His Life and Notions* by Shway Yoe, a book first acclaimed for its native author's masterly grasp of English. When it transpired that Shway Yoe, which means 'Golden Truth' in Burmese, was in fact George Scott – the 'jolly, fiery, football-loving head-master of St John's College' – the book was praised anew, this time as an intimate and remarkably detailed portrait of Burmese life by a gifted young Scot who had only briefly called the country home.

The Burman remained in print over a century later, and was still consulted by Burma scholars and plundered by travel writers. Every time I opened my dog-eared 1963 edition I found something new and surprising – like the fact that a Burman can tell the time by looking at his shadow, or that the young Thibaw liked to play cricket, or that a poultice of pulverised gecko feet and cock's dung is an excellent remedy for sores. The book began with a Burman birth, when the infant is smothered in turmeric to drive out noxious spirits and his horoscope is recorded on a palm-leaf; before an event of any consequence – a journey, a marriage, a visit to the barber – this horoscope will be consulted to ensure that the stars are propitious. Scott displayed his keen reportorial skills in first-hand evocations of Burmese rituals and celebrations, like festivals and plays, or the funeral of a venerated abbot whose pyre was lit by giant, unstable fireworks which guaranteed that one or two unlucky spectators joined the monk in the afterlife. *The Burman* was as illuminating on the gentler arts of lacquerware and silk growing as it was on winning strategies in Burmese chess or the correct method of crucifying criminals. An entire chapter was devoted to *ngapi*, the ubiquitous Burmese condiment made from putrid fish and so offensive to British nostrils that in 1880 the assistant commissioner of Yandun blamed its stinky vapours for a cholera epidemic in Lower Burma, and banned the substance outright.

The book was written with a passion seldom found in colonial works of the period, when identifying too closely with 'the natives' could ruin career prospects. Scott's vision was essentially romantic. 'If any one has escaped the curse of Adam it is the Burman,' declares his literary alter ego, Shway Yoe. 'Riches having no attraction for him, when his patch of paddy land has been reaped, his only concern is how to pass the time, and that is no very difficult matter when he has plenty of cheroots and betel-nut.' The author constantly poked fun at uptight Englishmen who failed to appreciate this simple life. 'The best thing a Burman can wish for a good Englishman is that in some future existence, as a reward of good works, he may be born a Buddhist,' Shway Yoe wrote, 'and if possible a Burman.'

Scott didn't know it, but *The Burman* described a country on the brink of immense upheaval. The hapless King Thibaw was about to pick a fight with his powerful British neighbours that would alter the course of Burmese history and change Scott's destiny forever.

It started with another massacre. In 1884, convinced that his prisons were infested with political enemies, Thibaw engineered a 'break-out' during which 300 escapees were butchered. The bodies were thrown into shallow graves outside the palace walls, where the omnivorous pigs swarmed and feasted on the putrefying flesh. The slaughter caused outrage in Rangoon, where the merchant community was agitating for the British annexation of Upper Burma. Ultimately, however, it was a trade dispute over royal timber revenues that Britain would seize upon as the pretext to invade Thibaw's unstable kingdom.

On 20 October 1885 the wife of Lord Dufferin, viceroy of India, made the following entry in her diary: 'We breakfasted at eight o'clock. At a quarter past the Viceroy signed the declaration of war with Burmah.' And by half past eight the breakfast things were cleared away and all Burma was in British hands. Or so it seemed. Imperial warships steamed up the Irrawaddy, and Mandalay was taken with less than 1,000 troops. Thibaw's last sovereign act was formally to surrender to what a Burmese historian would call 'those trousered creatures', the British. The annexation of Upper Burma was announced on 1 January 1886, as a New Year's present for Queen Victoria.

King Thibaw left his palace in a covered bullock cart, with Queen Supayalat at his side. Flanked by Welsh Fusiliers, the cart bumped along an unpaved Mandalay street lined with weeping Burmese women. The sun had set by the time this sad procession reached the river bank, and the royals boarded a British steamboat in darkness. Then they were shipped down the Irrawaddy to Rangoon, and from there across the Bay of Bengal to eventual exile in the coastal town of Ratnagiri, south of Bombay. This was the first time the king had ever left the palace; and it was the last time he ever saw Burma. The white elephant died ten days later and, without ceremony, was hauled onto an enormous sledge built by British military carpenters and dragged from the palace for burial. Its death marked the end of the old regime – and, it seemed, an inauspicious start for the new one.

At first the British occupation of Mandalay Palace – now renamed Fort Dufferin – brought little stability to the city. The ease with which Thibaw's puny army had been swept aside left the British unprepared for the fury of the Burmese resistance that came after. The following weeks saw an alarming increase in disorder. Thibaw's scattered troops forged new careers in armed gangs led by princes, patriots or thieves which robbed civilians and attacked British patrols. While walking in the palace grounds one day, Dufferin asked his general how far British power in Burma now extended. The general pointed to a sentry on the ramparts and replied, 'Up to that man and no further, sir.'

Two months later, in April 1886, George Scott returned to Mandalay – not as a journalist this time, but as a member of a hand-picked cadre of British administrators set up to carry the great imperial gift of civilisation into the Burmese wilderness.

The city must have seemed scarcely less chaotic than during his first visit, six years before. In the month he arrived, several police officers were hacked to death and a portion of the city was set ablaze by rebels loyal to an exiled son of King Mindon. The climate added to the apocalyptic atmosphere. It was just before the monsoon, the hottest time of the year, recalled Scott, when scorching winds scoured the dirt streets and 'sudden dust-storms made the sky dark at midday'.

The British response to the growing chaos in Mandalay was merciless. In the first few weeks alone, dozens of Burmese were summarily tried then publicly executed by firing squad at Fort Dufferin. But it would be years until the city was at peace. News of one insurrection reached Scott as he enjoyed after-dinner coffee and cheroots at the Upper Burma Club, the social focus of colonial life in Mandalay, housed in a sumptuous teak pavilion that had formerly served as Queen Supayalat's private quarters. An old monk claiming to be the reincarnation of a long-dead Burmese prince was marching upon the palace's south gate to reclaim the throne. He was accompanied by a band of devotees, most of them unarmed, who were convinced that the venerable monk possessed the supernatural ability to make them invisible to their enemies. Hadn't he already proved this by walking three times around his monastery and vanishing himself? In the event, Burmese voodoo was no match for Major Dobbie of the Indian Army, who opened fire on the approaching band, killing the monk and four of his highly visible followers. Scott, who had abandoned his coffee and dashed to the scene, arrived to find the palace walls splashed with blood. Ten more people were rounded up in the days that followed, tried, then hanged publicly as a warning to anyone else tempted to pit his occult powers against British Maxim guns firing 600 rounds per minute.

As the British imposed order on Mandalay, Scott found that the so-called 'City of Gems' was losing its sparkle: 'Mandalay is a vastly less interesting place than it used to be,' he wrote:

> The pigs have all been eaten up and the pariah dogs poisoned by municipal order; A, B, and C roads testify to the unromantic stolidity of the Military Intelligence Department; electric trams make it easier for the Burman to move to the suburbs and leave the town to the hustling foreigner. There are no agreeable scallywags. The Palace, instead of being tawdrily magnificent, smells horribly of bats.

Fortunately, Scott's work lay in the rugged Shan mountains that rose darkly to the east of the city. 'There is in this particular region', he observed, 'a collection of races diverse in feature, language and customs, as cannot, perhaps, be paralleled in any other part of the world.' Scott would spend a quarter of a century exploring this vast, landlocked nowhereland. Acutely aware of how British influence erased the ancient societies it touched, he would study the tribes he encountered in intimate detail, record their beliefs and rituals, learn their languages, and photograph their way of life.

And everywhere he went he brought a gift – not the great imperial gift of civilisation, as it turned out, but a game of two halves, and a crudely stitched sphere of Indian rubber to play it with.

3

My taxi headed east, negotiating a ribbon of crumbling tarmac that unfurled across parched rice fields and up into the Shan hills. It climbed steeply through cool, verdant forests, and soon, through a clearing, I caught a last glimpse of Mandalay shimmering mythically in the heat haze far below. My destination was the former colonial hill station of Maymyo on the edge of the Shan plateau, where I planned to revisit a reclusive and largely forgotten Burmese called Taw Paya – the grandson of King Thibaw.

I had company. In Mandalay I had engaged the services of a young Shan guide called Hseng. He needed the work, and I needed someone who knew the Shan hills and the Shan language. What I didn't find out till later was that Hseng had spent nearly all his life in the Burman lowlands and, while he spoke Shan fluently, he had never been to northern Shan State before. I would never have guessed. Hseng wore his Shan identity like a coat of armour. He believed the Shan were a blessed race. He believed the most beautiful woman in the world was his Shan mother. He believed in the Lord Buddha, and took pains never to step on the shadow of a passing monk.

He feared nothing and he feared no one.

'You see, I am Shan,' he explained in the car. 'I have no fear. When I was a boy I slept in the forest under a very big tree. My friend said to me, "A bad spirit lives in that tree. If you sleep there it will come at night and squeeze your neck. You will be dead on the spot." But I was not afraid, because I paid my respects to the Buddha and to my mother.'

He leaned out the window and spat. 'And I bring with me the knife of my grandfather. No, not knife – something you put on the end of a gun.'

'A bayonet.'

'Yes I bring the bayonet of my grandfather. In the war he killed many Japanese with it.' He ruminated for a second or two. 'I think I inherited my bravery from my grandfather,' he concluded, 'like you inherited your bald head from your grandfather.'

I liked Hseng enormously. He had the stocky build of a highlander and the disreputable good looks of a gangster. His flattened nose was the souvenir of a reckless youth he was trying to put behind him. The son of a farmer, Hseng had dropped out of high school to devote his teens to watching kung-fu videos and getting smashed on palm toddy. Then he ran an illegal lottery and took part in a timber racket. His latest reincarnation as a tour guide was part of a promise to his mother to clean up his act. 'She told me, "Hseng, watch out, you are walking around the edge of the prison,"' he said. Overnight he gave up gambling, brawling, chewing betel nut and smoking cheroots – but not drinking. Hseng insisted on being my *guide*, rather than my *translator*: the latter word in Burmese had connotations of 'traitor' dating back to colonial days, he claimed. He was fanatical about appearances. Much later, after a reunion at a Rangoon restaurant, Hseng hailed a taxi to take us to a nightclub less than 200 yards away. As he explained, 'If you arrive by walking everyone will think you a small man.' He was amazed I didn't know this.

Our route into the hills led past a quarry where a road crew was breaking down boulders, a process that began with a grinding machine and ended with a mother and child armed with tiny pickaxes, grimly absorbed in the Sisyphean task of rendering pebbles into gravel. Women in bright sarongs bore away the gravel in baskets on their heads to fill in holes on the Burma Road, which was pulverised daily by hundreds of overloaded trucks. We were travelling in what could be considered Burma's national car: a second-hand Toyota Corolla estate with beefed-up suspension, which still bore the logo of the Japanese firm that had recently owned it. The cars are right-hand drive, because in Japan you drive on the left. The same was true of Burma until General Ne Win, apparently on the advice of his personal astrologer, decreed that motorists should drive on the right. Driving on the right in right-hand-drive cars has made overtaking a perilous art. Happily, our driver was a master. First he pulled up close behind the truck, honking his horn repeatedly. As attention-grabbing devices go, this was as effective as pelting a stegosaurus with Smarties. So the driver swung right, rumbling along the stony verge, to snatch a peek at the road ahead; it was all clear. Then he violently swung the wheel to the left and gunned the engine, hooting maniacally at the truck until we were safely past. Sometimes, just as we pulled alongside, the truck driver would sound his horn, and my eyeballs would rattle in their sockets.

It was with some relief that we stopped at a roadside shrine to pay our respects to Ko Myo Shin, the chief nat or spirit of the Shan and a patron of travellers. Ko Myo Shin was rendered in English as 'Lord of the Nine Towns'. In Shan State, said Hseng authoritatively, nine passengers will never travel together for fear of angering him, although he can be fooled if a doll is brought along to make the number ten.

The shrine was a substantial one-storey building, where Ko

Myo Shin took pride of place on an altar milling with figurines. His golden statuette was wrapped in billowing robes of pink taffeta and garlands of jasmine; on a pedestal below was a sumptuous arrangement of votive coconuts and sprigs of holy eugenia. A male custodian, chanting softly, stuffed banknotes between the statuette's fingers. Nats were worshipped as the spirits of dead nobles or folk heroes. Those who had not died violently – for example, burned at the stake, savaged by a tiger, devoured by leprosy, or poisoned by a viper – had died improbably. One nat called Lady Golden Flanks expired from grief caused by her errant lover. The inaptly named Lord of the Swing died falling off one. The Lord Minhkaung of Taungoo was killed by an overwhelming smell of onions. The manner of their deaths made nats wicked and vengeful, and lavish offerings were required to placate them. The eleventh-century King Anawratha declared there to be only thirty-seven nats, but local folklore added hundreds of so-called 'outside' nats to create a baffling, constantly evolving pantheon. Connoisseurs identified nats by their costumes, or by the weapon or instrument they carried, or by their posture – triumphantly astride an elephant, for instance, or, in the case of a Burmese king who joined the nat realm after a fatal bout of dysentery, bent double and clearly in some distress. The cult of nats enjoyed a revival during King Thibaw's reign, and when the British took him away the gilded nat images at Mandalay Palace were said to have shed human tears.

'I know this one,' said Hseng.

He was pointing to a sword-wielding figure on a horse guarded by gremlins with hefty mallets. It was U Min Kyaw: rogue, rogerer and opium smoker. Hseng knew him better as the nat of gambling. Burma's underground lottery was based on the result of the bimonthly Thai lottery and run by a vast network of brokers, and before each draw Hseng would visit his local nat shrine to propitiate U Min Kyaw with a bottle of Johnnie Walker. The nat never repaid the favour. Hseng was almost bankrupted by several huge pay-outs, and narrowly avoided a seven-year jail sentence for illegal bookmaking.

'The pure Shan man does not believe in nats,' pronounced Hseng bravely. 'Thirty-seven nats inside, thirty-seven nats outside – it's very confusing. I believe in Buddha only.' A Buddha image sat in an alcove next to the nat shrine, and while Hseng knelt and prayed before it I wandered off to take photographs. When I returned he was standing in front of the nat shrine, reverentially wafting the figurines with a bamboo fan.

'Hseng, I thought you said you didn't believe in nats.'

'I don't,' he said cheerfully. 'But my mother says, even if you believe or not, you must be very careful. Some nats are very dangerous.'

Two hours after leaving the sweltering plains we arrived at Maymyo to the most English of welcomes: drizzle. Hseng and I checked into a government-run hotel, which in colonial times had been a company lodge. It must have been a company of giants, because my room was Brobdingnagian. I could have practised pole-vaulting in it. The bathroom was slightly smaller, but had an even higher ceiling; I felt as if I were relieving myself at the foot of a missile silo. The toilet had not been disturbed for months, and made angry, roaring noises when it flushed. I quickly learned to depress the handle at arm's length and make a sprint for the wide open plains of the bedroom.

I hired a bicycle at the hotel, and set out along Circular Road. It made sense that Taw Paya, a living relic of Burma's royal past, stayed in Maymyo. Much of the town had the oddly deserted feel of a museum. Odder still, all the houses seemed to have been fashioned after my aunt's place in Reigate. Instead of building airy colonial bungalows, the British put up street after street of red-brick mansions with mock-Tudor facades and strategic privet hedges – middle-class dream homes rising from the jungles of South-East Asia. Now many were owned by military top brass – General Ne Win was said to have a summer house here – or by the dubiously rich, which often amounted to the same thing. The houses looked unlived in or unloved, and cycling past their weed-choked driveways felt eerie and dislocating, like visiting Guildford after a mass evacuation.

Few houses had been built when Beth Ellis, a late-Victorian adventurer and contemporary of Scott's, cycled intrepidly along Circular Road in the 1890s. She called it 'this poor new road, wandering aimlessly in the jungle, leading nowhere and used by no one', though prowled by ravenous tigers and giant cobras and gangs of merciless dacoits – or so Ellis secretly hoped. Like later travellers, she found Maymyo a little dull. There was the Club House, of course, but this was a male-only preserve, lodged in an imposing building perched high on a hillside. Squatting at its foot was a tiny one-roomed shack known as the Ladies' Club. 'Here two or more ladies of the station nightly assemble for an hour before dinner,' recalled Ellis, 'to read the two months old magazines, to search vainly through the shelves of the "library" for a book they have not read more than three times, to discuss the iniquities of the native cook, and to pass votes of censure on the male sex for condemning them to such an insignificant building.' A more suitable venue was found as Maymyo developed, for the British would eventually hack from the wilderness a golf course, rugby pitches and, with the help of Turkish prisoners of war, a botanical garden – while all around the jungle frothed and seethed, waiting for a chance to invade again.

It waited in vain. The town had grown considerably since colonial times. It was now home to the Defense Services Academy, Burma's answer to Sandhurst, and sober young cadets in violently shined boots strode past me on brisk R & R tours of the streets. Maymyo's centre had the hard-scrabble cosmopolitanism of a Wild West town that the railroad didn't pass through any more. Along the shabby main street I half-expected drunken cowboys to come tumbling out of doorways – except that these weren't saloons but cake shops run by Indian and Nepali Gurkhas, descendants of the imperial troops who subjugated Upper Burma back in Scott's day. They now operated the dairies that supplied Maymyo's milk and yoghurt, as well as the looms that produced the multi-coloured cardigans festooning many downtown shops. The clock tower near the market was built in honour of Queen Victoria, and was said to chime like Big Ben (although I never heard it).

It was not only Britain's past that was preserved at Maymyo. Sitting at a drinks stall, I watched in amazement as an old Chinese woman tottered past me on tiny bound feet, a relic of a feudal practice outlawed in China when Mao Zedong's Communists had swept to power over half a century earlier.

I had met King Thibaw's grandson for the first time two years before. Taw Paya lived in a decaying mock-Tudor mansion just off Circular Road. I had been welcomed at the gate by his middle-aged daughter, who showed me into a dim, high-ceilinged room sparsely furnished with rattan armchairs and a few elephant sculptures. A single light bulb dangled from a crumbling ceiling rosette. Above the disused fireplace I saw a large black-and-white photograph of King Thibaw and Queen Supayalat. The gilt frame was carved with a peacock and a rabbit, both symbols of the Burmese monarchy.

The woman disappeared through a curtained doorway, and I settled in for a long wait. I remembered what Scott had written about Taw Paya's great-grandfather, the pious King Mindon. He liked to make his foreign visitors sit on the floor and wait for so long that their legs went numb; many had to be carried from the court.

The stoical few who remained had the honour of being scrutinised by Mindon through field glasses from twenty feet away.

But then the curtains on the doorway parted and a bemused-looking old man with a few wisps of grey hair scuttled into the room, still buttoning up a pristine white shirt over his deep-purple sarong. He stuck out his hand. 'Hello,' said Taw Paya in a clipped British accent. 'What can I do for you?'

To my relief, he seemed pleased to receive me. Many visitors weren't so welcome. Now in his late seventies, Taw Paya had found that being the oldest living descendant of Thibaw – being the man who, under quite different circumstances, would have been king – had turned him into something of a one-man freak show.

'In the past I was always being trotted out for the Burmese military,' he said. 'Officers would stand there and just gape at me. People like you who come for research, that's fine. But those who come to gape – I just tell them to go away.'

I asked him about the photo of Thibaw on his wall. Wasn't displaying a picture of the old king, even in private, supposed to be illegal in Burma? 'Yes, some military chaps came round and complained,' Taw Paya sniggered. 'But I said to them, "What? You don't have pictures of *your* family on the wall?" They didn't bother me after that.'

A Burmese-speaking friend had told me that the Burmese are the Italians of Asia. This certainly seemed true of Taw Paya, who grew more animated by the minute, gesticulating wildly and punctuating sentences with volleys of chuckles. By the time his daughter set down a lacquerware tray of tea and biscuits on the table between us, he had launched into a spirited defence of Thibaw's first massacre.

'Imagine!' Taw Paya enthused, his eyes brightening. 'There are thirty-seven male heirs who can claim the throne; they won't go quietly; they'll be at each other's throats. And what will happen? The country will suffer.' He shook his head and smiled to himself 'Those were the wild days . . .'

While he spoke, I tried to associate this genial old man with his tyrannical grandfather – but failed miserably.

'Do have a biscuit,' smiled Taw Paya.

King Thibaw arrived in exile with nothing. Well, almost nothing. There were a few trunks containing a diamond-encrusted cradle, a set of solid-gold spittoons and some solid-silver toys for the children, and a dazzling assortment of gems and jewellery which the royal couple pawned off over the years to supplement their British government pensions. Their new home in India was hardly

British officers guide Thibaw onto a steamship at Mandalay.

British officers and Indian troops parade by Mandalay Palace (c. 1890).

palatial, but nor was it spartan. It was a sprawling mansion with 160 staff – none of whom, lamented Thibaw, knew how to roll a cheroot properly.

Isolated from his homeland, the king lived out his days brooding over his fall. You can almost plot the slow extinguishing of his pride by the letters he wrote in India. In his earlier correspondence Thibaw demanded the immediate return of household items left behind in Mandalay, including 'one large sofa made entirely of gold' and 'four complete sets of trappings for elephants decorated with rubies'. These letters were signed defiantly 'From His Most Excellent and August King Thibaw of Burma'. By 1911 he was reduced to making a grovelling appeal to George V for an increase in his monthly allowance of 5,500 rupees – 'a small pittance for a former sovereign', he humbly ventured. Bowing to British pressure, he now signed his letters 'Ex-King Thibaw.'

Thibaw died at the age of fifty-eight of a heart attack, possibly brought on by the news that one of his four daughters had eloped with his private secretary. In 1916 Queen Supayalat returned to Rangoon, where one of the remaining daughters married a Buddhist scholar and gave birth to six children, one of them Taw Paya. He spent some of his early boyhood in Mandalay. 'When I was young we used to go and play in the palace. We used to go every weekend, until my parents made a fuss about Thibaw's private property and the British sent us to Moulmein. Exiled us!' He and his siblings were monitored closely by the British, who feared that the fledgling royals could become rallying figures for increasingly vocal Burmese nationalists. The colonial authorities separated Taw Paya from his parents and educated him in various boarding schools across the country.

'We were always shunted off here and there,' he recalled indignantly. 'The British had no concern for what today you would call human rights. We were told what to do and what not to do. Even if we wanted to go shopping we had to apply to the sub-divisional officer and he would take us around everywhere.'

The full injustice of these restrictions first struck home when Taw Paya and two of his brothers were chosen to play for their school football team at an away match. 'One brother was a good left-footer, which was very rare in those days,' he said. 'The other was a centre forward, a very good player, although a bit on the short side.' Taw Paya played on the left wing – or would have done if the district commissioner had not forbidden the young princes from travelling. The away match was cancelled. 'We got a real cursing from the rest of the players,' he said.

When he left school Taw Paya had to fend for himself. Gone were the privileged days when all rubies above a certain size found anywhere in Burma automatically belonged to the royal family. Taw Paya went into the jade business, calling his company the Thibaw Commercial Syndicate.

'I thought if we could start selling Burmese jade we'd make a killing,' he said. 'Burmese jade is the best in the world. It's the hardest, you see. Chinese jade is like wax.' And for a while the Thibaw Commercial Syndicate thrived and life was good. 'In those days we had servants galore,' he said dreamily. 'Servants, gardeners, cooks . . . '

At that moment the single light bulb above us blinked out. A power cut.

Taw Paya ignored it. 'But then we ran out of luck,' he sighed. So did Burma. It was 1962, and General Ne Win had just seized power.

The Ne Win regime nationalised industry as part of a disastrous economic programme called 'The Burmese Way to Socialism'. Only state-run enterprises could now deal in jade. The Thibaw Commercial Syndicate went out of business overnight.

Taw Paya has no royal inheritance – no elephant trappings to pawn, no golden spittoons tucked away in the attic. 'I have nothing of my grandparents,' he said. 'The British considered us absentee landlords, so all our property was confiscated. Even the palace sweepers got some land. We chaps, the descendants, we got nothing.'

Like Thibaw himself, Taw Paya wrote angry letters to the British, including Churchill, Attlee and a young Queen Elizabeth, protesting that he and his siblings had 'lost their rightful prerogative and dignity of birthright and suffered all sorts of indignities and inconveniences'. He sought information about a host of missing heirlooms that he still insisted had been swiped by a British colonel after annexation. He received no reply. He also claimed that the British destroyed documents in Mandalay Palace which would have proved his family's entitlement to various properties and land. 'The British annexed Burma in the cold season, you see, and the Indian soldiers who guarded the palace felt the cold. They burned all the royal manuscripts to keep them warm.'

'Do you feel bitter about how the British treated you?' I asked.

'At times we felt the British were a bit unkind to us,' he replied. 'But it's no use crying over spilt milk.'

I wondered, would the monarchy still be around if the Brits hadn't removed it?

'No,' said Taw Paya firmly. 'One way or another, someone would have come and taken this little country away. If not Britain, then France. And perhaps we were lucky. Look at Vietnam today. Or Cambodia. The French were worse. At least the British had good administration. And their diplomacy takes the cake.'

Taw Paya did inherit something less tangible yet utterly unique from his royal forebears: he and his children still communicate with each other in a special form of courtly Burmese that outsiders find completely unintelligible. This means that in Taw Paya's household, as in Thibaw's court, nobody goes for a walk; instead they 'make royal progress'. Nobody eats either; they 'ascend to the lordly board'. Taw Paya was clearly quite tickled by all this. 'Nobody else can understand us,' he chuckled.

King Mindon had been less amused by an English mill manager who, while fluent in everyday Burmese, forgot about its courtly variation during an audience with the King. Scott recounted the anecdote with relish: 'This gentleman, in replying in the affirmative to some remark of the king, horrified the court by saying *hokde* instead of the prescribed *tin-ba payah*, meaning "I think with your majesty." This expression was much the same as if someone were to say to His Majesty the King of England, "Right you are, old cockie." '

The mysterious fate of Thibaw's crown jewels was still a favourite topic of propaganda issued by the Burmese regime. At a Rangoon bookstall I picked up a pamphlet entitled *Cruel and Vicious Repression of Myanmar Peoples by Imperialists and Fascists and the True Story about the Plunder of the Royal Jewels*. It was published by a branch of government with a truly Orwellian name: the Committee for Propaganda and Agitation to Intensify Patriotism.

Thibaw's lost trappings were of great personal interest to General Ne Win. The old despot always claimed to have some royal blood, and was even married for a while to a genuine Burmese princess called June Rose. In the 1960s, during an official visit to Britain, Ne Win persuaded the Victoria & Albert Museum to return 140 items of Burmese royal regalia, including crowns, costumes and ceremonial yak-hair whisks. When he returned to Rangoon, I was told, Ne Win descended the aircraft steps like a returning conqueror, triumphantly bearing the great sword of Alaungpaya – a weapon which, according to legend, was blunted by the slaughter of Burma's many enemies. The regalia were now displayed behind iron bars in the National Museum in Rangoon. Or were they? One Burmese historian insisted to me that the regalia were fake, and implied that Ne Win had spirited away the genuine articles for his private collection.

Taw Paya would not be drawn on this, but it was clear what he thought of the 'treasures' in the National Museum. 'Ach, those are the rubbishy regalia!' he said, throwing up his hands. 'Only a few little things are of any value.'

Of more value, perhaps, was the very concept of royalty in Burma. The post-war years saw a campaign to bring Thibaw's remains back from India. It came to nothing – Burma still had no memorial to its last king – but people had been known to pay their respects to Thibaw's throne, which was also in the National Museum. Even now, over a century after the Burmese monarchy fell, Taw Paya received visits from descendants of Thibaw's ministers. Despite his protests, these men always sat respectfully at his feet.

'I tell them to sit up, sit here!' cried Taw Paya, slapping the empty seat beside him. 'But they are not comfortable, so they sit on the floor.'

Taw Paya received another astonishing show of respect in the northern town of Shwebo, the ancient birthplace of many Burmese kings. Back in the 1960s the Burmese military had ordered him to speak at an anti-Communist rally there. As Taw Paya stepped from his car to walk to the podium, awe-struck local women knelt down and spread their long black hair on the ground to form a carpet for him to walk upon. Taw Paya was whisked away by soldiers, and never addressed any more government rallies. The regime wanted a supine propaganda tool, not a popular rival to its authority.

'There is some sentimentality about the old kings,' admitted Taw Paya, but when I suggested that a serious restoration movement might gather steam in a free and democratic Burma he started shaking his head. 'Royalty has gone out of fashion,' he said solemnly. 'It's not the time for despots to rule over the country.' I looked at him. He blinked.

'Of course!' he cried. 'We've got despots now!' He dissolved into high-pitched giggles. 'Worse than despots!'

Taw Paya was wrong about one thing: royalty had not gone out of fashion in Burma. If anything, the opposite was true. Small pictures of Thibaw with his queen were still sold as lucky charms at temples and lottery booths across the country. As for the generals, they adored royalty, or at any rate the pomp and ritual associated with it. At a diplomatic reception in Rangoon an 'abasement dance' had been performed before the generals – a type of homage not seen since Thibaw's last days. Recently, too, with the help of Chinese

Convicts at Mandalay Palace build a road for foreign tourists. (Nic Dunlop)

Lt-Gen. Khin Nyunt, once Burma's despised spy chief. (Dominic Faulder)

film-makers, the regime had made a sweeping, three-hour costume drama about Thibaw's fall. It was called *We Shall Never be Enslaved*. Residents of Mandalay were drafted as extras, and some of them reportedly wept real tears during the filming of the climactic scene in which the British escorted Thibaw from the palace.

This royal epic was a smash at the box office, and was described, inevitably, as Burma's answer to *Titanic*. It could also be described in another way. Young Burmese embraced Western culture whenever they could, while older Burmese often recalled British rule with nostalgia. Both these trends enraged the junta. Lieutenant General Khin Nyunt, Burma's despised secret-police chief and de-facto leader, was famous for his tirades against the corrupting influence of Western culture, and had even publicly disowned his son for marrying a foreigner. *We Shall Never be Enslaved* was an anti-British film made to stir patriotic pride in Burma's heroic past and remind its people of the evils of colonialism.

In the same spirit, the generals had built a replica palace not only at Mandalay, but also at Pegu and Shwebo, both former royal capitals. At Pegu an archaeological site which held many clues to life in the ancient town was tragically ruined when tons of concrete was poured on top to create a foundation for a replica of dubious historical accuracy. But then these projects had nothing to do with preserving Burmese history. Their primary purpose was to 'revive and maintain national patriotism', as the regime's propagandists put it. They also served to legitimise the military's self-appointed role as the undisputed guardian of national identity. Having conquered Burma's present, the generals now wanted to conquer Burma's past.

The most extraordinary example of this was the strange case of the Pondaung Bones. At Pondaung, a place not far from Mandalay, two Burmese geologists had unearthed some very old fossils which seemed to suggest that a very early form of humanoid had once lived in Burma. The wily Khin Nyunt realised that, potentially, the Pondaung Bones had immense propaganda value. What if they were actual proof that all mankind originated in Burma? Such a discovery would, he announced, 'greatly enhance the stature of the country in the world'. An archaeological team was immediately dispatched to Pondaung under the direction of Khin Nyunt's spies. Their findings were inconclusive: while millions of years old, the fossils hardly proved that the first man was a Burman. But why let science get in the way? 'It can be assumed that human civilisation began in our motherland,' the regime declared. For the generals, the bones had the totemic value of a Buddhist relic, and were subsequently enshrined at the National Museum. Tellingly, the other prominent exhibit was King Thibaw's throne.

The regime had shown less interest in Thibaw's bones – they still lay in a dilapidated tomb at Ratnagiri in India – although dead monarchs did have their uses. The junta was promoting as a new national hero an ancient king called Bayinnaung, whose forces plundered Thailand in the sixteenth century. The regime had erected sword-brandishing statues of Bayinnaung outside the National Museum and (rather undiplomatically) at two places along Burma's border with Thailand.

The sudden popularity of King Bayinnaung was puzzling. Why delve so deep into the past to find a national hero, when the country already had one? He was Aung San, the architect of Burma's independence from Britain, whose assassination in 1947 marked for many Burmese the moment their country began to fall apart. But Aung San was also the father of democracy leader Aung San Suu Kyi – which was precisely why the junta was so keen to erase his memory. He was rarely mentioned in official speeches now, and his face had disappeared from all the banknotes.

While dead royals were valuable to the junta, live ones were more trouble than they were worth. Taw Paya's usefulness ended on a carpet of human hair in Shwebo; his younger brother had spent many years in prison for his Communist sympathies, for which he had earned the nickname 'The Red Prince'. The military government, like the British before them, still feared the residual sway that Burma's royals had over the people.

Taw Paya had attended the Rangoon premiere of *We Shall Never be Enslaved*. He wasn't impressed. 'It's just a story, that's all,' he shrugged. But later I heard that he had sat in the darkened movie theatre with tears rolling down his cheeks.

It had been nearly two years since that first encounter with Taw Paya. I took longer than expected to find his house again. The garden had been chopped back for the winter and was almost unrecognisable. Taw Paya appeared slightly reduced too – a little frailer, and with fewer teeth. Otherwise he was on good form, and his eyes had lost none of their sparkle.

'So,' he smiled, leaning back in the same armchair in the same dim room decorated with family portraits, 'you came back.'

Since our first meeting I had come across another claimant to King Thibaw's throne. He was a vulpine Burman in a pinstriped suit who called himself Shwebo Min. I had met him, at his request, at the unlikely venue of the Latvian Welfare Club in Bayswater.

While we talked, his foxy French assistant, Véronique, sat nearby patiently studying her Gothic fingernails.

Taw Paya was not surprised to hear of a potential rival. 'People are very ignorant of Burmese royal history, and will believe everything if you can put on a good show,' he said cheerfully. The name 'Shwebo Min' – it meant 'Shwebo King' – certainly smacked of showmanship. The 'Taw' in 'Taw Paya' was a subtler signifer of royal status. 'If I use my name in the countryside, crowds will come and sit down to listen to what I have to say,' said Taw Paya. 'One of those Communist chaps said he didn't want to call me by my royal name.' His face suddenly darkened. 'I said, Look here, call me anything, just don't call me a dog or *I'll punch you in the face.*' He smiled again. 'One Burmese official,' he mused, 'used to call me Tommy.'

I had brought Taw Paya a gift – Kitty Kelly's sensational biography of the British royals – and this got us talking about the fall of the House of Windsor.

'It's a pity,' he remarked. 'Modern values have entered the family – the children can't behave. Now Edward is the only bachelor left.'

'Actually, Edward's married now.'

'Really? When?'

I told him. 'Oh,' he said, a little crestfallen. 'I didn't read it in the newspapers.'

I once asked Taw Paya if he had visited Mandalay Palace in recent years. He said he had, several times, although it was usually a frustrating experience.

'When I go to the palace, I always clash with the military chaps,' he frowned. 'They say I can't go here, I can't go there. I tell them, "This is my grandfather's place! Don't you know your own history?"'

I left Maymyo with that image in my head – of Taw Paya, the uncrowned king of Burma, striding into that stronghold for the all-powerful Burmese military and getting all bolshy and proprietorial. He was the only man left in all Burma who could possibly get away with it.

4

Later that evening I met up with Hseng and got stupid-drunk on thick damson-fruit wine, a local speciality. On the way back to the hotel we stopped off for a few plates of barbecued pigs' tails – Burma's answer to a late-night kebab, I suppose, except crunchier – and in the morning I found myself swaying with nausea on a station platform, waiting for a train, my stomach feeling as if I had swallowed rubble. Hseng, who had his Shan pride to think about, sat in a nearby teashop manfully eating sticky cakes dipped in condensed milk to prove how fantastic he felt.

Someone hammered on a fragment of rail hanging not far from my fragile head, and then the train slowly emerged through a curtain of wood smoke. Old women squatting on the betel-splattered platform heaved baskets of tomatoes and onions onto their heads and bullied their way on board. Their baskets safely stowed, they removed the load-bearing scarves from their heads, rewrapped them loosely around their necks, and curled up around contemplative cheroots. The luggage racks were stuffed with bundles of purple-and-white flowers, another Maymyo speciality, and their delicate scent filled the cabin – until the toilets reached critical mass. The train gave an animal shudder and then moved off. As we picked up speed, the man in the seat behind me held his pet monkey out of the window until it chattered with terror.

A monochrome morning etched with pine trees unscrolled outside. High on a hillside I could make out a large tin shed which one would never guess held one of Burma's most revered Buddha statues. The enormous statue was on its way to China on the back of a truck when, just outside Maymyo, the truck skidded and the statue fell off. Rather than blame this on execrable driving, the accident was widely interpreted as a divine message: the Buddha loved Burma so much that he didn't want to go to China. A crane and a platoon of monks were required to coax the statue into an upright position and then persuade it to move to the purpose-built shed, which was named Pyi Chit Paya – literally, 'Country Love Pagoda'. I saw photographs of the Buddha all over Burma. Worshipping the image was an act of both religious devotion and patriotism. It was also, I suspected, a private protest against the mainland Chinese who had come to dominate commercial life under the generals. There were now plans to move the Buddha statue to a grander temple nearby. 'But whether or not he wants to move,' Taw Paya had told me, 'nobody knows.'

A plum vendor swept through the carriage dispensing free handfuls of his produce in the hope someone would buy a few pounds. Next, a thin man with a haunting face stood at the centre of the carriage holding aloft the wrinkled pit of another fruit, which, he declared in a sombre chant befitting a Greek chorus, cured muscular aches and bad skin and a hundred other maladies. Vendors constantly plied the aisles with snacks of all descriptions – sticky rice roasted in bamboo, tongue-numbing chilli and sour-tea salads, rice crackers as big as your head. I was happy to note that the Shan shared the same passion for snacks as their ethnic cousins the Thais, who consider it madness to embark on even a short trip without enough sustenance for a journey of intergalactic distance.

At the far end of the carriage sat the soldiers: armed, sleek, hostile. I guessed that some were recent graduates of Maymyo's military academy. Earlier I had watched them on the platform. Some had stood alone, while others had grouped into silent conspiracies of khaki; none of them had mixed with the civilians. I wondered what the academy had taught them. 'They spend four years getting brainwashed, and when they come out they expect all civilians to behave like soldiers,' a Burmese dissident told me later. 'But of course we don't want to behave like soldiers. *That's why we chose to remain civilians.* But they think they are the greatest people in Burma. They think they know what's best for the rest of us. They don't.' Casual visitors to Burma are unaware of the visceral hatred most people have for the military, particularly among ethnic minorities. The same dissident told me how a group of Kachin farmers stood by and watched as six young Burmese soldiers writhed in agony in the wreckage of a crashed army truck. When the dissident's sister, who had witnessed the crash, pleaded with the farmers to do something, one of them chillingly replied, 'Why should we? They will only live to make our lives worse. It is better to let them die.'

As far as I could work out, the military seemed utterly unaware of its unpopularity, although its guardians were alert to any potential blots on the escutcheon. I had heard, for example, that Burmese cartoonists working for newspapers or magazines were forbidden to draw men in trousers. This was because the only Burmese men who wore trousers were soldiers, and soldiers could not possibly be allowed to appear in such an undignified and dangerously satirical art form.

The train trundled through fields of sugar cane and scorched paddy towards distant hills patched with cloud shadow. Hseng spat messily out of the window, wiped his mouth, grinned, and slapped his forehead theatrically.

'What a dickhead,' he said. It was a phrase I regretted teaching him.

Our destination was the Shan town of Hsipaw. Since Hseng had never been to northern Shan State before, the prospect gave him a patriotic kick. He had already chatted up two young women who had got on at the last station and now sat opposite us, giggling.

'Now the Burma ladies,' he said to me, 'They love the Shan men. Why? Let me tell you. Because the Shan men are very honest and open and have soft skin.'

'What about the Shan ladies,' I asked, nodding at the girls. 'Do they love the Shan men?'

'The Shan ladies?' asked Hseng in mock astonishment. 'Of course they do.' He grinned winningly at the girls. 'Shan ladies, they are very beautiful also, because their mothers teach them to walk slow and gracefully and stepping softly, just like an elephant.'

Scott spent the early months of his colonial career in the gruelling pursuit of elusive dacoits through the monsoon-lashed jungles around Hlaingdet, on the edge of the great Shan plateau our train was now crossing. Hlaingdet had been a Burmese outpost against bellicose Shan highlanders for over 700 years. It was a god-forsaken place, stalked by disease, and Scott marvelled that the imperial troops stationed there 'did not all die of the badness of the water'.

But Hlaingdet was also the starting point for the Shan States Expedition of 1887, the first major British foray into Shan territory. The force that left there in January that year under Colonel Stedman included 250 men of the Hampshires, 50 Bombay Sappers and Miners, and a battalion of Gurkhas, along with an army of coolies, mule drivers and elephants. Scott, who reconnoitred the expedition's route through the uncharted hills, joined as assistant political officer. The 'pacification' of the Shan had begun.

While few Europeans had travelled in Shan territory, the British already knew something of the Shan. They used to call themselves Tai, and enjoyed their first apogee in the seventh century with the founding of the Tai kingdom of Nan-chao in what is now China's Yunnan Province. The capital of Nan-chao was a formidable walled city called Talifu, where the Tai monarch ventured forth in the shade of a parasol of kingfisher feathers accompanied by dignitaries cloaked in tiger skin, and where women (according to Scott's interpretation of a disapproving Chinese chronicle) 'were very easy previous to marriage' and were executed for any infidelity during it. However, none of this much impressed Kublai Khan, whose Tartar hordes flattened the Nan-chao kingdom in 1253. By now the Tai were on the move. They swarmed south and east into what is now Laos, northern Vietnam and – the greatest of all Tai kingdoms – Thailand. (The word 'Shan' is actually a Burmese corruption of 'Siam', the old name for Thailand.) The Tai who migrated westward began to populate the plateau of rugged hills and lush valleys that would be called the Shan hills.

Here they formed themselves into over thirty states, each with a hereditary ruler called a saopha or 'lord of the sky'. Even today the saophas are lesser known than their princely counterparts elsewhere in the British Empire – the maharajas of India – although the two sets of feudal rulers resembled each other in a number of ways. Like the Indian princes, many Shan saophas maintained opulent courts with arcane ceremonies and well-stocked harems. Both sets of rulers were feared and revered by their rural subjects, over whom they traditionally wielded the power of life and death. Both would submit to British power in return for limited self-rule, then set about emulating their new overlords. Both, ultimately, would be defeated by history.

By the time Scott arrived on the scene the saophas held sway over a landlocked region larger than England and Wales combined. The Shan states were neither united nor wholly independent: each saopha paid tribute to either Burma or China, depending on whether his fiefdom lay east or west of the ferocious Salween River, which roughly bisected Shan territory. The states varied vastly in size and power: Namtok was a pint-sized hamlet of 100 or so peasants, while Kengtung was a rich and influential principality the size of Belgium.

The British could not plot the boundaries of these states with any certainty, and knew even less about the many tribes who lived among the Shan. Nor could they grasp the shifting alliances and endless feuds between the various saophas. The ostensible mission of the 1887 Shan States Expedition was to rescue the besieged saopha of Yawnghwe State from rival Shan forces. Internecine wars in the Shan states had razed villages, destroyed farmland and laid waste whole states. A year before the expedition set out, a man-made famine in the Laikha area had killed 3,000 people, a pitiful state of affairs for a land so fertile that, as the saying went, a farmer tickled the earth with his hoe and it laughed a harvest.

The Shan States Expedition wound up into the hills, leaving the sweltering Burman plains far below. Now there were pine trees and crisp air and frost in the mornings – a climate that might have reminded Scott of his native country. Indeed, a colonial traveller to the Shan hills described them as a 'tropical Scotland'. Not that

Scott had much time to appreciate the scenery. Shan resistance fighters had blocked the expedition's route with felled trees and bamboo spikes. Even with the Sappers to cut paths, shifting the mountain guns and other supplies through the hills required patience and effort – and, added Scott, 'much bad language'.

Official reports, written with the usual Olympian detachment, made the expedition seem like a stroll to the pub. A more vibrant account was provided by Scott's jungle diaries in the British Library. I had spent many afternoons (and much bad language) trying to read them. Scott recorded his impressions in microscopic handwriting on the rice-paper pages of duplicate books. (A doting son, he always sent a carbon copy to his mother – 'The Mum', he called her.) 'Most valuable and interesting,' fudged a Shan saopha to whom Scott gave them to read, 'but oh, my dear fellow, why write with a pointless pencil in a dark room?' The diaries were written in a breathless shorthand that captured the cut and thrust of Scott's mission:

(2 Jan. 1887) Col. Stedman of the Gurkhas very energetic. Likely to hurry the expedition up. Dined with Tucker in the evening; Vyse and Joseph there. Got on very well. Capital dry sherry.

(15 Jan.) Thick jungle. About 12 started up the gorge. Terribly blocked with trees but apart from that boulders make it impassable. One man shot on the right flank; then Gurkhas got sight of them, killed two and wounded another. Evg., bother about dinner.

(27 Jan.) Nankon. They opened fire on us at about 700 yards, bullets about. Yelled defiance at us. Fled at first shell. One friendly killed. I saved a village full of them. Afterwards got the Colonel to give the dead man's wife Rp. [rupees] 100. Camp dined off my stores again.

Although Scott had orders to avoid fighting whenever possible, villages which resisted the British advance or were suspected of harbouring rebels were mercilessly shelled or put to the torch, while Gurkhas fanned out from the main column to hunt down gangs of dacoits. The hills grew increasingly tough to climb as Scott's party penetrated deeper into Shan territory. 'The Gurkhas did it easily,' Scott recalled, 'as they are born hillmen. I wasn't going to be beaten by Gurkhas. So just to show it was nothing to me, I used to go up as fast as they did, and smoking my pipe all the time.' Most Shan villagers offered no opposition to the British. They lived to hear the deeply perplexing news, delivered by a short, bearded Scotsman wearing a pith helmet as big as a washbasin, that they were now subjects of a queen who lived over 6,000 miles away. 'Assembled all the villagers,' Scott wrote in his diary, 'men, women and children, about 30 in all, and made them an oration, and gave the smallest baby a rupee, which it promptly swallowed.' So the battle for hearts and minds was won.

Five weeks after setting off the Shan States Expedition approached the town of Yawnghwe, where it was met by the saopha. 'Thick-set short man, freckled face,' Scott noted. 'Small half-closed bright eyes, but unpleasant looking. Professed great delight at our arrival.' The saopha rode a magnificently caparisoned elephant shaded by five gold umbrellas and flanked by palace guards 'armed with comic opera weapons, tridents and pikes and spears festooned with horse hair dyed red'. Later, Scott rode into Yawnghwe on one of the saopha's elephants, an honour that almost ended in disaster when the beast was startled by a new and terrifying sound: Gurkha bagpipes.

Not all Shan rulers professed such delight at the British arrival. The saopha of Lawksawk had vowed to raise a man from every household in his state to resist the British. His forces were dug in at a mountain-top stockade, ringed with booby-trapped trenches. Scott's advance party stealthily approached by moonlight, hoping to catch the rebels unawares, but 'found most of them much more wideawake than I had expected'. British artillery began blazing, and the one-sided assault ended with twenty-four Shan dead and three soldiers of the Hampshire Regiment wounded. 'Had some sandwiches,' Scott recorded in his diary, 'and then went on.' During another assault on a Shan stockade, Scott blundered into the firing line and, once there, decided he 'might as well' do something dramatic. Pausing twice – first to extract from his puttees a bamboo spike which almost took his foot off, then to relight his pipe – he walked up to the stockade and delivered a brief speech to the rebels which began with that Great British plea for reasonableness 'Look here . . .' The rebels gave up soon after. 'Got in just after dark,' Scott wrote that night – 'doosed fagged.'

The British established a frontier post at Yawnghwe called Fort Stedman. This was the springboard for Scott and his men to plunge deeper into Shan territory. He sought out other chiefs and persuaded them of the wisdom of swearing allegiance to the Queen Empress. At the town of Thaton, at the saopha's bidding, Scott ran a British flag up a makeshift bamboo flagpole and the entire population bowed before it. At Mawk Mai he arrived to find the saopha lying in state with musical boxes at his head and feet playing 'There's Nae Luck Aboot the Hoose' and other tunes then popular in Britain, while a bevy of palace maidens fanned the corpse to keep the flies off. Scott swore in the dead saopha's son.

The most serious challenge to early British rule in the Shan states came in the unlikely guise of Prince Limbin. He was the handsome, foppish son of a Burmese crown prince and a palace dancing girl. He had escaped King Thibaw's massacre in 1879 by fleeing Mandalay Palace disguised as a woman – shades of Bonnie Prince Charlie there – and dreamed of one day claiming the Burmese throne for himself. Still in his twenties, and not renowned for his smarts, Limbin forged a strategic alliance with several dispossessed Shan saophas whose combined forces had devastated northern Burma. But, as the rainy season began, rumours percolated down from the hills that Limbin had tired of jungle life and the rough company of the saophas, and was ready to surrender – if the price was right. Fortunately, Scott already knew the man who now styled himself 'King of the Ninety and Nine Gold Umbrella-bearing Rulers'. He had tutored the prince at St John's College in Rangoon. 'He was a lymphatic person and little inclined for war and camping,' was his unsparing appraisal. Scott assembled a contingent of fifty or so men and made a seventy-mile dash along unmapped paths to the war-ravaged town of Mongnai, where the prince now sat in state.

And what a state that was. Limbin's palace was a mat shed decorated with shiny paper, his throne a rough wooden dais disguised by a German rug. After heated negotiations with Scott, the prince agreed to surrender, but only if he could have his ceremonial gong regilded – a privilege reserved for royalty – and ride back to Fort Stedman on an elephant. Scott agreed. So Limbin left Mongnai on a swaying golden howdah shaded by a royal white canopy and flanked by Indian troops. 'All this finery was to throw dust in the eyes of the poorer sort and make them think this a Progress instead of a Submission,' explained Scott. 'The Prince looked on the sepoys who were put over him on guard as a personal distinction.' The journey was punishing, and, with the elephant travelling at a leisurely two miles per hour, took over a week – the prince 'grumbling like a baby' all the way. From Fort Stedman he would follow King Thibaw into exile in India, where the British nobly permitted him (as Scott put it) 'to vegetate in Calcutta, on an allowance'.

With the surrender of Prince Limbin, and the break-up of the Shan alliance he nominally led, all the southern Shan states were firmly in British hands. While the rest of Burma – or what the Brits called 'Burma proper' – came under direct colonial rule, the saophas were granted the same system of limited self-rule as India's maharajas, and continued to run their own affairs, albeit under British supervision. They could raise taxes and dispense justice, but – and here was the catch – all the natural resources of their states now belonged to the Crown.

It wasn't much of a deal: you get to keep your royal spittoon bearers, your umpteen wives and your ceremonial yak-hair whisk; we get all your teak, jade, gems and silver. But then that's colonialism for you. And the Shan saophas, fatally enfeebled by centuries of in-fighting, had no strength left to argue.

The train arrived at Hsipaw in the late afternoon, and Hseng and I strode into town along the deserted main street – trailing long, thin shadows and feeling like gunslingers. We refueled at a Chinese restaurant, then found beds at a cheap rest house on the Burma Road, where the room partitions shuddered with trucks rumbling past to Lashio or Mandalay. I was awoken before dawn by the high moan of sticky-rice sellers, carried with haunting clarity through the damp air. Then began the morning chorus of Burmese truckers hawking and gobbing at the wash area downstairs.

It was an awesome performance. A decade before, while interviewing people in post-revolutionary Eastern Europe, I had come to suspect there was a connection between spitting and dictatorship. It was not entirely implausible that the way in which people spat in some way reflected the kind of government they'd endured. For example, the Romanians gobbed seldom but copiously, punctuating their political statements with great phlegmy commas of disgust; the Albanians spat little but often, as if trying to get a nasty taste out of their mouths, a nervous tic developed over years of mad-house isolation; and so on.

But this idle hypothesis fell to pieces in Hsipaw. The Burmese truckers had no single method of evacuating their tubes. There was nothing immediately political about their vastly differing styles either, unless you interpreted them as unfettered expressions of individuality. Because these men – they were *artists*. They not only put the oyster in the sink; they put mussels, they put clams, they put the whole prawn cocktail. One man summoned a bath sponge from his gullet; another, after much effort, successfully ejected a loofah. Somebody gurgled marbles, then shot them one by one into a metal basin with a mulled *ping*. Somebody else impersonated an ageing cappuccino machine. The combined effect was symphonic.

I strolled down to the market in search of breakfast. Hsipaw was an attractive place with a deceptive air of tranquillity. The town was badly bombed during the Second World War – first by the invading Japanese, then by the liberating Allies – but a few of its old teak houses had survived to slumber in the shade of hallowed rain trees. The town's eastern boundary was marked by a river the colour of antique jade, the feathery profusion of bamboo along the banks reflected perfectly in its undisturbed depths. At the market, women in conical hats laid out unfamiliar vegetables and herbs on fresh sheets of banana leaf. There was a traditional Shan chemist selling colourful sachets of powder purporting to cure everything from flatulence to malaria. Another stall sold nothing but flip-flops made from car tyres, a type of universal peasant footwear that Vietnam War reporters knew as 'Ho Chi Minh Specials'. On a table nearby a butcher carefully arranged a variety of animal innards into something that resembled an exploded anatomy diagram, then ruined the whole effect with a large, still-bleeding buffalo leg.

Breakfast, when I found it, was unusual. I chose a bowl of Shan sticky noodles with scraps of meat and a sweet, glutinous sauce. This was topped with crushed peanuts, chopped coriander and a dollop of syrup-like jaggery. I'd never tasted anything like it. It was a sort of collision between a main course and dessert – like eating spaghetti alla carbonara and custard at the same time.

At the market, I had hoped to spot members of the hill tribes who lived around Hsipaw. I was out of luck. The only man I saw wearing traditional ethnic dress was an old farmer in baggy Shan trousers, and he was eyeing up a pair of tracksuit bottoms from a Chinese soccer strip. The most prominent tribe were backpackers. There were never more than a dozen foreigners in Hsipaw at any one time, but it was a small town and we stood out. Hsipaw had been erratically promoted as a destination for hill-tribe treks, but the authorities had forbidden foreigners to stay overnight in nearby villages, thereby removing one of the chief attractions of trekking. If they wished, tourists could travel further east to Lashio, their last permitted stop on the Burma Road, but the people of Hsipaw seemed actively to discourage this. 'Lashio?' I was told repeatedly. 'That's just a Chinese town.' Yes, I thought, and so is Shanghai.

So the tourists just hung about. I saw the same bored posse constantly circulating the dusty lanes of Hsipaw. They shuffled along the sun-baked main street and past the shady corner where the rickshaw-wallahs snoozed and along the Burma Road for a bit, and then back to the main street again – all in the evident hope that they might discover a new suburb, or perhaps a Tesco Metro, or just something unnoticed during the previous circuits.

Hsipaw was actually a fascinating place, although very little of its often tragic history was meant for tourist consumption. It was one of the five great Shan states, given strategic value by the Burma Road that ran through it. For centuries Hsipaw had been both a bridge and a barrier to relations between the Shan people and their lowland overlords – be they Burman or British. Hkun Hseng, the great saopha of Hsipaw, was the first Shan ruler to submit to British rule. He could trace his family's origins to 'fairy princes and vampire ogresses', wrote Scott, and, like many Shan royals, was brought up in Mandalay Palace. But Hkun Hseng apparently did something to displease the easily displeasable King Thibaw, and wisely fled for Rangoon in 1882. There, rather less wisely, he shot two of his followers for suspected betrayal and, to his astonishment, was arrested by the British and sentenced to death. He was later released on condition that he never again set foot on British soil, whereupon he returned to Hsipaw to rule. After the fall of King Thibaw, Hkun Hseng marched down to Mandalay to formally submit to British rule. He was welcomed with an honourary cavalry escort and a military band.

Hkun Hseng was a shrewd man. He calculated that by bowing to the inevitability of British rule he would receive certain privileges, like new weapons to pester his Shan neighbours with. Scott, whose job it was to warn the incorrigible saopha to use his privileges responsibly, found him exasperating: 'He had fits of madness brought on by disease of the eyes and the savage remedies, red pepper among others, employed by native doctors to cure him.' Later Hkun Hseng traveled to London for medical treatment and became the first Shan chief, and maybe even the first convicted murderer, to meet Queen Victoria.

With Hsipaw safely nuzzled in the imperial bosom, Hkun Hseng's son and successor reigned in an era of unprecedented tranquillity. Sao Hke – later Sir Sao Hke – set about perfecting a lavish and benevolent form of feudal rule which preserved on a smaller scale the glories of the Burmese court. He took about forty wives – sources disagree on the exact number – and sat on a jewel-encrusted golden throne modelled on King Thibaw's. The removal of Thibaw threw royal musicians and entertainers out of work, and many found patrons among the Shan saophas. Whenever Sir Sao Hke's volcanic tantrums sent his officials fleeing from the Hsipaw throne room, his young Mandalay-trained singer was frantically searched for and then pushed through the door. Her divine voice would unfailingly restore the good humour of the great man.

An official portrait reveals Sir Sao Hke to be – surprisingly, perhaps – a slim, bookish, rather harmless-looking fellow. But his moustache has villainous twirls, and his eyes stare out through small, gold-framed spectacles with the calculating iciness one would expect from a ruler with the power of life and death over his subjects. In the photo he is wearing Shan national dress – a flamboyantly knotted turban, a fancy embroidered jacket, and billowing Shan trousers – but with a symbolic addition: Oxford brogues. For Sir Sao Hke and many other saophas had only one eye on the court of King Thibaw; the other was on the Court of St James's and the life of the British.

Sir Sao Hke built an enormous neoclassical palace called Sakandar for his wives and children, and in British imperial style he administered his state from there during the hot season, while leopards and tigers padded through the surrounding forest. His son and heir was educated at Rugby, where he was Scott's ward, then went up to Oxford – 'and speaks English like an Englishman', approved Scott (a Scotsman). Other saophas would also live in stately homes, wear bespoke English suits, and send their sons to England's best schools. Their wives learned the piano, ordered stockings from Rowe & Co. in Rangoon, and dreamed of being addressed as 'Lady'. The time-honoured Shan practice of polygamy began to fade out under the British. Only a few saophas braved the withering looks at garden parties to keep the tradition alive. The saopha of southern Hsenwi had fifty wives and was called 'The flower round which the ladies flutter'.

Every March Sir Sao Hke put on his full ceremonial costume – all 100 pounds of it – and hoisted himself upon an elephant to open the famous festival at the Bawgyo Pagoda. People fell to their knees as his splendid procession passed. The festival, one of the biggest in the Shan states, lasted ten days, and drew hundreds of thousands of people – not just Shan, but Kachin, Palaung, Lisu and Pa-O in their dazzling hill-tribe costumes. Village headmen came to honour the saopha and listen to his advice, and perhaps to marvel at his demonstration of the phonograph; thus the affairs of state were run. Then they retired to the state-authorised gambling tents to blow their hard-won income on the four-animals game. There were Indian-rope-trick artists, Chinese cinemas, Shan theatres, music, dancing and drinking, as well as fireworks provided by the saopha. There were endless shops where villagers could buy a year's worth of supplies, such as English cotton, tinned milk, scissors, betel boxes, enamelled plates and – never forgotten among all the worldly fun – gold leaf to plaster in veneration on the pagoda's Buddha image.

The most spectacular event Sir Sao Hke attended was his own funeral, in 1927. His body, probably embalmed in honey like the bodies of other exalted Shan, lay in state for seven days, and thousands came from afar to pay their last respects. His funeral pyre, crowned with a seven-tiered spire, was extravagantly lit by Shan rockets – bamboo packed with gunpowder. The urn with his ashes was transported by his favourite elephant in gem-studded trappings to an elaborate tomb on a hill outside town. Leading the procession was a black horse which, an attending British official might have churlishly remarked, was without a rider; but Shan mourners knew that Hsipaw's powerful guardian nat sat invisibly in the saddle. Behind Sir Sao Hke's elephant came columns of barefoot monks, a squadron of Gurkha bagpipers, and twenty-four of the saopha's widows cooling themselves with long-stemmed fans. Bringing up the rear was a vast fleet of black limousines belonging to various Shan chiefs.

The oddest ritual took place at the tomb. A portly British official read aloud a solemn declaration which formally released Sir Sao Hke from his allegiance to the Crown, almost as if the soul of a mighty Shan saopha remained earthbound until a plump agent of a distant monarch stepped forth to set it free.

I met a grand old dame in Hsipaw who had the faintest memory of attending Sir Sao Hke's funeral. 'It was a *very* grand occasion,' she said in the kind of beautifully accented English that nobody in England speaks any more. 'So many people. We all wore white, if I recall. I was only a little girl at the time...'

We were having tea and biscuits in her huge ramshackle house when I noticed a poorly patched hole in the wooden floor.

'A Japanese bomb did that,' she explained. 'It hit the roof and went clean through the floor. Thank goodness it has never exploded.'

'You mean, it's still down there?' I asked with alarm.

'You know,' replied the grand old dame airily, 'I really can't remember.'

It took me ages to realise she was joking.

Hseng was standing outside the cinema looking deeply troubled. 'Very strange,' he said distantly. A tuft of hair stuck up at right angles from the back of his usually well-groomed head. He had obviously been rubbing it in some bewilderment. I had never seen him like this before, and for a second I worried that the local MI had been hassling him for associating with a foreigner. But it was worse than that. It was the women.

'Very strange,' he said. 'The ladies in Hsipaw say they are Shan, but they have very round faces. And they have hair – here.'

'You mean moustaches?'

'Yes,' said Hseng. 'They have moustaches.' He started rubbing the back of his head again. 'Very strange . . .'

And it was not just the women he objected to. The men hadn't been that friendly either. We had half-planned to go trekking together, and Hseng had been asking around for an experienced guide who might take us off the beaten path.

'Even though I'm Shan, the people don't trust me,' he said. 'I told them, "I'll pay you for three days' guiding." Some of them don't have work, but even they say no. I think they are very scared of foreigners.' To his confusion and dismay, Hseng's gangster charm had hit a brick wall – and on his first ever visit to his home territory.

But he was right. I don't mean about the women (they seemed all right to me), but about Hsipaw. It was a bit of a strange place. Behind its happy tourist facade – behind the huge billboard in Burmese and English instructing townsfolk to welcome international travellers – were ethnic tension and a history of unforgotten wrongs.

Hsipaw was a famous recruiting ground for Shan nationalist rebels, who first emerged from the hills in the late 1950s to launch guerrilla attacks against Burmese army units. Apart from the Shan State Army on the Thai-Burma border, which I had visited with Philip the Miracle Monk, the Shan rebels had signed ceasefire agreements with the Rangoon regime in the 1990s. It was unclear how ironclad these agreements were. Only two weeks before, not far from Hsipaw, a number of cars and trucks had been held at gunpoint by unidentified Shan rebels, who threatened to torch the vehicles unless the drivers coughed up money.

Two Shan groups who had signed ceasefire agreements had bases not far from Hsipaw, and I often saw bands of former rebels in exhausted khakis sloping around town. The years had not diluted Shan hatred towards the Burman overlord. It wasn't surprising that Hseng – a proud Shan, but one who had lived his entire life among the Burmans – was treated with caution.

Hsipaw's long history of resistance continued in other ways. People in the area were still solidly behind the National League for Democracy, the party of Aung San Suu Kyi, and the NLD's representatives in Hsipaw were harassed without interruption. The previous year, I was told, one of them had been locked up in a military prison in Lashio for no other reason than his opposition membership. Another had endured not one but two spells behind bars, after which he had resigned from the NLD. This was not because he feared further arbitrary jail sentences, but because his wife was a teacher, and therefore an employee of the state, and the local authorities had threatened to sack her if he did not comply – a favourite tactic of the regime. Both men were now effectively under 'town arrest', forbidden to leave Hsipaw without official permission, which of course was never granted.

Hsipaw's transition to British colonial rule had been relatively peaceful. But the Burmese military announced their arrival in 1962 with an act of signature brutality the townsfolk have never forgotten. Here is the story of the eighty-eighth and last saopha of Hsipaw.

It was told by a remarkable Austrian woman called Inge Sargent in her book *Twilight over Burma*. Inge arrived in Rangoon in January 1954 on the *SS Warwickshire* with her new husband, an earnest and unassuming Shan man called Sao Kya Seng. She had met Sao while studying in Denver, Colorado, and they had been married for ten months. As the ship prepared to dock, it was approached by a flotilla of small boats with people waving WELCOME HOME banners and tossing flowers into the river. 'Somebody very important must be on board,' Inge remarked excitedly to her husband. He suddenly looked uncomfortable. This was the moment that Sao Kya Seng finally chose to tell Inge that he was not a lowly mining engineer, but the hereditary ruler of Hsipaw, a remote Shan fiefdom the size of Connecticut, and that his name was short for Saophalong, or 'Great Lord of the Skies'. And the welcoming party in the boats below – well, he said, that was for them.

As you can imagine, Inge gave the Great Lord of the Skies a right earful.

When the couple arrived in Hsipaw, thousands more people filled the streets to greet them. At Sao Kya Seng's palace – an eccentric British-style mansion with large bay windows and deep verandas – Inge was formally installed as the mahadevi or 'celestial princess' in a ceremony solemnised by three Shan ancients blowing conch shells.

Inge, or Thusandi, as the court astrologer propitiously renamed her, quickly grew to love her new life. She mastered Shan and Burmese, bore Sao two daughters, and stood beside him at formal events like the opening of the great Bawgyo festival, at which the First Couple now arrived not on an elephant but in a Mercedes. Sao Kya Seng was a thoroughly modern saopha. He gave away portions of his estate to local farmers, lent them equipment to cultivate it, and experimented with different crops. Hsipaw prospered. Sao and Inge were so popular that their wedding portrait hung in many homes.

Then one day in March 1962 Inge awoke to find the palace surrounded by troops. General Ne Win had seized power of the country. Within hours, Sao was arrested on his way home from Rangoon and imprisoned at an army camp many miles from Hsipaw. Inge couldn't be sure he was even alive until an intermediary smuggled her a letter. 'Liebling,' it began, 'I am writing this secretly . . . I am still okay.' Then she heard – nothing. For eleven desperate months the palace was Inge's prison. She was eventually allowed to take her daughters to Rangoon, where she continued to pester the regime for any news of her missing husband. In return she was watched, threatened and stonewalled, and cruelly misled by alleged sightings of Sao in Mandalay and elsewhere. A year later, as Burma's atmosphere grew ever more repressive, she took her girls and fled the country while she could.

But she never stopped searching for Sao. In 1966, with her daughters in tow, Inge marched into a luxurious private hotel in Vienna and demanded to speak to 'The general'. She knew Ne Win was seeking medical treatment in Austria and had rented the place outright. She was told he was too sick to meet her. This was a lie. Before Inge left, she caught a glimpse of a tall Burmese man ducking into a doorway on the upper floor – General Ne Win himself.

This much is known about the fate of Inge's husband, Sao Kya Seng, last saopha of Hsipaw. He was arrested, locked in a bamboo cage for a few days, then executed. The regime has never acknowledged his death.

Sao Kya Seng's palace still stood in Hsipaw. His nephew lived there. The tennis courts were choked with weeds, and the manicured lawns of Inge's days were vegetable plots. Visitors were welcomed with an old-world charm, but otherwise the palace had an air of embattled seclusion. Sir Sao Hke's summer palace, Sakandar, was still standing too, but only just. It was derelict and scrawled with graffiti, a glorious piece of Shan history being dismantled brick by brick by impoverished locals, who were forced to plunder their past to build homes for their own wives and children.

The Bawgyo festival was going strong, and was still one of Shan State's biggest. Now it was officially opened by the regional commander. He arrived not on an elephant, nor even in an antique Mercedes, but in a heavily guarded military convoy driven at high speed from the army base in Lashio.

I wanted to pay my own respects to the saophas of Hsipaw. At dusk I set off on a bicycle to look for Sir Sao Hke's tomb. I had

Sao Kya Seng, the last saopha of Hsipaw, with his Austrian bride Inge Sargent.

been told it was on a hillside about two miles away, on the road to Mandalay. I pedalled out of town past the old teak school, built in Scott's time, with the smoke of evening cooking fires catching at my throat. Candles were being lit at household shrines inside the tin-roofed bamboo shacks along the roadside. I reached a parched football field dotted with enormous turds in a rough four-four-two formation and two buffalo shambling off for an early bath at a nearby watering hole.

Just beyond that was the hill. Far up on its heavily overgrown flank I could make out a domed structure with a lopsided spire supported by a colonnade. It looked like a lost fragment of the Brighton Pavilion. I left my bike at the roadside and, armed against snakes with a length of bamboo, began thrashing my way through the dense undergrowth. Twenty minutes later I was scratched and filthy, and a wall of tangled vegetation still lay between me and the tomb. Then I realised with a jolt that I was standing on a road – vastly overgrown, but a road nevertheless: the same one built for Sir Sao Hke's magnificent procession all those years ago. Emboldened, I slashed my way to the tomb.

Vandals had got there before me, but I had expected that. The tomb had been cracked open by thieves looking for gems and other valuables sealed in with the saopha's ashes; the urn was gone. Still, it was a lovely spot. You could see the whole of Hsipaw, surrounded by ochre paddy fields with dark mountains in the distance.

The light was starting to fail. I grabbed my stick, pounded back down the hill, and freewheeled into Hsipaw on flat tyres.

I found Hseng at the outskirts of town, with a sleepy-looking Shan man called Boon. The confused, distant look I had seen in Hseng's eyes earlier had melted, and his trademark big-kid grin had thankfully returned. He had found a friend. Hseng carried a bag with a clear liquid inside, and looked a bit like a boy who had lost his goldfish on the way home from the fair. Always eager to sample the local hooch, he had bought some rice wine off a Shan farmer.

Shan rice wine is a rough cousin to sake, a substance whose unique inebriating qualities I knew all too well from my years of living in Tokyo. The main problem with sake is that it is weaker than wine but stronger than beer, and so, for the uninitiated, judging your alcohol intake is close to impossible. One minute you're sitting at a table, discussing Yamazaki's thesis on the spread of samurai values after the Meiji restoration, and the next minute you're under it, gibbering about your childhood and telling everyone within hugging distance that you love them.

With this in mind, I joined Hseng and Boon at a basic Shan restaurant. It would be our farewell dinner. The next day Hseng was returning to Mandalay, while I was heading deeper into the hills.

The heavily tattooed owner of the restaurant decanted the rice wine into a bottle and put three glasses and a plate of deep-fried chickens' feet on the table. Boon splashed a finger of firewater into each glass and we tossed it back in one. It was like swallowing hot pins.

'Good?' asked Boon.

'The best,' I croaked.

I got talking to Boon about some of the old Shan traditions that Scott and other early observers had written about. I was happy to hear from him that many had endured. Shan builders still spat betel juice into the foundation holes of a house to destroy tiny devils that live there and can, if ignored, wreck the house's stability. And it was still widely believed that cutting your nails in another man's house brought poverty upon him. Traditional trials by ordeal also fascinated me. These were used to determine guilt in a man or to prove his strength over a rival – a bit like an ancient tribal version of the Japanese game show *Endurance*. Scott wrote of a Kachin ordeal in which a man immersed his hand in boiling water; if his skin peeled off afterwards he was guilty. A more inventive but equally painful Shan trial was licking hot metal. The winner was the first man whose tongue returned to its normal size.

I asked Hseng if he would prove his Shan manhood in this fashion. He extracted a chicken foot from his mouth and stared at me.

'You think I'm stupid?' he asked.

We ate a little more – a sour mustard-leaf soup, a noodle salad made with another bitter herb and, oh, why not, another plate of chickens' feet – and we drank a little more. Boon had started saying something when the lights went out, but he didn't even pause, just kept right on talking, as if the difference between a brightly lit restaurant and a pitch-dark one were purely academic.

A generator throbbed to life somewhere and the lights came back on. The owner produced some more rice wine, and then rolled up his sleeves to show us his tattoos. Shan tattoos are punched into the skin by hand, using a foot-long steel rod with a blunt nib – a fantastically painful technique. The owner's entire upper body was covered with them. Here was a man worth putting money on if Hsipaw ever had a hot-metal-licking contest. We toasted him loudly.

Then Boon and Hseng fell into a heated discussion about who was stronger, King Bayinnaung (r. 1551-81) or King Alaungpaya (r. 1752-60), much as one might discuss the relative merits of Michael Owen and David Beckham. 'In a past life,' Hseng told me suddenly, 'I was a Shan soldier and you were a British soldier and we were good friends.' Only half of him was joking. The other half was steaming drunk. We toasted each other.

It got late. The generator puttered and died. There was only one more toast to make – a toast to be muttered only in the murky back room of Shan restaurants after a plastic bag of moonshine. Hseng raised his glass and cried:

Mai soong moeng tai,
Hpai mai moeng man!

– or 'Prosperity in Shan land, fire in Burma!' The owner smiled indulgently, then glanced around quickly to see who had heard.

We exchanged drunken farewells, and I climbed on my bike – and realised that, while I had been eating, someone had kindly pumped up the tyres. Feeling a great surge of warmth towards the restaurant owner, the residents of Hsipaw, the whole Shan people, I cycled unsteadily back to my hotel – on the wrong bike, as it turned out, obliging its owner to spend the night racing all over town on flat tyres trying to find me.

5

'Scott was a natural imperialist,' wrote Geraldine Mitton, his third wife and biographer, and this was just as well, since he spent the next few years tramping restlessly along the unmowed touchlines of the British Empire. He dodged bullets, came down with fevers, braved mosquitoes the size of light aircraft and – 'what annoys me most' – lost a pair of horseshoe cufflinks during a freak hurricane, which also carried off his shirt, his chair and his tent. 'The work was arduous,' trumpeted *The Times*, 'but before the end of 1888 the mission had succeeded in transforming some two or three millions of excited and rebellious Shans, scattered over an area of nearly 80,000 square miles of difficult country, into loyal subjects.' Scott summed it up more succinctly: 'Awfully fagged.'

The 'pacification' of Upper Burma and the Shan states was not really achieved for another decade. During this time Scott would play a central role in convincing the Shan to accept British rule. 'If there was little bloodshed it was largely due to Scott,' wrote the historian G. E. Harvey. 'He had an iron physique and a quick, masterful temper, but he also had a warm heart and he seldom failed to win men over.' Scott would note how the arrival of the British forced the feuding saophas to meet and bury the hatchet, and how his favourite sport played its part in the peace-making. 'It is great fun watching them,' he wrote in a letter home, describing one such meeting of the Shan chiefs:

> At first they all camped separately, scattered about over the wide paddy stubbles round about here; now they are beginning to gather closer together, and some of them are actually quite chummy. When we have a football match, or when the band plays, they all of course gather round, and then even the most standoffish of them are bound to meet.

Scott was now based for longer periods at Fort Stedman. There he studied Chinese, penned unattributed front-line reports for British newspapers, and began to acquire what would become the largest collection of Shan manuscripts outside Burma. He also played a lot of football with the officers, and sometimes with the Gurkhas too, despite what he felt was their 'vile selfish habit' of hogging the ball. There were always visitors to greet – the garrulous saopha of Yawnghwe being a regular caller. 'Sawbwa [Saopha] in, stayed as usual a couple of hours,' recorded Scott. 'Wanted to know what hats English merchants wore, heard they were of gold.' The father of the saopha of Lawksawk was less welcome: 'Old nuisance. Gave him a tin of corned beef, four empty beer bottles and 25 rupees, and handed him over to be taken back to Lawksawk. He has not long to live. What time he has to do so I want him to be somewhere far away from me.' On another occasion, 'Old Mawkmè [Mawk Mai] churchwarden round in the morning with some fruit and a petition that he might be allowed to look at me. Had come back to the place four months ago, and has never had a good look at me. Would like one now. Indulged him accordingly, and then sent him to scrutinize Fowler.'

Scott spent a lot of time absorbed in official paperwork. He fired off letters, full of thinly veiled threats, to encourage saophas to stop fighting and bow to British supremacy. His patience with this hands-off approach was limited. 'Bold decision and not the writing of letters was in fact what was wanted,' he declared. Whenever there was derring-do to be done, Scott did it, while his immediate superior, an unhappy chap named Hildebrand, remained at Fort Stedman tending his strawberries.

A welcome reprieve from unloved paperwork was provided by a defrocked monk called Twek Nga Lu, whom Scott had once met at Fort Stedman. Twek Nga Lu had turned nasty after being ousted from the chiefdom of a small Shan state, and his raiding parties pillaged and torched with seeming impunity. Scott had seen their handiwork: the previous year he had trekked through abandoned villages where even monasteries lay in smouldering ruins. Like other Shan men, Twek Nga Lu was not only heavily tattooed, but had penny-sized discs of gold and silver inserted beneath the skin of his arms and back. These talismans were rumoured to have extraordinary protective powers, and in the popular mind perhaps explained why soldiers of the Great White Queen had not caught him. It was this impression that Scott was determined to change. After Twek Nga Lu seized the town of Mongnai, Scott set off from Fort Stedman with a column of 150 soldiers. 'You see, the British flag flies at Monè [Mongnai],' he explained, 'and it won't do to let that be pulled down by a wretched creature like Twek Nga Lu.'

With the monsoon already begun, it was a hazardous journey. 'Very violent storm between three and four,' recorded Scott. 'Had to hold on to my tent poles like grim death.' The air was thick with mosquitoes and flights of white ants, and giant stinging centipedes wriggled across the forest floor. Finally the column approached Mongnai. The *St James's Gazette* described what happened next as 'as successful an example of prompt daring as is to be found out of a lady's romance'.

Scott assembled six Tommies and a lieutenant and set off to catch the dacoit in a lightning dawn raid. Galloping up to Mongnai Palace, a teak building where the British flag once but no longer flew, Scott spotted Twek Nga Lu on the balcony. He ran up the wooden stairs and, before the bandit could grab the Winchester rifle lying on his bed, seized the man and held him until the Tommies arrived. Then Twek Nga Lu was tied to the bedpost.

Meanwhile, outside, twenty of the bandit's armed ruffians approached. 'I walked straight up to the first man,' recalled Scott, who was unarmed, 'and told him to kneel down. He did not do so, so I promptly knocked him down. The men half raised their guns whereupon I shouted that they would be shot if they did not lay their guns down, and grabbed the nearest man's. It was pure cheek, but it settled them.'

Six or eight of the leaders were sentenced to death by the Mongnai saopha. In a traditional execution the men would have been lashed to a crucifix and dispatched with a single knife thrust through the heart; their bodies would then have remained on the cross until carrion birds had picked the skeletons clean. But Scott intervened, and they were shot instead. Twek Nga Lu was brought alive to Fort Stedman, where he was later shot dead trying to escape.

But such was Twek Nga Lu's reputation for being a 'slippery fellow' that afterwards Scott went to investigate the shallow grave where he had been buried. Rather eerily, he found only a long lock of hair. The corpse had already been dug up by some Shan men, who had hacked off the head so that it could be triumphantly displayed in a nearby town that Twek Nga Lu had terrorised. Once the potent talismans beneath Twek Nga Lu's skin had been winkled out with knives, the rest of the body was boiled down into a nauseating broth, which was then decanted into glass phials and sold at exorbitant prices as a potion for bravery. One phial was even offered to Scott, who, despite his boyish mania for collecting memorabilia of every kind, apparently refused to buy it. 'Twek Nga Lu,' he could confirm with grim satisfaction, 'was very completely disposed off.'

I hitched a lift from Hsipaw with an Indian truck driver, a tiny, silent man with a permanent half-grin of contentment lurking in the shadow of the most stupendous nose I have ever seen. The road was a cratered dirt track with a few scabs of tarmac left over from colonial times. The only worse road I had travelled was Route 10 to Pailin, the former Khmer Rouge stronghold in western Cambodia, and that had had the excuse of having been recently bombed. The truck clawed its way up the mountain at walking pace, the gearbox weeping for mercy, and wherever there was a stream we got out to throw buckets of water on the engine's steaming underbelly.

We stopped just as often at checkpoints. These were usually attached to army or police bases, and in total extorted from drivers a small fortune in bribes – otherwise known as 'wheel tax', 'gate tax' or 'tea money'. The checkpoints were also the regime's radar. Travellers in Burma must register their names and ID numbers with the authorities several times during even the shortest of journeys. This practice was so ingrained by decades of military rule that several Burmese friends were astonished when I told them that Britain and America did not have similar systems. The checkpoints were an extremely effective system of keeping tabs on people and – get this – *the people paid for it*. Self-financing oppression: it could be the generals' only brilliant idea.

'Eat?' asked the driver, pulling up beside a solitary teashop, a mop of thatch and bamboo cringing at the roadside. It was the first of just two words he would address to me during the entire eight-hour journey. The other was 'Piss?'

Our destination today was Namhsan, a remote tea-producing town stranded high in the northern Shan hills. From there I planned to trek into the wilderness to get a taste of the conditions that Scott endured on his numerous expeditions. I also hoped to encounter hill people who seemed to shy away from bigger centres like Hsipaw – specifically, the elusive Palaung tribe known as the Golden Palaung. But after the teashop there were no houses at all, and no people, only enigmatic stacks of chopped wood marking footpaths that led off into the forest. Hidden springs turned the road to mud, and our route through the mountains soon looked as if a child had dragged a dirty finger across a still-wet landscape painting. Night came. An unseen moon softly backlit the ridge we were climbing, and fireflies fell like cinders. At corners, the truck's headlight beams swung out into nothingness, devoured by the darkness. Soon I could see a messy collection of lights on a far-off hill which I initially mistook for stars. This dim constellation was Namhsan.

Arriving at night was eerie. The houses lining Namhsan's deserted main street were made of darkly varnished teak or pine, and were spookily lit by fluorescent strip lights suspended from wooden gantries. The doors were fastened shut to keep out the chill; in the old days they also kept out leopards and tigers. Scott recounted how a hungry tiger once followed a dog into a house and mauled the owner.

I checked into a large wooden guest house full of murky corners and creaking floorboards. The landlady was a tiny but clearly formidable woman with neat Palaung features framed by a pink woolly bonnet. She was solicitous in a businesslike way, like a nurse with too many patients, and sent me to a cold room upstairs with a candle and an enamel mug of steaming Palaung tea. I slept beneath three dusty blankets. As I drifted off I could hear her praying musically at a large household shrine in the room next door, and then, through a half-dream, there was an urgent voice at the door saying, 'Goodnight, goodnight!'

Maurice Collis, a former colonial judge who visited Namhsan in the 1930s, likened the town to 'a lamasery in the wastes of Tibet', such was its sense of isolation and solitude. Seventy years later it still felt remote. During the next three days I would meet Namhsan people who had never visited Hsipaw, less than fifty miles away. Many townsfolk were gratifyingly gobsmacked to see a white face. One old man followed my movements so intently that I wondered whether, by darting behind him, I could make him fall over.

Scott described the Palaung as a rough, industrious people who were both profoundly superstitious and zealous Buddhists. He also called them 'quiet and peaceable', two racial characteristics that my Palaung landlady had evidently failed to acquire. The next morning I was woken by the noise of her tapping a drum before the household shrine. It was still very dark outside. The drum beat got faster and louder and then stopped, and a murmuring prayer began. Only when the landlady had finished her devotions did dawn break and the cockerels dare to crow.

Outside there was a small morning market where women from the villages sold vegetables and herbs laid out on tarpaulin. (By 9 a.m., as the sun rose, the women packed up and vanished like the dew.) The Palaung landlady was there, her pretty face disfigured by an enormous quid of betel nut stuffed in one cheek. She flitted between the stalls, bellowing instructions through a petite mouth that frothed red with beteljuice. For a tiny woman she had a shockingly loud voice. It was loud enough to carve bas-reliefs into granite. As I sat on the guesthouse steps, a village woman wandered up, squatted a few yards away, and hoisted her sarong to urinate. The landlady spotted this, and let off a deafening volley of abuse. The woman dropped her sarong as if she'd been struck by a blow-dart.

I went out for breakfast. The doors on the houses were open now, and women were slapping dust off the shelves and laying out their goods – pots and pans and other essential hardware, Shan

The Palaung town of Namhsan in Scott's time.

medicines, gaudy Chinese fabrics – while pigeons scratched noisily
on the tin roofs. Drying outside in woven trays were squares of
tofu furry with fermentation, or dark Palaung tea – the best tea
in Burma, it was said. I found a tea shop and had breakfast: a
chapatti, a bowl of oily dhal, and some sickly-sweet instant coffee
served with an inch of condensed milk in the bottom of the glass
– enough sugar to make my teeth stampede around my mouth in
panic. Afterwards, on a surge of carbohydrates, I climbed up a hill
to the town hospital. Namhsan was laid out with almost allegorical
logic, watched over by the two institutions that dominated its
existence. The hill to its left had a monastery with rusting roofs
and a listing silver spire; the hill to its right had a transmitter and
a neat grove of houses belonging to Military Intelligence. The town
itself lay in the purgatorial gorge between.

The hill from which I viewed this was once a centre of influence,
too. Namhsan used to be the capital of Tawngpeng, a 'Shan'
state ruled by a dynasty of Palaung saophas. The last saopha of
Tawngpeng took five wives, although not all at the same time, and
sired thirty children. They included Albert, Joseph, Clive, Eddie,
Wendy, Barbara, Patrick, Shirley, Noreen and the twins – Peggy
and Joyce. The hospital was formerly his rambling palace. Sections

of it were boarded up and semi-derelict now, but one could still see the long, deep veranda that the saopha had built for his numerous children to play on during Namhsan's interminable rainy season.

As I stood in front of the saopha's former palace, a hospital orderly appeared on the balcony and tipped a bucket of slops over the railing. Inge Sargent, the Austrian mahadevi of Hsipaw, came here in the 1950s. 'Every room had a fireplace,' she recalled, 'and even during the hot season they were all in use.' She was treated to a Palaung feast of crunchy pig's ear and a piquant salad made from ant eggs.

Sadly, no such delicacies were served in Namhsan any more. The town had only one restaurant, I discovered, run by a Chinese man with an inexpertly bandaged head. It closed at 5 p.m. But the tea shop stayed open until eight, so for dinner I ate a whole loaf of sponge cake.

Namhsan was said to be the best place to see Golden Palaung women dressed in their tribal finery. But the village women I had watched carrying heavy baskets of firewood through town had dirty, ragged clothes, and wore blank expressions of utter exhaustion. What had I expected to see? Streets full of exotic Golden Palaung dancing a ritual of immeasurable antiquity? It would have been a bit like turning down a back road in the Scottish Highlands and finding a group of kilt-clad clansmen practising with their claymores.

Namhsan received power from 6 to 8.30 p.m. each day, and the street lights flickered to life as I walked back to the guesthouse. A teacher who lived in a room on the ground floor was holding English lessons while the light lasted. She was a stout, cheerful widow with an aristocratic air – her late husband had served as the saopha's retainer – and was determined to take me under her wing. When her two students had left, I asked her if there was anyone who could take me on a long trek into the interior, staying in villages along the way, so that I could meet the Golden Palaung.

'Overnight stays are impossible,' said the teacher curtly. 'They won't allow it.'

This was a disappointment. What about the Golden Palaung, I asked – did they even exist any more?

'Only the old women wear such costumes now,' she replied, 'and they live far away.'

So was it possible to hike into the hills to see them? I explained to the teacher that I was ready for some hard trekking to the remotest hills, but she just didn't seem to register what I wanted. At that moment the Palaung landlady, who had been flitting around outside, stuck her head through the door and, ignoring me, started gurgling something through a mouthful of betel. A long discussion began.

Finally the teacher turned to me and nodded. It was decided, she said. Tomorrow we would all walk to a hilltop temple where the Palaung landlady was very anxious to pay her respects to a venerable old abbot. It would take three hours, perhaps more. The teacher had an undiagnosed heart condition, you see, and so we would all have to walk quite slowly. She hoped I understood. And would it be all right if she brought along some students, so they could practise their English? Of course it would. So few foreigners came to Namhsan after all . . .

I gave up – this woman knew how to bargain. We arranged to set out at six the following morning. I went upstairs. The Palaung landlady was sitting cross-legged at a low table in front of her candlelit shrine. She was studying a scrap of paper so intently it might have been a long-lost love letter.

'Goodnight,' I said.

'Hmph,' she replied, without looking up.

I slunk into my bedroom to listen to the BBC on my short-wave radio. For the Burmese, foreign radio broadcasts were the chief source of news about their own country. All branches of the domestic media were censored; overseas phone calls were prohibitively expensive and routinely tapped; and the Internet was reserved for a select few and strictly monitored. For me the radio also helped to temper the feeling of being utterly cut off from the rest of the planet, an isolation felt even more keenly in faraway Namhsan. But I was listening not just for news of the outside world, but for news of Burma itself, for while travelling there I was always pursued by a nagging sense of cluelessness. Decades of military rule made the Burmese naturally cautious about talking to foreigners, even in private, so I often heard about events only long after they had happened – the Golden Land haunting in Rangoon being a good example. Whenever I returned from Burma to my Bangkok home, my first ritual was always to plough through the foreign pages of a month's worth of unread *Bangkok Post* newspapers, in the hope of discovering what had actually happened in Burma while I had been there.

I pressed the radio to my ear, thinking of the thousands of information-starved people across this huge country who were doing exactly the same. But there was no news about Burma tonight. So I read until 8.30 and then put down my book, expecting the town's electricity to shut off. But for some reason we were given an extra fifteen minutes of power. When darkness finally came I lay back on my bed and thought, Well who's a lucky Namhsan then?

Later I learned why we had received extra power that night. A week or so before, Lieutenant General Khin Nyunt had lectured a meeting of coaches, sportswriters and retired footballers on the importance of 'uplifting the standard of Myanmar soccer'. How, he asked, could the national game return to its post-war golden age, when Burma had been one of the strongest teams in Asia? None of the assembled experts pointed out that the golden age of Burmese football died along with democracy after the 1962 military coup. At one point in the 1960s official neglect of the sport was such that the entire country ran out of footballs.

National trials to select Burma's best players were now under way, and were being televised in full. Last night's game had run over, thus the extra fifteen minutes before lights out. But Khin Nyunt's sudden passion for soccer alarmed some people I knew. What was he up to? What did he *want*? It wasn't as if the generals even *liked* footie. In 1962 the only people allowed through the cordon of tanks and troops encircling Rangoon were golfers – the city's best course lay on the other side. But Khin Nyunt wasn't interested in the game itself. For him it was a potentially valuable tool for what he called 'enhancing the nation's dignity'.

The trouble was, Burmese football was not very dignified. George Scott's students had loved it for being 'just like fighting', and little had changed since. In the post-war period, matches often progressed through player punch-ups into full-on stadium riots in which even Buddhist monks were known to put the sandal in. Matches between universities and the military – bitter political enemies off the pitch – were notoriously prone to violence. Students were now banned from competitive football, but the Burmese game was still robust. I saw a match in Mandalay where the referee showed his yellow card thirteen times and sent five people off. As far as I could work out, this was considered quite normal.

Burmese league football was bad, but the national team was worse – possibly the worst in South-East Asia. Its consistently dismal performance abroad was a source of acute embarrassment to the generals. Two years before, when Burma was trounced in a match in tiny Brunei, all reporting about the national squad was banned when a disgusted senior general declared that he 'didn't want to hear another word about it'.

Later, when Burma conceded a crucial goal during a nationally televised game against Indonesia, the state-run TV Myanmar actually went off air for a few minutes – in shame, apparently. Interestingly, the manager of the national team was an Englishman called David Booth. His pedigree was unknown, although one Burmese trainer described his management style as – ironically enough – 'very dictatorial'.

After Khin Nyunt's golden-age lecture, an editorial in the *New Light of Myanmar* reminded readers that supporting Burmese football was a way of 'expressing their patriotism'. To which your average Burmese soccer fan, drawing on his nation's rich stock of peasant vocabulary, might respond, 'My arse.' No one I talked to had a good word to say about Burmese football today. But go to a match – particularly a match between two military teams – and you realise that that's the whole point. Gatherings of more than five people are technically illegal in Burma, and even an innocuous remark can lead to a spell of hard labour. But a thousand football supporters can sit together and scream abuse at the players until they're hoarse, and if there's a five-star general in the VIP box they shout even louder.

I had discovered this for myself a few weeks before, at the final of the Aung San Shield – the Burmese equivalent of the FA Cup. I arrived at Rangoon's Thuwanna Stadium to find about 5,000 people crammed into the shaded west stand. The rest of the stadium was empty, and pariah kites made graceful, swooping orbits above the silent terraces opposite. The spectators were young, male and rowdy. They were squatting Asia-style on the concrete seats, with their sarongs tucked up round their crotches. They were smoking sweet-smelling cheroots, gobbing betel juice between their flip-flops, and passing round hard-boiled quail eggs and dodgy-looking kebabs – just lapping up the pre-match atmosphere. They had each paid about forty pence to see this game, and were expecting to get their money's worth.

I had two friends with me. Sein Da was a cheerful, soft-spoken Arakanese student with a million-watt smile. Tin Mya was his emotional opposite: an intense young Burman whose father, an opposition politician, had spent over a decade in prison. We bought some pumpkin seeds and sat down near the double helping of barbed wire that ran the length of the terrace.

The players trotted on to the parched turf and began to warm up. At this point I would like to report that the teams had romantic names like 'Mandalay United' or 'Rangoon Rovers'. But I can't. The team in the yellow strip was the Ministry of Finance and Revenue; the one in blue and white was the Ministry of Home Affairs. It could have been worse: the final of another tournament had been fought out by the No. 323 Supply and Transport Battalion and the Defense Services Orthopaedic and Rehabilitation Hospital.

I asked Tin Mya if teams in Burma had any nicknames. After all, 'Ministry of Finance and Revenue' was a bit of a mouthful.

Tin Mya frowned. 'What do you mean?' he asked suspiciously.

'Well, for example, Manchester United are sometimes called Man U. or the Red Devils. Don't teams here have similar nicknames?'

'No,' replied Tin Mya sternly. 'No nicknames.'

With a carpet of pumpkin-seed husks at his feet, Tin Mya gave me his pre-match analysis. Basically, he said, Home Affairs was about to get thrashed. Finance was a relatively wealthy ministry where officials had plenty of opportunities for graft. (Most foreign investors in Burma bribe Finance officials at some point – an envelope of hard currency here, a Rolex there.) Everyone wanted to work there, and the ministry picked the best footballers from among the applicants. Finance was the holder of the Aung San Shield. Tin Mya was in no doubt that it would win again today.

A clinical header, a goalmouth scramble, a low, unstoppable volley – Finance was soon three-nil up, and the crowd had grown increasingly raucous. They scented a massacre. They roared with glee when a Home Affairs defender fell from a mid-air tussle into a lifeless, stretcher-ready heap by his own goalposts. They screamed with laughter when a desperately cleared ball almost knocked the Aung San Shield from a taffeta-fringed table near the dug-outs. When Home Affairs blundered into yet another offside trap, a man in front of us sprang to his feet and launched into a virtuoso abuse of the linesman.

I nudged Sein Da. 'What's he shouting?' I asked.

Sein Da grinned. 'He is saying, "Hey! You! What the hell is going on? Pisses on you!"'

The man in front of us was still screaming. 'And now?' I asked.

'Now he is saying, "Fuck your mother!" '

'You mean "motherfucker".'

'Yes, yes,' said Sein Da excitedly. '"Fuck your motherfucker!"'

Finance won four-nil – no surprise there. Afterwards, the pariah kites returned to circle above the electronic scoreboard, which registered a flurry of meaningless pixels. A flock of mynah birds descended upon the threadbare penalty area to feast on worms brought to the surface by the relentless pounding of the Home Affairs goalmouth. A portly colonel in uniform stepped out to present the awards, and it was then, much to my surprise, that the jeering really began.

First the Home Affairs team was given its runner-up trophy. This was accepted not by the team captain, but by a uniformed policeman. A growl of annoyance went through the crowd. The policeman accepted the trophy, then saluted the colonel – and the crowd roared with derision.

'There is no need to salute the colonel,' explained Tin Mya. 'They are just civilians. But that policeman has saluted, and now – look – the whole team has to do the same.'

'What a shit!' someone nearby exclaimed in perfect English.

Many more trophies were handed out. One fell apart in the colonel's hands, and the crowd hooted with laughter. Then a player called Aung Moe Oo came forward. He belonged to the much-loathed Defense Services team and was himself a military officer. A low, whooping sound rose menacingly from the terraces. It sounded to me as if the crowd were making monkey noises, but in fact they were saying a Burmese word over and over again, with increasing volume and venom. By the time Aung Moe Oo took his trophy from the portly colonel, that single word was booming maddeningly around the stadium.

'*Ayu, ayu, ayu, ayu, ayu* . . .'
'Fool, fool, fool, fool, fool . . .'

This open ridicule of the military astonished me. But, as Tin Mya explained, beyond arresting 5,000 rowdy fans, the authorities could do very little to stop it. The crowd dissolved into gleeful, schoolboy laughter. Then, almost as one, people got up, retied their longyis, and began filing towards the exits. This bewildered me, too. It all seemed so abrupt. Wasn't anybody going to watch the Aung San Shield itself being presented?

But for everyone else the afternoon was now complete. They had smoked a few cheroots, they had watched some eventful footie, they had hurled abuse at various members of the police and military. For ordinary Burmese, that's just about the most fun you can have in public without getting arrested.

The prospect of seeing the venerable old abbot cheered the Palaung landlady enormously. She was up and singing at amazing volume well before dawn.

I stumbled downstairs in search of coffee. It was misty outside, and very cold. The landlady was waiting, her dark eyes gleaming with religious devotion. She wore a woolly bonnet over her funny little head, and her cheeks were liberally daubed with thanaka. She reminded me of a commando prepared for a mission of some danger. I said good morning. She scowled.

It was about this time that I suddenly became aware that I was really quite smitten by the Palaung landlady. I don't know when it happened, or why – blame it on the altitude, or the lack of sleep. She just fascinated me. It didn't matter that we barely understood each other. It didn't even matter that she didn't seem to like me. In fact the less she liked me, the more smitten I became. Every time she scowled I felt all warm and fuzzy. I was a sucker for it.

The teacher arrived with two of her female students. So here we all are, I reflected glumly. So much for a grueling trek into deepest Shan territory. A typical jungle march by Scott might include a battalion of Gurkhas or Baluchis, an artillery piece, scores of coolies and mule drivers, and maybe a couple of elephants to impress the natives. And my first expedition into the Shan hills? A pocket-sized Palaung landlady, an old dear with a dicky heart, two students in their Sunday dresses, and me – the big girl's blouse.

Sulky and a little lovesick, I followed them along the main road winding up out of town. It was rush hour in Namhsan. A boy in a grubby white sheet marched down the hill striking a bell-shaped gong to announce the imminent passage of a dozen monks hugging their alms bowls. They were followed by a herd of donkeys ferrying panniers of tea from the more remote hills. Then came a torrent of schoolchildren in green sarongs, rattling their tiffin boxes.

The English students now walked one stride behind me, riffling through phrase books and pelting me with questions.

'What is your weight?'

'Do you like Burmese food?'

'How many children do you have?'

'What is the chief production of your country?'

We passed a small British-built reservoir, then the first of many immense banyan trees with age-twisted branches propped up by a number of forked sticks. These were placed there by locals in the hope that the tree's spirit would cure a particular illness. Nearby was a nat shrine – not an elaborate shed full of gilded idols like the one I'd seen en route to Maymyo, but a rudimentary country version: a beehive-like box, ragged prayer flags, a few sprigs of eugenia, and two (to my mind) empty cushions.

The landlady saluted the invisible nats and then scampered onward, plucky and splay-footed, keeping up a loud monologue in choppy Palaung and occasionally turning round to screw up her nose at me. And what a lovely nose it was.

As our path meandered gently up the mountainside, the scenery grew ever more spectacular. I was now high on the Shan plateau, and deep-green hills dotted with whitewashed pagodas tumbled off in every direction to misty horizons. The Palaung were thought to be the earliest inhabitants of this land – earlier even than the Shan who gave the hills their name. When Scott entered this territory over a century ago, the population was sparse and the great hunger for land and firewood had not yet begun. The steep hills were more thickly forested then, and rhinoceros and barking deer roamed the deep, shadowy gorges. Local people drew maps for Scott during his travels. A few months earlier I had sat in a reading room at Cambridge University Library marvelling over some that had survived. They were as big as bed sheets, and thickly painted on rough paper or mould-speckled linen which crackled as I unfolded it. Some were quite beautiful. The rivers were painted ruby-red; the mountains, which were often given strange, curly peaks, were done in electric greens and purples; pagodas were painted gold. The maps were surreal, magical, like illustrations from a Dr Seuss book, yet utterly true to the wonder inspired by the real scenery now unfolding before me.

The teacher shuffled up and took my arm. 'Oh,' she panted, 'I wish I'd brought my walking stick.'

The monastery was a scattering of white buildings and stupas clinging to the highest peak for many miles. The sound of gongs echoed down the hillside as we approached. The famous abbot was a toothless pixie of a man. The landlady put a silver tray with flowers and several thousand kyat on the floor before him. 'He is a very honest monk,' whispered the teacher. 'He always hides donations in different places, so the novices can't steal them.' The women knelt and bowed, touching their foreheads to the floor. The abbot took the money, folded it into a thick gangster wad, and tucked it into a secret pocket beneath his left armpit.

While the English students prepared our lunch, an old woman appeared from nowhere. With a little shock I realised she was Golden Palaung – in full traditional dress. It was a stunning ensemble, almost Elizabethan in its multilayered complexity. She wore a light-blue jacket with a small V-neck delicately embroidered at the front, the sleeves of a golden velvet undergarment showing beneath. Her skirt was really a kind of smock, split at both sides and hemmed with bright squares of blue and orange velvet, and beneath that she wore a plain sarong and ankle-length leggings. A number of black-varnished bamboo hoops were loosely stacked around her waist. Her head was shaved – the sign of a married woman – and covered with a black skullcap, over which she wore an elaborate pointed hood of blue-and-white cotton. She had a square, manly face, and a muscular neck. Three betel-stained teeth, as big and black as dominoes, stuck from her gums in three different directions. She was an ugly old bird with spectacular plumage.

Palaung national dress is supposed to carry echoes of the tribe's folkloric origins. The Golden Palaung are said to have descended from a boy hatched from one of three eggs laid by a lovelorn she-dragon for a wandering prince, then flung in rage into the Irrawaddy River. The Palaung's peaked hood had reminded Scott of the cowls worn by Franciscan friars, but it was meant to resemble the she-dragon's head, while the squares of velvet were her scales. It amazed me to think that these were everyday clothes, in which a Palaung woman is expected to gather firewood, harvest tea and prepare food.

Not for much longer, though. The old woman started talking, and the teacher translated. It was very sad, the old woman said, but her daughter wore Palaung dress only on special occasions now. I asked how well other traditions had survived, and the answers were mixed. In many villages, after his wife had given birth, a Palaung man still washed the placenta and umbilical cord, placed them in a section of bamboo, and buried them beneath the house. But other time-honoured ceremonies seemed to have disappeared. I had read that Palaung women often took their pestles and pounded down cracks in the earth around the house which were caused by restless earth monsters. Yes, said the old woman, she'd heard of such a thing, but in the old days. She had never witnessed it herself.

One of the oddest Palaung rituals was the *Prüh* or 'Taming' ceremony. Scott described this coming-of-age rite as 'a means of teaching polite behaviour between the sexes'. Bands of small boys would visit the home of a particular girl and, while her parents slept in an adjoining room, pinch and pummel her for at least ten minutes. Although it was refereed by a village elder, the ceremony could be used by horrid little boys to settle grudges, and many girls lived in terror during the three nights when the *Prüh* took place. After this the boys and girls were paired off by drawing lots. A young couple then exchanged love tokens and recited traditional love rhymes that their elders had taught them. These were sensual and rather beautiful. The boy might begin:

In the daytime, when the sun is young,
My heart aches for thee.
I take a flute and blow it.
I go out wandering.
Taking a long sword,

I go away into the night;
I go away under the dark sky.
I fear nothing . . .

And the girl might bashfully reply:

I have been preparing myself
I put on my clothes.
I looked into the water as I dressed,
I looked into the water as into a mirror.
My heart ached in my body;
I longed to be with thee . . .

They sang to each other every night for six weeks, after which the couple might eventually be betrothed. The whole courtship was really quite sweet, apart from the pinching and pummelling bit.

I described all this to the old Golden Palaung woman, but it didn't seem to register. Perhaps the teacher's translation wasn't clear enough. Or perhaps the old woman had never heard of the *Prüh* ceremony. There are at least a dozen types of Palaung, spread across an enormous area, and each had varying customs. Maybe it had died out years ago.

The Palaung landlady seemed to sense my disappointment. With the teacher's help, she began to explain that many tribal practices had survived. For example, when she was pregnant she had bathed in water with a magnet in it. Sometimes she had drunk this water, too. I had heard about this. The Palaung believed the magnet acted as a strengthening agent for the fetus. The landlady was convinced it was the reason her children were all born so healthy.

There was another practice I wanted to ask about: Palaung curses. One such curse I had read about was carefully digging up your enemy's footprint, wrapping it in leaves, and baking it over a fire. It fascinated me that, over 10,000 miles away, the fearsome Yanomami tribe of Venezuela – once described as the most violent people on earth – had developed a near-identical voodoo to use on their enemies. Perhaps the Palaung weren't always as 'quiet and peaceable' as Scott believed, although he did note that they were distant cousins of the headhunting Wa, whose guttural language uses many of the same words.

But the teacher didn't want to talk about Palaung cursing. 'Only evil people do that,' she sniffed. I took this as a non-denial denial.

Lunch was ready, and we sat down to eat at a low table overlooking the valley. The landlady sat beside me, eating noisily with her hands. She would grab a handful of sour curry, vigorously squeeze it into her plate of rice, then push the fistful of soggy food into her delicate little mouth. She talked loudly throughout, spraying the table with rice fragments.

I was still sitting with a plate of lumpy rice. When the landlady saw I wasn't eating, she did something so thoughtful that I dared to think that perhaps she liked me after all. Between mouthfuls, she reached over with a greasy but petite hand and one by one massaged all the lumps from my rice.

6

In 1891 Scott began work on his great five-volume *Gazetteer of Upper Burma and the Shan States.* Brick thick and turgid with detail, gazetteers were the blunt instruments of colonial administration. Today they squat, massive and many-volumed, on forgotten shelves in library basements, dusty reminders that the Empire was won not just by force of arms, but also by sheer tonnage of paperwork. They are psychotically fastidious. Scott's *Gazetteer* records every man, woman, child, bullock, buffalo, cow, pig and pony in the Shan states, along with the geography, ethnicity and chief produce of even the most pifflingly tiny village. Nothing escapes its omniscient sweep. It knows, for example, that the saopha's revenue from opium and liquor licences in Hsipaw State in 1897-8 was 18,132 rupees. It knows that in Kengteng five annas will buy you four duck eggs and still leave change for a custard apple. It just knows.

But Scott's *Gazetteer* was much more than a dry imperial stocktaking. It was a fathomless resource on the origins, customs and languages of Burma's ethnic peoples, written not in the stilted prose of a bureaucrat, but with the flair and passion of an experienced journalist. Even a century after its publication, the *Gazetteer of Upper Burma and the Shan States* still had an almost biblical authority. In Burma I met an American gem dealer and a Canadian Red Cross worker who both swore by Scott's *magnum opus*.

I bought my treasured copy of Part I, Vol. I, at a Rangoon bookshop. It was a 1980s reprint by a New York publisher, photocopied in Burma and skilfully bound, like so many books sold in Rangoon. (English-language originals were far too rare and valuable to sell.) The *Gazetteer* wasn't great bedtime reading; that would be like propping the Ten Commandments on your chest. But with a firm table, and some quality time, it was endlessly absorbing. I now knew that Kachin warriors usually make war just before the moon rises, and make love in purpose-built 'bachelors' huts' – the love hotels of the jungle. I had learned the crucial difference between the Banyôk people (who worship their dogs in an annual ceremony) and the En (who eat them). I had followed Scott's brief exegesis on the Karen's use of chicken bones to divine the future. I knew that the Kachin believe that the movement of giant subterranean crocodiles causes earthquakes, while the Eastern Tai are convinced that eclipses are the work of a moon-swallowing frog who must be frightened off by gong-beating and gunfire. I no longer confused the Yindu people with the Yaw, the Yao or the Yo.

Even the index was a rewarding read. Looking up one eye-catching entry – 'Headhunting, rules for its conduct' – I read that, among the Wa, 'to behead a man from a community even on the same range of hills is looked upon as unneighbourly and slothful'. The *Gazetteer* also scotched the myths of earlier observers, disagreeing, for example, with Lieutenant Master's flamboyant contention that the Ling tribe solves the problem of coping with elderly relations by eating them.

The colonial gazetteers exhibited an almost pathological obsession with separating the native population into religious and ethnic categories. It has been argued that the British set out to understand ethnic differences so that they could better exploit them – the classic divide-and-rule model of imperial control. I preferred to think that a scholar-administrator like Scott had less cynical motives. As he knew only too well, ordering a region of such baffling human variety into water-tight ethnic categories was a mug's game. Many minority peoples in the Shan states identified themselves not by the language they spoke, or by the beliefs they held, but simply by the area in which they lived. Others happily answered to four or five different names, depending on who was addressing them. 'The names of the Kachin tribes or clans are bewildering beyond endurance,' complained Scott, 'and the sub-tribes of the Karens recall a history of tartans.'

It took Scott ten years to complete the *Gazetteer* – 'a stupendous task', he immodestly conceded. He seemed to have no fond memories of compiling it. 'I didn't want to do it,' he recalled in his twilight years. 'Was ordered. Had no choice. They said they would give me 2,000 rupees.' He wrote it at a furious pace in what little time he could spare from his main official duties, which in those years would include a spell as British chargé d'affaires in Bangkok, several expeditions among the Wild Wa, and delicate negotiations with Chinese mandarins on Burma's eastern border. Scott was eventually granted six months' leave in Rangoon to finish what he would later call 'that confounded *Gazetteer*'. This he did, although he never received his 2,000 rupees. 'They never even thanked me,' he sniffed.

The *Gazetteer* became my constant companion in Burma. When I wasn't hefting around the tome itself, I was carrying notes and photocopies from it. Its learning seemed inexhaustible.

A few days after leaving Namhsan I was back in Mandalay again – but not by choice. I was heading for southern Shan State, where

I hoped to encounter many of the ethnic groups that Scott had described so colourfully in the *Gazetteer*. However, getting there meant laboriously retracing my route to Mandalay, then looping south across the burning plains to connect with the road winding up into the hills towards the town of Kalaw. There was a mountain road that led directly from north to south, but foreigners were not permitted to use it. This was not because it was a poor road (which I'm sure it was), or because Shan guerrillas were active in the area (which they were). It was because the road passed through central Shan State, where the Burmese army were kicking hundreds of thousands of farmers off their ancestral lands in the latest attempt to pacify the Shan. I would learn much more about this later.

In his diary, Scott described the approach by horseback to Kalaw as 'very beautiful but most infernally rocky...the very dickens'. An erratically paved road now snaked through the gorge he had reconnoitred back in 1887, and nearby ran a railway with one of those impossibly tortuous routes that only colonial engineers with coolie labour had the hubris to construct. Kalaw was a halting place for caravans plying the trade route between Burma and the Shan states. The British knew it better as a hot-season retreat, where pretty bungalows nestled among cool pine forests and the water was so pure that every month the train carried a fresh supply back down to the governor in Rangoon. Now the town had been self-consciously spruced up for the tourist trade. Its flowerbeds were framed with whitewashed bricks, and there were English signs everywhere indicating local points of interest. 'Image of Buddha made by bamboo strips about five centuries,' read one breathlessly.

If there had been a sign reading 'Superb young guide with encyclopaedic knowledge of the hill tribes around Kalaw' it would have pointed to Ben. Ben was a walking *Gazetteer*. He was the only man I'd met who had attended both a Palaung wedding, which takes place before dawn, and a Pa-O divorce, where a couple formally dissolve their union by eating tea leaves. Ben's knowledge was the result of his perplexing pedigree – he had Shan, Pa-O and Palaung blood – and of his enthusiasm for hiking faster and further into the hills than other guides. He had a ragged smile, a hypnotically soft voice, and the quiet self-possession of a much older man. Without the sign, I was lucky to find him.

The following morning, after a pall of freezing mist had lifted, Ben and I walked past Kalaw's quaint railway station, its brick facade hung with baskets of petunias, and plunged into the surrounding pine forest. For a while all I could hear was the breeze whistling through the branches and the rhythmic crunch of pine needles underfoot, until we disturbed a large bird with an extraordinarily long tail, probably a drongo, which flew off shrieking as if its feathers were on fire. Kalaw's pine forests were still recovering from the 1970s, when a Japanese logging concern struck a lucrative deal with the Burmese regime to extract timber from the area. 'If they saw a tree and liked it,' said Ben, 'they cut it down.' It was now forbidden to chop down pine trees in the area. But presently we heard the creak of splintering wood and the crash of foliage, and a few minutes later came across three Burmese soldiers with machetes, poised to dismember a newly felled pine. They stared at us sullenly, and I stared back. Ben looked at his feet, and we walked on in silence.

We emerged from the forest on a ridge overlooking the valley. Rice terraces cascaded down the hillsides, looking from a distance like steps through an ornamental garden. For the rest of the day we walked in the baking sun. The area we were passing through was remote but not wild, for most trees had been cut for firewood and the denuded land then planted with crops in the slash-and-burn method of hill tribes everywhere.

A row of Palaung women with hoes worked their way through a field still dotted with charred and smoking tree stumps, the earth behind them brown and ready to plant. For a Palaung, a forest is just a field with lots of trees in the way.

The area had not only Palaung, but also Pa-O and Danu peoples. A hundred years ago Scott had noted that they 'keep themselves scrupulously apart', and there was still evidence of that. Ben told me which tribe inhabited which settlement, and it seemed to me that the Palaung villages were highest, the Pa-O claimed the middle ground, and the Danu seeped into the valleys. This separation was not only geographical, but also cultural. Ben explained that, if a Palaung took a spouse from outside the tribe, he or she would not be allowed to live in the village, although visits would be allowed. This was 'to keep the tribe pure', he said.

We stopped briefly at a ramshackle Danu village to take tea with its octogenarian chief. He quizzed me about the sea, which he had never seen ('Is it big like the Irrawaddy?'), and then Ben and I bowed our heads while he chanted an improvised blessing to protect us on our onward journey. I realised I knew almost nothing about the Danu people. Scott wrote little about them – possibly because, rather boringly, they dressed and spoke like Burmans; he seemed convinced that 'with buses and railway trains they are likely to die out before long'. Scott admired Danu women, however, judging them 'among the prettiest in the Shan States, along with some of the hill Karen clans and the Wa (when they have been recently washed)'.

I can only add that Danu villages, while ramshackle up close, were among the most picturesque from afar. From a hilltop I looked down upon one such Danu settlement. It was situated on a south-facing hillside, with a horseshoe of bamboo groves above and a neat orchard of pear trees at its foot. The simple thatched-roof houses tumbled down the slope with deliberate nonchalance, like bungalows at an exclusive country resort. The valley in which the village sat was a pleasing patchwork of brown fallow paddies and fields of brilliant-green pea plants. And standing at five-thirteenths across this scene of pastoral perfection, obliviously munching grass on the golden mean, was an artfully tethered water buffalo.

Around noon Ben stopped in his tracks. 'The land of the Pa-O starts here,' he declared with a sweep of his hand.

And at that moment, almost as if he had conjured it up, I saw fire in a nearby wheat field – no, not fire, but the flaming orange turbans of Pa-O women in plain black smocks cutting wheat with sickles. Some of them threw down their tools and came to greet us. Close-up I could see that the black smocks bore lines of multicoloured embroidery on the hems and seams, and the turbans were carefully sculpted around a top-knot of jet-black hair. The women had bright, intelligent faces coppered by the sun, and the most striking eyes – dark as an ocean, and curved into paisley swirls, like the kind of exaggerated eyes an occidental child would draw on an oriental face.

Many tapped their turbans and complained to Ben of headaches, doubtless caused by toiling all day under a fierce sun. Their demands rapidly diminished my supply of painkillers – a supply already plundered, it must be said, on the mornings after my sessions with Hseng and various local brews in Maymyo and Hsipaw.

An hour later we stopped for the night at a Pa-O village. The Pa-O were famous for building exquisite wooden monasteries, but I would never have guessed it. The village was a happy shambles of experimental carpentry. Built on stilts, the houses were barn-like, austere and virtually windowless, with wobbly steps and walls of scavenged timber. Sitting cross-legged on a mat outside the largest house was the chief, a magnificent figure with bronzed skin and thick grey eyebrows. He wore a huge white turban and a smile of secret joy. He looked like an Indian fakir after a particularly successful rope trick.

The chief invited us in for tea. His house consisted of one large room with a clay hearth built into the floor at one end and a small partitioned sleeping area. Village problems would be discussed in the room, and it was where we would be sleeping. I learned that he was the paramount chief for over 20,000 families in villages scattered across the hills. The chief smiled, cleared his throat, then leaned over to gob horrifically into a white enamel spittoon sitting on the floor between us.

According to my notes from the *Gazetteer*, the Pa-O 'are well known all over Siam and Cambodia and as far as the Lower Mekhong – about Bassac and the rapids of the Thousand Islands. In the Shan States they are cultivators. When they go abroad they are most commonly elephant and horse-dealers.' The Pa-O were the largest ethnic group in Shan State after the Shan, and grew as a cash crop the cordia tree, whose leaves were used to wrap cheroots. The *Gazetteer* then provided a primer for the amorous Pa-O male ('Love-making must not be carried on by stealth, though the proper time is after dark') before going on to note that, although nominally Buddhists, the Pa-O bury rather than burn their dead: 'When a Taungthu [the Burmese word for Pa-O] dies it is customary to tie the thumbs and great toes together. This is said by some to be intended to make walking after death less probable.'

'Less probable': it was a classic Scott touch. I suspected it was his way of putting some distance between himself and the often outlandish traditions he described. I recalled the tale of the missionary in South America who spent years learning a particular tribe's language and preaching to them about God, only to discover that the word the tribe had mischievously told him meant 'God' actually meant 'Satan'. The story was well worn and possibly apocryphal, but the lesson still stands: one is at the mercy of one's guide and interpreter. I'm sure this occurred to Scott during his compilation of the *Gazetteer*.

It had certainly crossed my mind with Ben. As night fell, and the temperature plummeted, we sat on the floor with the chief and ate the simple meal of curry and fried vegetables which Ben had conjured up from the contents of his tiny rucksack. Afterwards we gathered around the hearth with a group of young Pa-O women, their bewitching black eyes sparkling in the firelight, and Ben began to describe some of the customs and superstitions of the tribe. Apparently it was very bad luck for mushrooms to sprout under the house, but very good luck if hornets nested in the rafters – or had I got that the wrong way round? – and the mad could be treated by hanging a lock of their grandmother's hair round their necks.

'Wait a minute,' I interrupted suspiciously. 'What if both your grandmothers are dead and buried?'

'Then there is nothing that can be done for you,' replied Ben – a tad too quickly I thought. I mean, was that *it*? The Palaung, I knew, had a million and one cures for insanity, one of which was to discharge a hunting rifle next to the patient's head.

But Ben turned it back on me. The chief, he said, wanted to hear about a tradition of my own people. Fixed by half a dozen pairs of Pa-O eyes, I racked my brain for a suitable Great British superstition to rival, say, what Ben claimed was a last-ditch Pa-O cure for a man on his deathbed – a process of bewildering and frankly dubious complexity in which the patient's toenail clippings were wrapped in a fragment of his underpants and buried at a spot selected after impossibly arcane calculations involving his day of birth, his birth animal and the cardinal points – and finally, rather pathetically, I came up with this:

'In my country,' I ventured, 'when we spill salt, we always throw a pinch of it over our left shoulder to blind the devil. Otherwise, you know . . . it's very bad luck.'

Ben translated this dramatically and at great length. When he had finished, the chief gave me a weak diplomatic smile and turned away, muttering to himself, and somehow I knew from his expression precisely what he was saying: 'What absolute bollocks.'

I slept on the floor beneath three army blankets in a room so dense with wood smoke that my hand disappeared when I raised it above my head. The chief retired behind a partitioned sleeping area, and the animated fireside talk of Ben and the Pa-O women was punctuated by his titanic burps. It was a very long night – hard floor, cold feet, country noises – but eventually dawn leaked through the interstices of the bamboo walls to throw phoney starlight on the floor, and the villagers greeted a new day with an aubade of mild expectoration, and finally, blessedly, there was birdsong. And then a diesel-powered threshing machine started up beneath the house.

I folded my bedding and joined Ben by the fire, where he was frying eggs for breakfast.

'What was everyone talking about last night?' I asked.

'The women? They were just talking about what price they will get for their ginger at Nan Teng market today.'

'I thought you were talking about politics.'

'These people don't talk about politics,' said Ben, lifting a frizzled egg from the hot oil with a spoon. 'That is all far away from here. They talk about their crops. They talk about when the rains will come. Everything is very peaceful here.'

What Ben omitted to say was that this tranquillity was a relatively recent phenomenon. The Pa-O once deployed one of the largest armies in Burma, with thousands of insurgents operating in the hills around Inle Lake and the Shan capital of Taunggyi. After a series of blistering attacks by the Burmese army, a substantially smaller Pa-O force signed a ceasefire agreement with Rangoon in 1991. But it seemed that the Pa-O, through the Pa-O National Organization (PNO), still had some autonomy in how they ran their own affairs.

'There are no police or military in the area,' said Ben. 'The Pa-O look after themselves.' The PNO were the top authority, he went on, with the power to try Pa-O for murder and carry out executions. They were based in Nan Teng, where the market was.

'And the PNO – they're good men?' I asked Ben.

'Oh yes,' he replied. 'They are good men.'

'So what kind of criminals do they execute?'

'Drug dealers, mostly,' said Ben. 'If you are caught, they take you into the forest and shoot you immediately.' He seemed to approve of this rough justice. 'There are no drug dealers around here any more,' he said firmly. 'Everything is very peaceful.'

After breakfast we went to say goodbye to the chief. He sat outside the village shop, a shack selling cheroots and Chinese cigarettes, beturbanned and swathed in a blanket, doing a startling impression of Omar Sharif in *Lawrence of Arabia*. I pestered Ben to ask him more about Pa-O rural justice. As recently as a decade ago there were stocks in the village, the chief told us, where minor offenders were punished. These had since been moved to Nan Teng, and the chief referred most cases to the PNO leadership there. He rarely dispensed justice himself, unless you counted the drunken youths he sometimes lashed to a sturdy pole outside his house and left there for a few days to cool off. Alcohol wasn't permitted in the village.

But what, I persisted, was the punishment for, say, stealing a buffalo? The chief nodded his massive head wisely as Ben translated. A man caught stealing a buffalo, he smiled benevolently, might spend a month or more in the stocks at Nan Teng as a first warning. This seemed fairly lenient to me, considering the economic importance of a buffalo to a peasant family. And the second warning? Well, said the chief calmly, his smile unwavering, if a man was caught stealing another buffalo he was usually taken into the forest and shot.

Jesus, I thought, that's one hell of a second warning.

'So I bet there aren't many buffalo thieves around here either,' I said to Ben.

'Oh no,' he whispered monkishly. 'Everything is *very* peaceful.'

We planned to spend that night at a Red Palaung village higher in the mountains. It was the best part of day's walk away, and en route we passed cheerful columns of Pa-O women going to Nan Teng market. They were immaculately dressed, for the market was also a social occasion. It was a good place to find a husband too: bringing up the rear was a young single woman wearing shiny pink lipstick and dainty smears of thanaka on her cheeks and forehead.

The saopha of Yawnghwe State once offered to buy Scott a Pa-O woman 'for dispatch to England as a curiosity'. Over a century later, another grubby human transaction was on the cards. The regime was now looking for families to inhabit its 'Village for National Races', a sort of living museum of Burma's ethnic groups under construction on Rangoon's outskirts. Ben told me that twenty families from different ethnic groups in the Kalaw area had been instructed to 'volunteer' for two- or three-month stretches at the 'village'. They would receive no salary, just supplies of rice and other basics. 'None of the families want to go,' said Ben.

They would want to even less if they saw it, as I did when I returned to Rangoon. The compound consisted of a set of newly completed but already shabby pavilions raised on stilts and linked by walkways decorated with potted palms and bougainvillea bushes. These floral touches could not disguise the fact that the whole complex sat on a steaming, noxious swamp, an unhealthy habitat for anyone, but particularly for hill-dwelling peoples accustomed to cooler climes. At the riverside I found a single workman pounding nails into a half-built wooden jetty. Tourists would arrive from central Rangoon by boat, it seemed, presumably to avoid the less picturesque poverty and squalor of the nearby township of Thaketa.

An old woman, L-shaped, hobbled along the path towards us. She wore a red-striped smock and crimson rattan hoops around her waist: a Red Palaung, then.

'How are you today, grandmother?' I enquired in perfect Palaung. (Ben had been patiently coaching me for an hour.)

'Something something something something,' she replied in rapid Palaung, obviously flattered, and then added in English, 'Thank you' – which I felt was just showing off.

My shameful failure as a linguist was acutely felt while

researching the life of the polyglottal Scott. He picked up foreign
tongues with astonishing ease, and, if his third wife is to be believed,
he was first attracted to Burma by the difficulty of the language.
('The harder they were,' she wrote, 'the better he liked them.') I
had only a smattering of Burmese, but even that seemed like a
small victory over astounding linguistic odds. Burmese has the
perverse syntax of Japanese and the tonal complexities of Chinese.
Its writing system is based on a devilish series of interconnecting
circles. Apparently, it is a great compliment to say to a Burmese
person:

လက်ရေး သိပ်ဝိုင်းတာပဲ

This means, 'Your handwriting is so *round.*'
One of my favourite books was a collection of Burmese proverbs
I had bought in Rangoon. Burmese, I learned, had pleasing
equivalents to many English sayings and idioms. To throw pearls
before swine, for example, was 'to play a harp for a water buffalo';
to blow your own trumpet was 'to praise the pickling of your own
fish'; to bask in someone else's glory was 'to lean on the sacred
white elephant and suck sugar cane'. However, there was one
Burmese phrase with no direct English equivalent, and it involved
an extremely delicate matter. When a man was sitting in such a
way that his sarong was gaping open, how did you politely inform
him? Well, now I knew. You said cryptically, 'Excuse me, sir, but I
see your department store is open even on weekends.'
The *Gazetteer* also had a list of phrases in Burmese, Shan and
umpteen different ethnic languages, but it wasn't exactly practical.
(I presume that knowing how to say 'How old is this horse?' and 'Let
them go!' was vital in Scott's day.) Fortunately my friend Sarah, a
talented linguist who had studied Burmese in London and whose
handwriting was very round indeed, had taught me some more
useful sentences. These included 'What is your name?' and 'Very
hot today, isn't it?', as well as valuable restaurant phrases like
'Don't skimp on the chillies' and the not-unrelated query 'Where
are the toilets?'
Even with this meagre linguistic armoury, I was startled to
realise that I could suddenly *hear* Burmese. The people around
me were no longer speaking a string of unintelligible syllables
that I didn't understand; they were speaking a string of *intelligible*
syllables that I didn't understand. It made all the difference.
It also made me dangerously overconfident. Some Burmese
friends once challenged me to try out my skills on a taxi driver

during a fairly boozy night out in Rangoon. So I leaned forward and casually told him to keep driving straight ahead. In fact, due to some crucial tonal imprecision in my delivery, I had actually invited the driver to mount me roughly from behind. But this was only explained to me an hour later, when my companions had finally stopped laughing.

The Red Palaung village was nearby. Its houses were as big and sturdy as barns, and rested massively on tree-trunk stilts set in hollows laboriously chipped from a steep mountain ridge. These, said Ben, had once been longhouses where over a dozen families might have lived, but in the last twenty years they had been cut into smaller units – longish houses. The village's highest point was occupied by a temple so ramshackle it looked derelict, the lowest by the village pump and nat shrine, both lost in the dense shade of three venerable banyan trees with interlocking branches. Every other space was occupied by black pigs. Immense, grunting sows flopped in the afternoon sun like punctured inner tubes, while legions of piglets, as hyperactive as rats, rootled and squealed and scurried beneath the houses.

Ben, who had a reputation as a healer, was soon summoned to the chief's house. In a gloomy, smoke-filled room a sick old woman lay swaddled in blankets by the fire. The chief's son squatted nearby and began to talk while Ben took the woman's temperature. 'He says his mother has a fever because she ate too many papayas,' Ben sighed. 'It's a very old belief.' He had heard it all before: bathing too soon after eating, offending a vengeful earth ogre or water spirit, pissing under a sacred tree – for hill tribes like the Palaung, disease had a million improbable causes.

The old woman had a slight temperature. Ben dropped two aspirin into a cracked teacup, where they fizzed authoritatively. Eating too much papaya did not cause fever, he told the woman as she drank. In fact, Ben added, papaya was an excellent source of vitamin A (although he told me later that some tribes use the fruit's seeds and flesh to terminate pregnancies). I had bought some multivitamins in Kalaw, and Ben now counted out ten on to a scrap of paper and folded it up. The woman put the tiny package beneath her thigh and lay on it for safe keeping. Then she pulled the blanket around her and, staring at the fire with watery eyes, started muttering.

'What is she saying?' I asked.

Ben smiled with exasperation. 'She's saying she really shouldn't have eaten all that papaya. Otherwise she wouldn't be ill now.'

For the next two hours Ben spun around the village dispensing aspirin and multivitamins. There was a lot of illness. Old women in faded and grimy Red Palaung costumes swung round to show Ben even filthier babies, hot to the touch and breathing like frightened birds, slung from their papooses. Ben cooed and lectured and dispensed. I watched him, and was in turn scrutinised expectantly by a gang of small children, their stomachs pot-bellied with worms, bubbles of snot expanding and shrinking in their nostrils.

Aspirin and multivitamins would do nothing for Ben's next patient, a young man. He lay apparently dying of cerebral malaria in a shack clinging to a hill on the outskirts of town. There were over a dozen family members inside. A brother roughly wiped the man's face; a sister stroked his hands, while another hugged his legs. The man's already thin Palaung face was gaunt with malnutrition. His bony jaw hung open, cat's-cradled with spittle, and his bulging eyes made slow unfocused sweeps of the soot-blackened roof.

The man hadn't caught malaria in this village; it was too cold for mosquitoes here. He was an indirect victim of the Palaung's rapacious slash-and-burn agriculture. There was a shortage of timber in the heavily cultivated highlands, and the villagers were forced to travel some distance in search of firewood, often descending into warmer, malarial, forests to cut trees. This man had been chopping wood in just such a forest.

The man suddenly tried to sit up, his eyes rolling wildly. He was hallucinating. 'The house is on fire!' he screamed. 'The house is on fire, the house is on fire!' His siblings restrained and quietened him, and smiled weakly.

The family told Ben they had made an offering to the nats. Ben nodded but said nothing. Then he quietly but firmly told the family that they must take the man to the hospital in Kalaw. 'This is always the hardest part,' Ben told me later. 'The Palaung don't trust hospitals. They think they're going to die there.' It usually took the combined entreaties of Ben, the village chief and the local abbot to persuade them to go. They were also afraid of the cost: about 5,000 kyat, just fifteen dollars, for each week of drugs and treatment, which was way beyond what they could afford. Ben and I offered to pay the hospital fees. This didn't seem to make any difference. They were worried that the man would die on the stretcher during the five-hour trek to Kalaw. Ben told them he would die where he lay if they did nothing, and he would return in the morning to check they had left for town.

We walked back through the village. For the first time I registered a smart-looking wooden building with a heavy padlock on the door.

A sign outside announced the building as a medical centre for the United Nations Development Programme.

'Ben, hang on a minute,' I said. 'Isn't that a clinic?'

'No,' he replied drily, 'that is just a nice place for the UN people to sleep when they come to visit.' The clinic had been built over a year before at great expense. At the same time the village had been plastered with UN posters teaching basic hygiene with the aid of simple cartoons. Two rainy season later, the posters were washed out and peeling, and the clinic had yet to open. The best cure for a headache, the villagers now joked, was to go up to its walls of fine, factory-hewn teak, and sniff them.

Over the centuries, and with no assistance from the UN, the Palaung had developed an immense body of folk medicine, much of it indirectly inherited from Brahmin priests brought to the Burmese court as prisoners of various old wars. According to a 1920s study of the tribe, the Palaung have bizarre and inventive treatments for almost every common ailment. Rheumatism can be cured by scraping the aching body part with the horns of a buffalo which has been struck dead by lightning. A ring made from rhinoceros horn will ward off cholera and stop diarrhoea. One remedy for a malaise-stricken youth is marriage; if a suitable partner cannot be found, the youth will be ritually wed to a chicken (the mere threat of which, I imagine, would be enough to make the most miserable teenager perk up in a hurry). During colonial times, one Palaung chief wore beneath his turban a special root, tightly bound in cotton to stop the resident spirit escaping, which he believed rendered all his faults invisible to visiting British officials.

We retired to one of the longish houses. Two families lived there, about thirteen people in all, representing four generations, from the L-shaped woman we had met on the path to her gurgling great-grandchild swinging in a hammock improvised from a rice sack. One large room held the clay hearth, where Ben was rustling up some dinner, and sliding doors led to an even larger room. Most Buddhists in Burma distanced themselves from their animist origins by banishing the nat shrine to the outdoors. But, interestingly, in this house it was built into a corner not far from the flower-decorated alcove in which the Buddha images sat. I watched our host pray for half a candle's length to the Buddha. Then, still on his knees, he shuffled around forty-five degrees and bowed deeply to the nat shrine.

Darkness fell, and the temperature plunged with it, and after dinner we huddled around the fire.

Fifteen years ago the main crop in these parts had been *Papaver somniferum*: the opium poppy. Now the villagers grew tea, corn, peas, garlic and cordia trees, and Ben said they made more money that way. That didn't surprise me. As I would discover among the Wa, the only sight more sickening than the conspicuous wealth of Burma's drug barons was the wretched poverty of those who harvested the opium for them. And only recently, our host revealed, the villagers had performed a dark and ancient ritual to banish a mystery plague (cholera? smallpox?) that had killed over twenty people.

The preparations for this rare event were elaborate. First the villagers carved four wooden guns, four wooden swords, and four wooden bows and arrows. These were put into a monk's alms bowl along with four lengths of rope, eight charms made of paper or metal with magical inscriptions, some sand, and a few handfuls of uncooked rice. The alms bowl was placed at the centre of the village, and four monks came down from the monastery to chant incantations over it. Then the contents were split equally between four parties, each of which erected a 'nat gate' (as Ben translated it) on one of the paths leading out of the village to the north, south, east and west. (Plague never crossed fields or emerged from the forest but, rather obligingly, always entered along the path, just like everyone else.) First two holes were dug, with a charm placed in each, and the poles were raised. Then a rope was strung between these, and the wooden weapons were hung upon it. For the next twenty-four hours no one was permitted to enter or leave the village. During that time consecrated sand and rice was sprinkled on the floors of every house, and the walls were beaten with sticks to drive the plague-causing spirit from town. The nat gates ensured it would not return.

The ritual seemed to me to have at least some practical value. Beating the walls might flush out disease-carrying vermin. Forbidding anyone to enter or leave the village was a crude form of quarantine, although a single day was far too short to be effective. But, according to our host, it worked. The mystery plague vanished.

The fireside talk turned to the *kalabwa* – us foreigners. More and more of them were coming on tours to the once remote villages within a day's trek of Kalaw. The main draw were Palaung longhouses, and the two villages in the area where they could still be found now swarmed with tourists arriving in large parties on bullock carts from Kalaw, bringing T-shirts for the adults and pens for the children.

'In some villages the children won't go to school any more,' said Ben. 'They just wait around all day for the foreigners to come.' He blamed the guides. Most were Burman, he said, incurable lowlanders who spoke no more than a few words of any hill language, and had no understanding of the effect their visits had on remote communities – which, it must be said, benefitted little from the visits of foreigners once the novelty factor had worn off. Tourism was the next plague, it seemed, and any number of nat gates would not prevent its coming.

It got light early, but the sun would not rise above the ridge behind us and penetrate our gully for another hour. Instead, it lit up the surrounding hilltops like candles. We had breakfast, then did our rounds.

The woman who had caught a fever from eating papaya was much improved. The man with cerebral malaria was no longer clawing the smoky air and screaming fire, but his eyes were glassy and vacant and his breath rattled with phlegm. The family had finally agreed to go to the hospital, although they intended to take a roundabout route to Kalaw, since to head there directly was considered very bad luck. Ben was delighted. He felt there was every chance the man would survive the trip and make a full recovery. (And, as I later learned, he did.)

We headed north, on a path that would itself eventually take me back to Kalaw. Just outside the village Ben stopped and pointed into the vegetation.

'Look,' he said.

Almost invisible in the green was the paraphernalia of one of the nat gates. There were two wooden posts about eight or nine feet high, with holes at the top to tie a rope through. Nearby lay a wooden gun, a sword and an arrow.

'Is it OK to pick them up?' I asked Ben.

'It's OK,' he said, although afterwards I realised that he himself didn't touch them, not even with the toe of his jungle boot.

I picked them up and turned them slowly in my hands – the sword, the gun, the arrow. They were muddy and rotten, and pocked by the tiny excavations of insects, but I could see that they were simple and well carved, like a sturdy child's toy from a bygone era. Crouching in that sun-bereft nook, poring over this evidence of local sorcery, I got a shiver of excitement. The whole ritual had probably done more for the villagers' peace of mind than the UN clinic, and to stumble upon the charms seemed an apt farewell to a place where we had encountered so much sickness.

I wanted to take the imitation weapons with me, but one look at Ben made me decide otherwise. I laid the sword, the gun and the arrow back in the grass. Above us, in a sunny copse of trees on the hilltop, birds began their private conversations, and we hiked up towards them, into the light and warmth.

7

Back in Kalaw I said goodbye to Ben and headed further east by car for the nearby town of Yawnghwe. It was once the capital of an important Shan fiefdom of the same name, but was now better known as a base for exploring the picturesque Inle Lake. A market day was in full swing when I arrived, and Yawnghwe's canal was clogged with small boats loaded to near sinking point with vegetables grown on the lake's celebrated floating gardens. The market itself was the usual collection of makeshift stalls inadequately shaded by wildly flapping tarpaulins. Pa-O women with fiery turbans moved gracefully among the otherwise indistinguishable ranks of Shan, Palaung and Burmese shoppers. As dusk approached, the town emptied. By eight o'clock its deserted streets rang with the eerie, animal drone of amplified voices from a handful of late-night karaoke booths.

Scott arrived in Yawnghwe – or Nyaungshwe as the Burmans called it – as part of the Shan States Expedition of 1887, to discover one of the largest courts in Further India. The saopha's staff included over 170 guards, 4 elephant keepers and 12 umbrella bearers, as well as 60 oarsmen to pull an enormous golden barge in the shape of the mythical hintha bird. Despite the extravagance of his court, the saopha did not impress Scott, who dismissed the hereditary ruler of an area larger than Hampshire as 'an infernal old ruffian'.

The nearby Inle Lake was famous for the Intha, or 'Children of the Lake', a Tibeto-Burman people who arrived from southern Burma, perhaps as prisoners of war, during the reign of King Narapatisithu, or roughly the same time as the Fourth Crusade rolled into Constantinople. The Intha were popularly known for their curious ability to row with one leg while standing stork-like on the other. This freed up their hands to cast a fishing net, and to gesture furiously at passing tourist boats which frightened away the fish.

But the Intha were not the first ethnic group that tourists were likely to encounter in Yawnghwe. Menus, posters and calendars in restaurants and hotels across the town were plastered with images of Padaung women, still better known as 'giraffe women' or 'long-necks' for the heavy brass rings they wore around their throats. The Padaung were the most exotic and recognisable of all Burma's hill peoples, and in some ways the most emblematic of these peoples' plight. They hailed from Kayah State to the south, a land riven by war between Karenni insurgents and the Burmese army. Many Padaung fled over the border into so-called 'long-neck villages' in northern Thailand, where tourists paid them to pose for photographs. In recent years Padaung women had also come north to make a living along Burma's narrow tourist trail. I had heard that there was a 'long-neck village' in Yawnghwe, and one morning I set out to look for it.

Freak shows were hardly new to Padaung women. They had been paraded before the Burmese king at Mandalay, and, if one story is to be believed, had appeared at an exhibition in London which Scott saw as a teenager. The sight of these 'Brass-Bound Belles of Burma' (as one colonial travelogue quaintly described them) fired young George's imagination, and he vowed then and there that one day he would visit the faraway land where these magical creatures lived. Or so the story goes. I could find no evidence of Padaung women having visited Britain during Scott's youth. However, we do know that a troupe travelled in England in the 1930s as part of the famous Bertram Mills Circus, and were a huge success. Cyril Bertram Mills described them as 'the biggest side show attraction we ever had' – bigger, certainly, than the Plate-Lipped Women of Oubangichari, who had been a bit of a flop in London.

The Padaung show was so well received that a circus scout was dispatched to Burma to recruit a second troupe. He passed through Yawnghwe on his way south to the village of Pekkong. The journey was 'a series of nightmares', recounted Mills. 'The roads were no more than tracks through jungle, cut by the wheels of wagons drawn by oxen, and the only means of transport was an antiquated car with every ailment in the book, the hire of which cost seven shillings a mile.' At Pekkong the scout found a group of Padaung women who were only too eager to visit England. The first troupe had been treated well and had made a lot of money. Wrote Mills, 'When the women left Pekkong they were as thin as rakes, their clothes were rags and they had never worn shoes, so they had to be properly fitted out in Rangoon and on the ship they were stuffed with food so they would be presentable.'

The women toured England on a double-decker bus, refitted with three bedrooms on the upper deck and a kitchen and dining room on the lower. They had difficulty adjusting to the blandness of English food. Mills recalled how their demand for hot spices meant that 'the man who bought catering stores had to clean every town we visited out of cayenne pepper'. The foulness of English weather was another problem. Maurice Collis, the former colonial judge, paid sixpence to enter a 'giraffe woman' show at Piccadilly, to discover the Padaung seated behind a barricade 'being shown as freaks to a gaping crowd'. One of the women wore a fur coat she had bought at Barker's, and the rest were knitting woollen jumpers.

A Padaung girl will don her first ring between the ages of six and ten. An auspicious day is chosen by divination using chicken bones, then her neck is prepared with an embrocation of coconut milk and dog fat. The ring is about as thick as an adult's little finger, and more are added each year until the girl reaches adolescence. The brass coils do not lengthen the girl's neck but, as X-rays startlingly reveal, force her collarbones and ribs downward, creating only the illusion of an extended neck. Sometimes she will wear coils on her legs and arms too. The neck rings throttle her voice and give her a distinctive stooping gait; the leg rings make her waddle, as does the sheer effort of carrying around all this metal, which can weigh over fifty pounds – equivalent to four complete sets of Scott's five-volume *Gazetteer*. Yet the Padaung are not ornaments. They are hard-working country women who must fetch water, till the fields, lug goods to market, and bring up children. The rings are cleaned with tamarind or lemon juice and are never removed, not even while sleeping. Over the years the neck muscles atrophy. 'When a missionary once persuaded a Padaung lady to forgo her ornamentation,' recalled Scott, 'the sight of her neck hanging over like that of a dead hen was so painful that he reluctantly agreed to its replacement.'

Not even the Padaung knew for certain how this remarkable practice had originated. One theory was that the rings were worn to make the women unattractive to slave raiders, although the Padaung regarded the neck coils as signs of beauty. Or, went another theory, the rings were armour to protect the women against tigers and other wild animals. Or, as with the Golden Palaung I had met, the practice had its origins in the tribe's creation myth. The Padaung believed they were descendants of a dragon impregnated by the wind, and it was thought that perhaps their long necks were a tribute to the dragon mother.

The 'long-neck village' in Yawnghwe was run by a hotel called the Hupin. It was strategically located by a car park where buses disgorged Hupin guests on to boats for day trips on the lake, and cost three dollars to enter. One of the hotel's staff led me into a concrete compound occupied by a two-storey wooden house and a thatched hut.

'Traditional Padaung house,' explained the Hupin man, pointing at the hut.

A Padaung woman was sitting inside, working a loom with

Scott's portrait of Padaung 'giraffe women' in the 1890s.

Padaung refugees in Thailand a century later. (Nic Dunlop)

rehearsed absorption – A Padaung Woman At Work. Two little girls appeared. They wore neck rings, thick blusher and bubblegum-pink lipstick. Each smiled shyly from beneath a fringe of hair, cut in the Padaung's pudding-bowl style. They looked like dolls.

'You can take photographs, if you like,' urged the Hupin man, before breaking into a practised spiel. 'There are two families living here. This woman is thirty-seven years old, she has twenty-five rings. Twenty-five rings is the maximum. This girl is five, she already has twelve rings; the other girl is fourteen, she has seventeen rings.' He took a breath. 'You want to take photo?' The girls giggled obligingly. The woman did not look up from her loom. 'She is making traditional Padaung bags,' apologised the Hupin man.

'How long have these families been here?' I asked.

'They came about two years ago,' he smiled. He was very smiley.

'But Padaung women don't come from around here, do they?'

'No. They come from Kayah State. In the south. We bring them here so tourists can see them.' He explained this cheerfully; he had no nose for controversy.

Another Padaung woman emerged from the wooden house and shuffled up, listless as a zombie. The embracing coils made her head hover a full foot above her shoulders. A striking feature of any Padaung woman is her expressive black eyes, which rove constantly to compensate for the immobility of her neck, but this woman stared blankly into the distance. 'She also has twenty-five rings,' chirped the Hupin man. 'Wait here . . .' He disappeared, and returned moments later with a spiral of brass and put it in my hand. 'See? It is very heavy. This woman's rings they weigh over twenty pounds.'

Unbidden, the woman turned around and pulled down the collar of her shirt to show the full extent of her rings. She bowed her head slightly as she did so, and stood with the awkward stillness of a long-suffering child showing a bruise to a social worker. Protruding at right angles from the lower neck coils was a small ring which had reminded Scott of 'the handle of a teapot'. He theorised that it was used to tie the women up, although I heard a story that contradicted this. During the Second World War four Padaung women were taken prisoner by Japanese soldiers and secured by a bamboo pole pushed in turn through each of their small rings. What the Japanese didn't know was that the small ring can be unthreaded from the neck coil, just as a key is taken from a keyring. In the morning the bamboo pole was empty – except for four small rings.

121

'Why do you not want to take photo?' The Hupin man was getting worried.

I asked him whom I should give my three dollars to.

'You can give it to me,' he smiled. 'I am the caretaker.'

'Why don't I give it to her?' I said petulantly, gesturing towards the miserable Padaung woman.

The caretaker's smile creaked wider.

'As you like,' he said.

It troubled me that I couldn't ask the Padaung women if they were happy with their strange new life. The grinning caretaker probably spoke their language, but I could hardly trust him to interpret. By sheer chance, however, I later met a social worker who not only had talked to the women, but was Padaung himself. The first thing he did was correct me.

'Padaung is what the Burmese call us,' he said. 'It is a Burmese word only. We call ourselves Kayan.'

I asked him if the Kayan women in the Hupin compound were happy. 'They said they were happy,' the social worker said. 'They were glad to be making money. But I asked if the children were going to school, and they said they weren't. In fact none of them were allowed to leave the compound.'

'Not even to walk around town?'

'Especially not to walk around town. Then the tourists would see them for free. The family I talked to had been there five months already. I said to them, "What about your future – what about your *children's* future?" But they wouldn't listen, and I can't force them to leave.' He shook his head sadly. 'We need to convince them it is not money that is the priority, but their dignity.'

The social worker said there was another tourist compound with four Kayan families on the west shore of Inle Lake, and yet another back in Kalaw. By contrast, he knew of only one village in Kayah State itself where girls still wore neck rings. The whole practice was fading away, he said.

I found this sad, not least because it allowed those who ran this growing number of 'long-neck' attractions to claim that they were helping to preserve a dying culture. Were they really? In her native village a Kayan woman's neck rings were symbols of beauty, wealth and status; they were a living part of her ethnic identity. For a girl growing up as a semi-captive in a human zoo, far from the rituals and rhythms of village life, what cultural significance could the rings have? They were simply the means by which greedy Burmese hotels like the Hupin could extract money from ill-informed tourists.

Across the border in Thailand the 'long-neck villages' were not preserving Kayan tradition but distorting it. What most tourists didn't realise was that those villages weren't villages at all, but annexes to camps packed with thousands of rather less photogenic Karenni refugees who had also been driven from their native soil by Burmese troops and largely forgotten by the world. There was evidence that adult Kayan women there were donning neck rings for the first time – something not usually done, for very practical reasons. Nobody pretends that Kayan girls feel no pain from their rings – look closely at postcards of them sold in Chiang Mai and you can spot weal's around their throats – but their still-growing bones have a chance to adapt to the unyielding brass embrace. An adult woman who stacks her fully grown neck with coils goes through agony.

At first it puzzled me that Burma, a country run by a rabidly anti-colonial regime, should update and legitimise the Victorian freak show for the entertainment of foreign tourists. But actually it made perfect sense. While attending a party in Rangoon, a travel agent I knew had met Lieutenant General Kyaw Ba, a former regional commander, who as Burma's minister of tourism gained a reputation for operatic venality. The travel agent tried to engage Kyaw Ba in a conversation about his country's ethnic minorities. 'The only thing I know about minorities,' the minister of tourism cheerfully replied, 'is how to kill them.' The remark was barbaric, but wholly accurate. The Burmese army, which was overwhelmingly made up of ethnic Burmans, had spent decades fighting different ethnic insurgent groups: Karen, Kachin, Palaung, Arakanese, Shan, Pa-O, Chin, Mon, Wa. It didn't care about their customs or their needs. Now that ceasefires had been brokered with nearly all the insurgents, the Burmese regime was concerned only that ethnic groups observed these agreements and provided enough of their number for state-orchestrated displays of national unity – and for money-spinning tourist shows. In other words, the regime wanted its minorities to be seen but not heard, and the freak-show format was perfect for this.

I would see a bigger and more wretched human zoo before my travels in Scott's footsteps were over. But the 'long-neck village' in Yawnghwe depressed me more profoundly. I just felt there had to be more to the destiny of Kayan women and girls than being forever gawped at – being, quite simply, professional freaks.

'They wear rings around their neck and colourful costumes,' the social worker told me, 'but that is not what matters. Inside they are still human beings.'

*

Yawnghwe owed its existence neither to tourism nor to trade, but to the inhabitant of a rambling mansion to the north of the town. This was the palace of the great saopha, and in the past nearly everyone in Yawnghwe had depended upon him for their livelihood.

The palace, or *haw*, was now a museum run by the Ministry of Culture. It was the strangest building: a happy confusion of English red brick and tropical hardwood, with a royal seven-tiered spire soaring from a gloomy stone arcade. A few arches enclosing the south courtyard had been damaged by a British incendiary bomb, which happily did not detonate and was heaved into the lake by the saopha's men after many prayers to the town's guardian spirit. Otherwise the palace was remarkably intact considering the years of neglect. The main entrance was reached by the Dragon Stairs, presumably named after the shape of their handrails, which unfurled like giant serpents. At the foot of the stairs, inscribed with the knightly motto *'Honi soit qui mal y pense'*, was the cannon with which the saopha had given himself nine-gun salutes.

I entered by a side door – it was bad manners to use the front entrance – paid my two dollars entrance fee, and climbed a newly varnished staircase into a high, teak-panelled room. It was dark and lofty like an English country church. Even though large windows ran along both sides of the hall, it remained murky, as if the Shan hardwood absorbed light. This was the Great Hall of Audience, where Shan officials formally paid obeisance to the saopha as he reclined on a golden divan beneath royal white umbrellas. Nearby was an enormous painting of Sir Sao Maung, saopha from 1897, a bulldog of a man whose neck bulged over the collar of his ceremonial robes. There were wooden palanquins and peeling gold-painted howdahs, and some marvellous costumes, unfortunately exposed to direct sunlight, with heavy brocade, uncountable sequins, and bell-shaped folds so familiar from formal photos of King Thibaw.

In one room there was a magnificent long sword, gold-plated and almost as tall as the succession of portly Yawnghwe saophas who had symbolically wielded it. Hanging in the hall's eastern wing was a grand portrait of Sao Shwe Thaike, a British-trained army officer who in 1927 became – to give him his full title – the Very Just King of Great Lineage of Yawnghwe State Who is Full of Dignity and the Arbiter of Life. Plump, bespectacled and severe, Sao Shwe Thaike looked like a provincial bank manager with some very bad news about that loan you requested. But his *haw* was a magical place. Hassoldt Davis, an American adventurer who stayed there in the 1930s, felt as if he had 'stepped backward in time to the days of Marco Polo . . . Time in the Haw was not marked by the common minutes and hours of a clock. At three-hour intervals a group of musicians somewhere in the depths of the palace played soft Burmese songs, night and day, to indicate what time it was.'

During World War II, when Japan occupied the country, the palace's ground floor was requisitioned by the brutal Japanese secret police. As Patricia Elliott recounted in her book *The White Umbrella*, the saopha's young son, Tiger, entertained himself by dropping things on the Japanese through a hole in the floorboards, and had to be physically restrained from cranking up the phonograph and playing his favourite record, 'God Save the King'.

After the war, and after Burma gained independence in 1948, Sao Shwe Thaike, already a Shan politician of importance, became president of Burma. He spent much of his time in Rangoon, where he was ferried between appointments in a parting gift from the British, a Rolls-Royce Phantom. (I had seen the car displayed in a military museum in Rangoon. It had headlamps the size of woks, and a conspicuous hole in the bonnet where the silver lady had once stood.) Then came March 1962. In the dead of night Sao Shwe Thaike and his family were awoken by gunfire and found their Rangoon house surrounded by General Ne Win's troops. One of the saopha's sons was shot through the head – a 'mistake', the army would later admit. Sao Shwe Thaike was bundled into a waiting van and, to use the chilling officialese, 'expired' in custody before the year was out.

None of this dark past was acknowledged at the Yawnghwe museum, of course. In Burma, history stopped in 1962, and propaganda began. Nor was there any reference to Sao Shwe Thaike's formidable widow, Sao Nang Hearn Hkam, the last mahadevi of Yawnghwe and a Shan politician of some stature herself. Less than two years after the death of her husband, to whom she had been sold as a young girl, Sao Nang Hearn Hkam fled to Thailand to lead the war council of the Shan State Army. Sao Nang Hearn Hkam – whose name could be translated sweetly as 'Lady Golden Nest' – was soon advising young Shan rebels under her command on how to save ammunition: never kill a Burmese soldier with two bullets when only one will do.

The mahadevi was now in her eighties and lived with relatives in Canada. No doubt it would anger her to see the Yawnghwe palace today. There are rats' droppings in the meditation chambers and a nest of giant hornets in the throne room. But I found myself grateful just to find the *haw* standing at all. Elsewhere in Shan State an old palace had been demolished by the regime's bulldozers and its valuable contents stolen, sold off or buried beneath the rubble. So much of the saophas' history was now preserved only in the disintegrating photo albums or unpublished memoirs of exiled Shan aristocrats living unassuming lives in North America, Britain and Australia. Here, at least, a part of it had survived in Shan State itself. Critics could easily dismiss the museum as another way of removing hard currency from the bumbags of foreign tourists, but the only visitors I saw at the palace were locals, who paid only a few kyat to enter. Was this their way of paying respect to the late saopha, I wondered? And if not to the saopha then perhaps to notions of Shan nationhood he once enshrined?

From what I had learned of the mahadevi, I suspected she would regard this as overly romantic. ('One bullet, one man,' she warned her SSA fighters.) She would not be the only one. During my travels in Burma – I can't say where – I met a descendant of a great saopha, a man of courage and passion who was much respected by the people, and who, if the system of hereditary rule in Shan territory had somehow persisted, would now also be a Very Just King of Great Lineage Who is Full of Dignity and the Arbiter of Life. Dreamily – stupidly – I asked him if he ever regretted not being able to assume the saopha's title. His answer took me by surprise. It shouldn't have.

'Of course not,' he snapped. 'Why on earth would we want that feudal system again?' He looked at me with fire in his eyes. 'What we want is *democracy*.'

Fort Stedman, Scott's first headquarters in the Shan states, was built at the lakeside village of Myaing Thauk, about seven miles from Yawnghwe. Could any traces of it possibly remain after a century? I heard that there were some very old British gravestones at Myaing Thauk, and this seemed a promising start. I rented a bicycle and set off.

I set off too late. A low, hot sun was strobing through swaying brushes of sugar cane as I pedalled hard along a dusty cart track. At one point I rattled over a stretch of ancient cobbles, almost certainly laid by the British and plied by the Yawnghwe saopha and his myriad retainers on his way to ask Scott another probing question about life in Victorian England. Through the sugar cane I glimpsed the complex roof of a monastery silhouetted against the hammered silver of the lake. I reached Myaing Thauk an hour later, just as the sun was edging over the far hills.

'An old British cemetery?' asked a local man, who was a schoolteacher. 'It's up the hill near the pagoda. But you won't have time to get there before dark.' I persisted, and he wrote the

Burmese words for 'British cemetery' in my notebook. 'Just show this to people,' he said cheerfully. 'Everyone knows where it is.'

I cycled laboriously up the hill along a path that the teacher had indicated. My bike was one of those heavy-duty Chinese machines, built to carry a Yunnanese peasant, his family, a pig and a sack of rice. Soon the going was far too steep to pedal. People emerged from their huts to watch me push my bike past. When I showed them the words in my notebook they were incredibly friendly and would nod vigorously and point in various directions. I suspect I would have received the same enthusiastic response if the teacher had written 'Cydonia, Mars' in my notebook, or 'West Orchard Shopping Centre, Coventry'.

As I climbed, the lake spread out in the valley, its surface rippled black and red by boats as thin as pencil leads. Somewhere down there – possibly on the flat land where the village school now sat – had been Fort Stedman. I had seen photographs of it in Scott's files at the British Library. It looked like a Scout camp on steroids, with huge wooden mess halls and barracks set in the centre of a stockaded patch of denuded earth. The fort was an isolated place where the threat of disease was ever present; cholera killed thousands of people in Yawnghwe State during the rains of 1888. Letters from Rangoon took weeks to arrive at frontier posts, although Scott discovered that the process could be speeded up by bribing the mail runners with titbits of toast soaked in Worcester sauce.

There were no women at Fort Stedman, at least not officially. One of Scott's subordinates did have a pregnant Burmese wife, whom he later abandoned. Such alliances, and the children they inevitably produced, greatly troubled the colonial authorities. As early as 1872 the chief commissioner issued a confidential circular to warn civil servants against dallying with Burmese women. A measure of how seriously this was taken came at the Rangoon races, where one derby was contested by a horse called 'Chief Commissioner's Confidential Circular'. It was beaten by another horse called 'Physiological Necessity', much to the open hilarity of the racegoers. Meanwhile Rangoon's red-light area grew to be reputedly the largest in the Empire, attracting sex workers from as far afield as Germany, Russia, Japan and England. With the annexation of Upper Burma, and the stationing of tens of thousands of imperial troops there, prostitution boomed in Mandalay too. At a Christian meeting in the city the chief commissioner bemoaned 'the crying scandals of the open brothels that now disfigured some of the principal streets', and he was equally horrified by how fragrantly British men shacked up with Burmese women. It was his opinion that 'an officer, openly living with a Burmese mistress, not only degrades himself as an English gentleman, but lowers the prestige of the English name, and largely destroys his own usefulness'. By this definition, one useless Brit was Sir Harvey Adamson, a lieutenant governor of Burma, whose Burmese lover bore him an illegitimate son.

And what about George Scott? What did he get up to? I often wondered about this. True, Scott was a son of the manse (and two of his three wives were daughters of clergymen). But he always seemed to wear his faith lightly, and had lived for most of his adult years 'somewheres east of Suez', as Kipling put it, 'Where there aren't no Ten Commandments'. I found it hard to imagine him reaching his late thirties with his virginity intact – even harder when I recalled his passion for sampling all things Burmese. Scott once said that Burman women had 'the power of beauty without the possession of it', which seemed a coy way of admitting their undeniable attractions. Burma's ethnic peoples invariably had a free-and-easy attitude to sex, as Scott himself learned during an early foray in northern Burma. The area was largely populated by the Kachin tribe, whose menfolk had a formidable reputation as warriors. But Scott was more terrified by the over-amorous Kachin women. In one village he was mobbed by nubile young women, and as he bedded down in a corner of the chief's longhouse that night 'there were still three of them making eyes from under the fringe of hair that hangs down over the forehead and marks the Kachyen maiden . . . I did not dare go to sleep, matters were so desperate.'

As for other ethnic groups, in the *Gazetteer* and other books Scott displayed a subtle connoisseurship of tribal femininity, from the intricacies of a Pa-O woman's headdress to the pattern of tattoos on a Chinbok woman's breasts. Less subtly, he would later refer to 'the bouncing, strapping aborigine woman who is as full of sex impulse as those who write novels for a certain type of reader'. Still, I could find no evidence that Scott kept a Burmese mistress, or had any 'temporary connections' (as the euphemism went) with the ethnic women he so obviously admired.

All this became academic in 1890, when Scott galloped into Fort Stedman with his first wife. She was Dora Connolly, the daughter of the chaplain to Woolwich Dockyard. Scott had met Dora over four years before, and they kept up a correspondence during his early years of colonial service. Despite a long courtship, Scott does not mention Dora in his diaries until their wedding day: 'Sept. 9th, The long looked for day.' They were married in London and

Scott and his colleagues Mongnai in 1889; the intrepid Dora, his beloved first wife.

returned almost immediately to Burma, arriving at Fort Stedman in November. Only five days later, after less than three months of wedlock, Scott left for an extended jungle tour. He was away for nearly five months. Dora must have gone out of her mind with boredom and loneliness. At this time she was probably the only British woman living at Fort Stedman, a testosterone-rich environment where – after the novelty of watching the Intha glide over Inle Lake on one leg had worn off – the major recreational activity was the one her husband had introduced: football. During those five miserable months Dora evidently made up her mind: the next time her husband set off into the jungle, she was going with him – and to hell with the danger.

There is no record of Scott even trying to dissuade her. Indeed, her intrepid spirit was undoubtedly one of the qualities he found so attractive in her. He had already noted with admiration that Dora was 'quite a nailer at hill climbing'. When he was promoted the following year to superintendent of the northern Shan states, headquartered in Lashio, she joined him on a punishing six-month trek through the new territory. During her husband's tours Dora would sketch, indulge a passion for bird spotting, and endure random gunfire. On one occasion Kachin tribesmen rained poisoned arrows and bullets upon the Scotts and their party, which launched a ferocious counter-attack. 'Dora stood the fire splendidly,' Scott proudly recorded in his diary, 'and was much cooler than [Lieutenant] Martini.'

I had only one image of Dora Scott. It was a copy of a formal head-and-shoulders photo published in an 1895 issue of the pictorial magazine *Black and White*. Mrs Scott was no slender, swooning, porcelain beauty. In this photo anyway, she was a stout woman with scraped-back hair and the thin, impatient lips of a headmistress. She also had very bright, narrow, almost Burmese-looking eyes, and wore above the conventional ruffles of her dress a necklace of animal teeth. She looked as if she could eat a Kachin warrior for breakfast, and two for lunch. Scott adored her.

'The Adventures of Mr and Mrs Scott' would make headlines back home. Dora became the first European woman to cross both the Mekong and the Salween, two of South-East Asia's largest rivers, and her travels in deepest Shan territory would be compared to those of Lady Baker with her husband, Sir Samuel Baker, in Africa in the 1860s. 'Frail looking though the lady is,' enthused the *Pall Mall Gazette*,

> she makes light of trifles such as being three days without baggage, bedding, or food, except such as a native hut supplied; swimming her steed across a river wider than is the Thames above Oxford; or riding along jungle-paths where tigers cross in plain sight, and leopards have played with their cubs but a moment before; she has seen her sepoy guard shot down at her side, and gone through the ordeal of battle so splendidly that the Ghoorkas told her husband they wanted no better leader, in case he were shot.

Despite the privations of Fort Stedman, the days that George Scott spent with Dora on these shores were among the happiest of his life. He and his equally fearless wife would be inseparable in the years to come. Scott would penetrate the hilltop redoubts of the skull-worshipping Wa, and Dora would follow. Later he would present her at the court of the king of Siam. But in the end Scott would make a critical misjudgement about her failing health, and live out his very long life with the knowledge that he had almost certainly shortened hers.

There was a fork in the road, and then a man sitting smoking a cheroot beneath a tree. I showed him the Burmese words in my notebook, now hard to see in the failing light, and he smiled toothlessly with incomprehension. I decided to give up. Fort

Stedman was long gone. Its barn-like barracks, the stranded bones of its officers, Hildebrand's strawberry patch – all of it had been rightfully reclaimed by the jungle.

I cycled back down to the village, my face power-showered by millions of flying insects. I wasn't looking forward to pedalling seven miles in the darkness. Fortunately a long-tail boat was waiting on the jetty to take some visiting officials back to Yawnghwe. I gratefully heaved my bike aboard. The first stars were emerging as we chugged slowly out through a maze of floating gardens. These are fertile mattresses of mulched water hyacinth and mud dredged from the lake and fixed in place with a forest of bamboo stakes. According to an ancient omen, if Inle's surface appears dark, then great turbulence will hit the country. But for now the lake burned napalm-orange with the setting sun. The gardens fell away, the boatman opened up the throttle, and we shot out across the molten waters.

8

The following day I hired a taxi for the short journey across the valley and up the hill to Taunggyi, the capital of Shan State. I checked into a forgettable hotel, then went to a nearby tea shop for breakfast. As I sat there, a group of dark-skinned women walked up Taunggyi's main street in a kind of native dress I had never seen before. The women wore lime-green skirts, bright orange vests and wide-brimmed straw hats. I was intrigued. It took a full thirty seconds before I realised that this was not a tribal costume at all, but simply the uniform worn by all Taunggyi's municipal street-sweepers. Several days with Ben and all those hours poring over the *Gazetteer* had clearly taught me nothing.

Taunggyi meant 'Big Hill' in Burmese, but perhaps it should have been called Scottsville, or even Georgetown, for this was the town that Scott built. He arrived here in 1902 as superintendent of the Shan states, the highest position he would hold in Burma's colonial administration. 'There is no hill station in India where there is so much room,' Scott had enthused, 'not merely for house-building but for race-courses, polo-grounds and public gardens.' From my hotel roof Taunggyi appeared as a tightly packed collection of houses with shallow roofs of burnt-red tin, but it was still possible to discern its imperial topography. Built on a plateau at a celestial elevation of 4,700 feet, the town was dominated by a dramatic cliff studded with pagodas – the 'Big Hill' itself. In a grove of stately trees beneath nestled what was once the residency. From here a spacious boulevard, no doubt built with grand processions in mind, swept gracefully down the plateau to the town's northern tip, where military gardens offered a breathtaking panorama of the valley. The locals considered Taunggyi so distinct from the lowlands that it was said they still talked about 'going down to Burma'.

I had arrived on a Chinese holiday, which made it easy to judge to what extent ethnic Chinese dominated commerce. The town was dead. The main market was closed, and the iron grilles on the shop-houses opened only long enough to let extended Chinese families spill noisily into the afternoon sun. It was only the next day, when the Chinese community got back to work, that Taunggyi took on the appearance of a relatively prosperous provincial town. There were electrical shops, a supermarket selling HP Sauce and mayonnaise and other 'luxury' goods driven over the mountains from Thailand, and even a boutique selling golf equipment. It was unclear who these expensive shops catered to – certainly not the Pa-O women I saw selling wilted greens off soiled blankets behind the market.

As I wandered up the main street it struck me that Taunggyi was oddly blessed with banks. They were all shiny and new, as if they had been built only yesterday, and I never saw a customer in any of them. To drum up trade, one bank had stationed pretty girls in red miniskirts at its doorway, which lent it the appearance of an expensive brothel. A plethora of new banks with links to either the Burmese military or ethnic drug lords had opened in Burma in the previous decade. Their primary function, it was suspected, was laundering drug money.

I wandered along Circular Road, admiring from a distance the twin silver spires of the Catholic cathedral, which shone blindingly in the sun. Hanging in the sky like confetti were dozens of plastic-bag kites, jerking and swooping on invisible strings. Then I struck out to the west, to where the town seemed to tumble off the ridge, and suddenly everything went pastoral, with piglets and geese scratching around beneath the stilts of ramshackle houses and young women tottering back from the local well with heavy cans of water. Sitting peacefully in one back alley was a pristine Morris Minor. It was still in use, too, partly by grace of the blessed cotton entwined around its steering column. Later I saw a powder-blue Lincoln Zephyr cruise past, one of those monstrous pre-oil-crisis American pleasuremobiles, a double bed on wheels. Taunggyi seemed oddly blessed with classic cars too.

This was an important military town, and the military didn't let you forget it. There was a sprawling barracks on the north side, and Land Rovers carrying Burmese top brass roared along the main street accompanied by conspicuous security details, usually a truckload of soldiers holding automatic rifles at the ready. Outside the barracks was an enormous billboard which read, 'NEVER HESITATING ALWAYS READY TO SACRIFICE BLOOD AND SWEAT IS THE TATMADAW.' The Tatmadaw, or Burmese army, had erected hoardings with similar self-serving sentiments all along the road from Yawnghwe, and it took me a while to shake off the black mood they generated.

George Scott's reception in 1902 was a bit friendlier. The road was spanned by two triumphal arches bearing the legend 'WELCOME SIR JAMES GEORGE SCOTT, K.C.I.E.' (for by this time he had received a knighthood). Children waved Union Jacks, a marching band played, and pretty Shan girls showered the procession with scented water as it made its way up to the newly built residency. Noted Scott in his diary, 'Huge crowd, with the band, invaded the grounds and sat before the house while I gave the Sawbwa and the administrators and infants refreshments and moral sentiments.'

133

The only low point was to find that his belongings had been ruined by damp, and his books nibbled through by white ants: 'It is heart-breaking trying to keep things out here, and especially so for a person like myself who is hustled about from year to year.'

Many saophas took residences in Taunggyi, and sent their children to the Shan Chiefs' School. Scott, a former head-master himself, presided over its opening, which was marred when a pupil was struck by a door and died of fever less than a week later. Scott's fear that the ill-omened death would scare off mothers of prospective students proved unfounded. Modelled on a British public school and run by a British headmaster, the school would educate generations of Shan royals – once they were torn from the 'plurality of loafing attendants' (as Scott put it) whom their mothers fully expected to shadow them at all times.

Scott had a soft spot for pomp and pageantry, and the coronation of Edward VII in 1902 provided him with the first excuse for an imperial knees-up at Taunggyi. A grand celebration was planned, with fireworks, a traditional festival, manly sports, and musicians who arrived on a train of elephants. Scores of Shan worthies had gathered from afar when Scott received a wire announcing that the king was ill and the coronation was postponed. But instead of cancelling the celebration, and disappointing his distinguished guests, Scott turned the event into a vigil for the king's speedy recovery. A prayer was read out in a specially constructed Durbar Hall, before a brocade-draped shrine bearing portraits of the king and queen framed with flowers. Then everyone paid their respects: the Shan, Pa-O and other ethnic minorities shikhoed extravagantly; the Europeans rose stifly from their seats and bowed their heads.

The festival went ahead as planned. So, the next day, did the football. This was a much anticipated match between Fort Stedman and Taunggyi, and an excited crowd swarmed into the football ground to watch. Scott – now fifty years old – played in the Taunggyi team, which dominated the game. 'I got rather knocked about as usual,' he reported with masochistic relish – 'a kick on the thigh, a smash on the side of the head, and a chunk of skin off the temples. It was a very fast game.' The final score: Taunggyi 2, Fort Stedman 0.

Afterwards there was a rowdy dinner and a sing-song until the small hours to celebrate what was, after all, a symbolic victory. Fort Stedman had been only a foothold in the Shan hills; it belonged to an unsettled past. Situated at Olympian heights, Taunggyi was a citadel of the future, a monument to imperial supremacy, where each pukka new building proclaimed that the British pacification

A typical Burmese teashop, with a typical government billboard outside. (Nic Dunlop)

of the Shan states had reached its inexorable and triumphant conclusion.

A century later, the town one foreign overlord had built was occupied by another – the Burmese army – and the pacification of the Shan continued with unprecedented ferocity. While foreign tourists took day trips on beautiful Inle Lake, and enjoyed Kodak moments with long-necked Kayan women, less than twenty miles away at Ho Pong – a village very close to Taunggyi – people were being burnt from their homes. Less than sixty miles away, in the green valley of Nam Zarng, people were being raped, shot and beaten to death. They were all victims of an ongoing counter-insurgency campaign waged by Burmese troops – a campaign of such scope and savagery that I was amazed the world knew so little about it.

It had been well documented. Both Amnesty International and the Shan Human Rights Foundation in Chiang Mai had produced reports based on interviews with Shan refugees in northern Thailand. They were two of the most disturbing documents I had ever read. Tens of thousands of families had been driven at gunpoint from their ancestral land as part of a Burmese military operation known as the 'Four Cuts'. The purpose of this operation was to cut off supplies of food, funds, intelligence and recruits to the Shan State Army. What it amounted to in practice was a systematic campaign of terror against an unarmed civilian population, in which mass killings, gang rape and torture by Burmese troops were routine. Many of the worst atrocities had been committed by the Taunggyi-based eastern command, whose soldiers had demonstrated beyond a doubt that they were NEVER HESITATING ALWAYS READY TO SACRIFICE BLOOD – just not their own.

The first round of mass relocations had begun in March 1996, after troops loyal to Yawd Serk, the Shan commander I had interviewed on the Thai-Burma border, launched guerrilla attacks in central Shan State. Villagers were usually given only a few days to abandon their homes. Those who could moved in with relatives; those who couldn't scraped a living at army-designated sites at the roadside. Thousands more poured across the border into Thailand with eyewitness reports of their friends and relatives being beaten and shot by Burmese soldiers. By the end of 1996, it was estimated, over 100,000 people had been driven from their homes.

The Burmese regime must have considered this a strategic success, because the following year the programme intensified. This time, in many cases, no notice was given. Troops simply swept through and burned down houses with people still in them. Following the mass relocation in Laikha, a prosperous region famed for its fertile land, Shan human-rights workers reported 'scenes of social chaos in the town itself, with countless people begging in the streets, and camping in temples and under trees by the roadside'. In a matter of days, 40,000 people were made homeless in Laikha alone.

As many as 100,000 villagers were herded into relocation camps situated near Burmese army bases. Nothing was provided there – no shelter, food, water, or sanitation. At one overcrowded camp, forty people died of illness in the first month. I had seen photographs smuggled out of Shan State which showed the camps to be shanty towns stretching as far as the eye could see. Families arrived exhausted and hungry, only to watch helplessly as soldiers confiscated their precious stores of rice. This was supposedly done to prevent them from secretly supplying the Shan resistance; the real reason was to provide food for Burmese troops, who preyed on Shan farmers for basic supplies. Once inside the camps, forced labour was inescapable. Villagers were ordered to grow vegetables, gather firewood, and fetch water for the soldiers. They built barracks and other military buildings, as well as the walls, trenches and barbed-wire fences that protected them. Both men and women were drafted as army porters, carrying their own body weight in ammunition through dense jungle littered with anti-personnel mines – unimaginably gruelling and often fatal work. Relocated villagers were slaves for the Burmese army. They were also sitting ducks for military reprisals. One night in February 1997 a camp at Kho Lam was shelled by Burmese troops in retaliation for an SSA raid in the area. Two Shan families sheltering in a ditch were killed; three of the dead were children. Less than two months later shells rained down upon another camp at Tard Mork, killing three people.

I knew the name 'Tard Mork'. The refugees I had met at the SSA jungle base on the Thai-Burma border had fled from a village with that name after the Burmese army had set it ablaze to punish occupants for supposedly harbouring Shan rebels. There was the young woman whose sick grandfather had been burnt to death in their home, and whose uncle had been shot; there was the crippled girl with the wellington-boot prosthetic. I thought the reports might tell me exactly when this fire had happened. But it was confusing. Tard Mork had been deliberately torched more than once. On one occasion 200 houses burned down and at least four villagers died in the inferno. Incinerating what few possessions these wretched people had left was regular sport for Burmese soldiers.

Faced with the horrors of the relocation camp, many villagers decided to hide in the jungle. This was a perilous option. Depopulated areas were designated 'free-fire zones', and civilians who ventured into them to fish, collect honey or cut bamboo were shot on sight by Burmese patrols – or stabbed to death or blown up by grenades. On one occasion twenty-six villagers were caught foraging for food and decapitated; their headless corpses were left at the roadside as a grim warning to others.

A Shan teenager described how his family and four others hid in the jungle for a year. 'We stayed under trees and moved around all the time,' he said. 'If we stayed too long in one place, the paths we used became too obvious, and we were afraid the [Burmese] soldiers would find us. Finally, though, we found a cave, where we felt safe. So we stayed there.' This story struck me as bitterly ironic. While the generals bragged about creating a modern, developed nation, their soldiers in Shan State were turning prosperous farmers into terrified cave dwellers.

Some villagers were granted military passes to cultivate their fields for up to five days at a time. But these did not guarantee their safety. Villagers at a camp in Kun Hing had passes to retrieve food and other supplies from their houses, and on 16 June 1997 they set out in two convoys of ox carts. The first group was stopped by Burmese troops on its way back from the village. The villagers produced their passes and ID cards. To show their contempt, the soldiers rubbed these against their crotches and threw them in the dirt. Then they ordered the villagers to squat by the roadside, and shot them. Twenty-six of the thirty villagers in the convoy were killed. The carts were burnt, and the oxen slaughtered for meat.

A woman with an infant boy was spared. She later described the massacre in more detail to human-rights workers in Thailand. The soldiers first led away sixteen villagers – twelve men, four women – and then a second group of ten. 'Then to the west I heard bursts of machine-gun fire,' the woman recounted. 'In the group of ten my husband died. In the group of sixteen my younger sister and her husband died.' She went on, 'I was sure I would be killed too. I was shaking – shaking! I was sitting and shaking all the time. My blood was hot all over my body. I could not think properly . . . I think I would be dead if I hadn't had my son with me. One of the women who was killed had left her baby at home. She squeezed out milk from her breast to show she had a baby, but the [Burmese] commander said that her baby must have died.' Then she was shot.

The second convoy that set out from Kun Hing that day was stopped by soldiers not far from their village, where they had retrieved some rice. The villagers were detained for an evening – enough time for the soldiers to check the villagers' passes by radio, if they'd been so inclined – then taken to a forest, tied up, and executed. Twenty-nine people were killed.

How to make sense of this savagery? Burmese soldiers, many of them young and illiterate, were brutalised by their training and indoctrinated with a hatred for ethnic groups. This was reflected in what some soldiers told villagers. 'We don't want to see Shan faces – we want to kill all of them,' said one soldier quoted in the Amnesty report. 'You are Shan,' said another, 'you are not the same blood as us. We are going to kill you but before we kill you we are going to force you to work.' In Burma, as in Bosnia and Rwanda, rape was a key weapon. It was shockingly common in Shan State. In one instance Burmese soldiers raped a group of Lahu women whom they accused of 'cooking for the Shan soldiers'. Rape was institutionalised in the Burmese army, and published interviews with defectors suggested that soldiers were encouraged to regard the violation of minority women as a racial duty. 'Your blood must be left in the village,' they were told.

By 1998 over 300,000 people had been moved from an area covering 7,000 square miles – a 'conservative estimate', reckoned Amnesty International. This was like evacuating a city the size of Belfast, or depopulating an area almost as large as Wales. Possibly a third of this number had fled through malarial jungles into neighbouring Thailand. There a new set of dangers awaited them. While not considered refugees, Karen, Karenni and Mon people escaping war in Burma had at least some status in Thailand as 'displaced persons', and could receive assistance from international aid groups at official camps. The Shan, however, had no status – and no rights. It suited the Thai authorities to regard them at best as migrant workers. Many Shan refugees fed their families by taking low-paid jobs on construction sites, farms and orchards in Thailand's northern provinces. They were routinely harassed by Thai police, and women and girls were easy prey for sex traffickers. And when the Thai economy stumbled, as it did catastrophically in 1997, they were rounded up and booted back into Burma. Fugitives from ethnic terror in Shan State were expected to be thankful for this capricious hospitality.

And this *was* ethnic terror – an all-out assault by a Burman-dominated army on the Shan and other minority peoples. When you commit acts with intent to destroy a national, ethnical, racial or religious group, in whole or in part; when you kill members of that group, or cause them serious bodily or mental harm; when you deliberately inflict upon them conditions of life calculated to bring about their physical destruction – well, the civilised world has a word for that. The word is genocide.

The relocations in Shan State were still going on when I arrived in Taunggyi. The next day I met a number of Burmese people who at great personal risk were willing to talk about what they were seeing beyond the city limits – an army-designated 'black area', where outsiders were forbidden.

One man, whom I dare describe only as an unofficial health worker, told me how Taunggyi's orphanages were overflowing with the children of parents who were now too poor to look after them. 'When these people are moved, they have nothing,' he explained. 'They have no land. They are farmers. They can't work any more.' Then he gave me a report describing the plight of over 25,000 refugees inside Shan State, over a third of them children. Malaria and flu were endemic. There were no medicines, clothes or blankets beyond what hard-pressed local charities could provide; Burmese soldiers often blocked even this meagre aid from reaching the needy. Forced labour on military projects left people with little time to find food for their own families.

I spoke to a man who had just returned from Mong Pan. This was a teak-rich township less than 100 miles from Taunggyi as the crow flies; thirty-seven civilians had been executed there during the relocations. Our intermediary (and my interpreter) was a trusted community elder. We sat in a cramped, windowless room stacked with papers in a building not far from the famous Flying Tiger cheroot factory. I could hear a faint rumble of trucks on Bogyoke Aung San Road. The man from Mong Pan spoke quietly, although there was little chance of our being overheard. He said that six or seven Shan and Lisu villages in the area had just been forcibly relocated. 'The soldiers didn't burn the villages, but they killed off all the cows and pigs, and stole anything of value,' he said. 'Even people in villages which have not been ordered to relocate are moving, because they know one day the soldiers will come.'

Where did these people go? I asked. I had read that many now begged for a living, in Shan towns. 'It is true,' said the man. 'There are many people begging in the streets of Mong Pan. That never happened before. The military sometimes gives them a space in another village, but the people are often too scared to stay there. So they move to the nearest town or into the jungle.'

'Why are they scared?'

'They are scared the military will draft them as porters. But there's not so much portering as before. But they have to work for the army camp, making fences, fetching water for the soldiers, and so on.' The report I had been given by the health worker recorded how the Burmese army routinely forced villagers in the Mong Pan area to occupy sentry posts on key roads – to act, in effect, as human shields against Shan guerrilla attacks.

'Have any people tried to go back to their villages?' I asked.

'They dare not go back,' said the man from Mong Pan. 'They will just get chased out.'

'Have any villagers been killed?'

'Yes. People who have tried to return to collect paddy have been shot. I have heard of three or four instances of this.'

'Do the military give any reason for moving these people?'

'The only reason they give is that they don't want us supporting the rebels.'

'Do you support the rebels?'

'Yes,' the man replied. 'We have no choice. The insurgents also use the villagers as porters, take food – just like the Burmese military. There are several insurgent groups. Some of them speak Burmese, some are student groups –'

Our intermediary interrupted. 'You have to give food to the rebels,' he said, 'or else they too will shoot you. The people are completely trapped between the two sides.'

The area around the town of Mong Pan was almost deserted.

'There used to be so many villages,' said the man. 'But now some people have fled to the Thai border, others to Mong Pan town. The people who have not yet moved live in fear.'

The horror stories I heard in Taunggyi were disturbing enough. They also contained disquieting echoes from another age. Driving out villagers at gunpoint, torching homes, stealing precious livestock: all these tactics were vigorously employed by the British during the pacification of Upper Burma. Burning villages was an accepted way of imposing imperial authority. 'We simply wiped out the village and shot everyone we saw,' Scott blandly noted during one campaign. 'Burned all their crops and houses.' In some ways it seemed as if nothing had changed in Shan State for a hundred years.

The great irony here was that Scott's arrival in Taunggyi marked the start of what many people would recall as a golden age – a time when memories of the British pacification campaign were fading, and the Shan enjoyed a few precious decades of peace before the Japanese Imperial Army invaded in the Second World War and bombs began to rain down upon their towns and villages. 'There were great men in those days,' wrote the author F. Tennyson Jesse. 'Shans who were fine gentlemen, Burmese helpers and British. And not the least was Scott of the Shan Hills.' Foreign visitors during this period seemed to view the Shan states through soft-focus lenses. 'We lost our hearts to this fair princess of the peach-bloom skin and the almond eyes,' sighed Hassoldt Davis in his account of the mahadevi of Yawnghwe, the pugnacious Sao Nang Hearn Hkam, as he reclined on red velvet cushions in her private gondola skimming over Inle Lake.

Equally smitten by the Shan aristocracy was Maurice Collis, whose elegiac 1938 book *Lords of the Sunset* captured this period better than any other. He described the Shan States as 'an Arcadia of sorts, romantically far, the farthest off of all our land possessions, clean beyond India, on the high road to the world's end'. Collis waxed rhapsodic about the refinement and hospitality of his genteel Shan hosts – particularly the women, whom he found blessed with conversational charms 'which for repartee and fun could have been equalled in England only by clever women'.

But misty-eyed Maurice – who couldn't meet even the lowliest of Shan princesses without going all squiffy – was well aware that there was something rotten in paradise. By the turn of the century the British Empire was bloated, its resources overstretched. Its architects in London were content simply to occupy Shan territory so that nobody else could; there was little interest in developing the region. If the British Empire was like a rambling old country house, wrote Collis, then the Shan states were 'the imperial attic . . . Not one Englishman in ten thousand has ever heard of them.' However, the British were interested in the silver mine at Namtu, a place not far from Namhsan, where I had seen the Golden Palaung. Using modern techniques, they extracted more silver from the Bawdwin mine in twenty years than had been extracted in the previous one thousand. None of this benefitted the Shan – even the labourers were Indian and Chinese – and the profits poured into British pockets. (And American pockets: one Iowan built a very successful political career on a fortune made partly from Burmese silver. His name was Herbert Hoover.) As Collis put it, 'We went off with their silver.'

And so under the Pax Britannica the Shan states slumbered. Some would say they stagnated. The Shan historian Chao Tzang Yawnghwe – who, as his name suggests, is the son of the last great saopha of Yawnghwe – has accused the British of reducing the saophas from semi-sovereign rulers to 'elevated native tax collectors' who were taught that politics was 'ungentlemanly'. This left the Shan chiefs unprepared for the complex political times that lay ahead, particularly the turbulent years following Burma's independence, when the last vestiges of Shan sovereignty crumbled. In some ways the rot had already begun in Scott's time – and Scott knew it.

Partly he blamed the saophas. He found it next to impossible to enthuse them about technologies which might improve the lives of their subjects – particularly agriculture, which they considered a matter for peasants and therefore beneath them – although he wrote that:

> One or two of the Shan chiefs have taken up road-making as a pastime, to relieve the monotony of hearing pious works read to them, marrying new wives, or disposing of the older ladies, playing polo where both sides manoeuvre the ball so that the chief may hit between the posts, or going out on elephants to shoot doves; but a causeway which begins and ends in a mire is no use for communication.

While Scott was exasperated by the happy lethargy of some saophas, he was infuriated by the inertia of his own employers. When it came to the Shan states, he privately fumed, the government of India showed as much enterprise and energy as 'a sea-lion in the Sahara'. It was short-sighted, and throttled by red tape, and tight-fisted. 'The Government of India,' he wrote, 'can only be got to allot money to Burma with the very greatest difficulty and at intervals which imply the most enthusiastic belief in the longevity of the human race.'

On my last morning in Taunggyi I set out to visit the old residency building. Walking up the main road, I dropped into a small, two-floor museum dedicated to Shan State's minority peoples. It was ill-stocked and murky and, like the National Museum in Rangoon, crowded with evil-looking mannequins dressed in different ethnic attire. But two exhibits – a golden Palaung bracelet and a silver, conical Pa-O hairpin, both exquisite – showed an artistry I had not seen among the actual tribes, and made me wonder if such skills had died out. Another glass cabinet contained a hardwood opium pipe so enormous I initially mistook it for a walking stick.

Attached to the museum was something called the Shan State Library. I entered the building with extreme scepticism. The regime practises a rigorous system of censorship, and treats foreign books with particular suspicion. Years ago a large donation of English-language books had arrived at Rangoon port, bound for the country's book-starved schools and universities. I heard that the shipment was still there, held in storage while uniformed men with rulers went through each book page by page, ripping out any material deemed offensive. So imagine my surprise to find that the Shan State Library had quite the best public collection of English books I had ever seen in Burma, many of them potentially controversial. Among the bookshelves I found *Social Origins of Dictatorship and Democracy*, *History of Greek Political Thought*, definitive-looking tomes on the Sino-Soviet rift, all the Orwells (including *Nineteen Eighty-Four* and *Animal Farm*), and a complete set of Agatha Christies and Billy Bunters. There were even four smiling librarians poised to serve me. The only thing missing from this library was readers. Inexplicably, it was deserted.

Afterwards I walked a little further up the road and turned off along a peaceful lane shaded by stately eucalyptus trees. At the end of the lane, behind a big iron gate, with a big iron padlock, stood the residency; it was now a state guest house for VIPs. A truck approached and a gatekeeper materialised to unlock the gate. The truck drove through and I sneaked in behind it.

The garden was beautiful, and had been lovingly kept. Trying to look proprietorial, I sauntered across the pristine lawn, admiring the magnificent trees that had been planted in Scott's day and had now reached their maturity: Benguet pines, avocado trees, Burmese cassia with starbursts of pink blossom, an immense

Two shy Brè or Kayaw Women pose for Scott's camera. (British Library)

fig tree with spectacular fluted roots, and a Darjeeling gugertree with a girth not even three men with linked arms could embrace. A young Shan couple wandered through the still-open gate and began smooching in the shade of a jacaranda tree.

With its bay windows and original whitewashed facade, the residency struck Scott as 'something like a Metropole hotel at a seaside resort'. Now the woodwork was painted regulation grey, and the stone was dulled by some sort of treacle-coloured preservative. The four chimney stacks were still intact; fires had been lit almost daily, since the residency, situated in the shadow of Taunggyi's great promontory, was the last house in town to be warmed by the morning sun. Scott would spend eight busy years of his life here. 'All day long he was interviewing people, being terribly bored by many, settling disputes, smoothing down wounded pride,' wrote his biographer-wife. 'His fine new house was the centre of all the life in the place. When he arrived he had "dined" the whole station, and he seldom had less than half a dozen guests to dinner, and anyone passing through stayed with him as a matter of course. The servants grumbled and demanded extra bakshish.'

An iron gate blocked the residency's front porch. It was unlocked. With a crunch of pine needles it slid open a few inches, and through I squeezed. I walked up to the front door and tried the handle. It turned, and it seemed at first that the door wasn't locked, and I had wonderful visions of romping through Scott's rambling old house, lying on Scott's lumpy old bed, perhaps even relieving myself in Scott's crusty old water closet. But the door was bolted at the top. I made do with pressing my nose against the windows. There was a small entrance hall, with a dark wooden staircase doubling back on itself. It all looked very modest and homey.

I slowly made my way back to the garden. For me this was the end of the road – for now. Taunggyi had been only a thirty-minute drive from Yawnghwe, but in terms of Scott's narrative I had skipped an entire decade of his life. I now wanted to go back and retrace the most vibrant and dangerous years of Scott's long career in Burma. To do this I would have to travel to Kengtung, the capital of the Golden Triangle, which lay some 300 miles across the mountains of central Shan State. Due to travel restrictions, getting there would involve flying to northern Thailand and crossing the Burmese border at the town of Tachilek.

Before I left, I stood for a while on the residency lawn. Back in London I had turned the time-bleached pages of an old photo album recording one of the many exotic tea parties that Scott had held at the residency. On one occasion 10,000 people came, including –

at Scott's request – 'representatives of the wild tribes'. The lawn thronged with starched colonials in hot collars, and among them moved elegant Kayan women clutching champagne flutes, neck-rings gleaming in the late-afternoon sun; the Bre, waddling past in bulging knee coils, ear lobes plugged with silver, their chests garlanded with newly minted rupees; the mysterious Zayein in their simple white smocks and curious conical hats, their necklaces of silver-tipped boar's tusk drawing admiring glances from the plain English ladies.

I stood on that immaculate lawn and tried to picture such an afternoon, when a kind of peace reigned in the Shan hills, and for a moment I completely forgot the benighted hamlets beyond the residency gates. But only for a moment.

PART TWO

HEADHUNTING

9

It was precisely 8 a.m. in Mae Sai, northern Thailand, and for forty seconds or so the world stopped turning.

The traffic police climbed out of their booths and froze in mid-salute. Market women pushing barrows of fruit halted suddenly in their tracks. The *songthaew* drivers woke up and stood like salt pillars beside their cabs. Even a beggar struggled gamely to his feet. And for those forty seconds I stood with them, listening as the Thai national anthem reached its climax on loudspeakers and radio sets all across the town. Then it was over, and the frenetic border town of Mae Sai snapped back to life with the same abruptness with which it had stopped.

Every morning a similar public display of patriotism could be seen in provincial towns across Thailand. But the inhabitants of Mae Sai seemed to perform this daily ritual with particular attention. It was easy to see why. The six-lane highway that led into town ended abruptly at a two-lane bridge over a chocolate-brown river. On one side was a cluster of Thai checkpoints; on the other a set of imposing iron gates.

Beyond them, hidden behind a screen of immense trees, was the Burmese garrison town of Tachilek. This was the jittery interface between Thailand and Burma; between a maturing democracy and a regressive dictatorship; between two Asian armies who had had very little nice to say about each other since King Bayinnaung's war elephants thundered into the doomed Siamese kingdom of Ayuthaya in 1564. Thai soldiers regarded their battle-hardened Burmese counterparts as bellicose and slippery. They called them 'the ghosts'. The Burmese contemptuously referred to the peace-softened Thais as 'the girls'.

I had got up at dawn to watch the gates to Burma open. A crush of people poured through, mainly Shan farmers with baskets of fruit and vegetables to sell at Mae Sai market. A few empty lorries rattled in after them, to return a few hours later full of Thai goods bound for Kengtung, the capital of eastern Shan State and my next destination. Like the Burma Road through the northern Shan hills, the bridge was a lifeline for a stricken economy. Despite the impression of impregnability suggested by so many Thai and Burmese soldiers and officials, the border had always been hopelessly porous. Both upriver and down, a steady flow of people crossed illegally on small ferries with the tacit approval of officials on both sides, and all kinds of contraband came and went with them.

I was about to go to Burma too – or rather, go into Burma. Following the lead of my colleagues in the Bangkok press corps, I realised you never just *go to* Burma. Only tourists do that. Journalists, diplomats and aid workers always *go into* Burma, like you go into battle, or go into hospital – the suggestion being, I suppose, that you might not come out again.

After my passport had been stamped by Thai officials, I started to walk across the bridge. It was clogged with child beggars and cripples heaving themselves along on sticks. Walking across the no man's land between two countries is a rare event for jet-age travellers. Officially at least, I hadn't crossed a border on foot for years – not since I'd emerged from northern Albania to be faced with a sleazy Yugoslavian border guard who had asked, 'How many Albanian girl you fuck?' and then stamped my passport with violent derision when I'd answered, well, none actually. As I walked the last few yards into Burma that day I felt the same spidery unease, as if a rifle's cross hairs were trained on my chest.

I spent the next three hours at Tachilek's tiny immigration office. I surrendered my passport, dispensed the necessary bribes, and filled out forms in quadruplicate. While these were studied and shuffled about by cheerless Burmese officials, I strolled over to the nearby market to find a car and driver. Bewildered Akha grannies with coppered faces wandered past souvenir shops catering primarily to Thai day-trippers; one depressing stall sold nothing but leopard skins and tiger teeth. After some bracing haggling, I hired a taxi only slightly worse for wear than the road it had to travel. It was a Toyota Corolla, of course. The suspension had been beefed up, but otherwise the car was unadapted for terrain that would quickly reduce a Land Cruiser to a box of whimpering spare parts. I'd heard that during the rainy season, due to begin any day now, the road was often impassable. There were moments during the long trip ahead when I wondered whether I'd ever reach Kengtung – and, if I did, whether road conditions would allow me to return.

With the border formalities finally over, we set out for Kengtung, a drive of about 100 miles. As the car barreled along the bumpy road, nosed its way through fast-flowing streams, and juddered across disintegrating Bailey bridges, I bounced around helplessly inside like a hand grenade in a biscuit tin. We passed villages of stilt houses with thatched roofs, many announced by a white crucifix, the legacy of an evangelical assault by foreign missionaries which began in Scott's time. For one blessed stretch the road wound gently through a tunnel of dense foliage, following the natural contours of a picturesque tributary of the Mekong. The forest here was unmolested by loggers and swidden agriculture. Insects shrieked in the bamboo groves, and clouds of yellow butterflies corkscrewed in our wake.

But soon the construction work began. A mechanical digger now marked each passing mile, and the landscape had been scraped clear of vegetation and dynamited into submission. Then the road disappeared entirely into a hillside of soft earth being flattened by bulldozers. A long line of cars waited to pass. Some peasant women took advantage of the delay to sell the contents of their market baskets in the shade. I bought a can of warm Red Bull and waited for an hour until a semblance of a road had been constructed. Then we moved down the hill in a cramped, impatient convoy, the vehicle in front lost in the dust.

The trip from Tachilek to Kengtung took nine spine-fusing, ball-bruising, arse-tenderising hours. As night fell, the driver steered with his head out the side window, since by now the windscreen was mud-smeared and the wipers had packed up. Tired and travel-addled, and praying that a distant glow of lights was Kengtung, I had a weary line from one of Scott's letters home pop into my head: 'During the last two years there is not a man in Burma who has had so much bucketing about as I have.'

It was late evening by the time we entered the narrow, sinuous, ill-lit streets of Kengtung. I checked into a small hotel, where I was the only guest. A startled caretaker handed me two candles along with my room key, since there was no electricity; power reached Kengtung only one day in five. There was no water either, although I was naked and grappling with the coughing bath taps by candlelight before I found this out. While the caretaker disappeared into the hotel's jungly garden to torment some water-pumping equipment, I lay on my bed and reflected that in Scott's time water flowed through the 'primitive' villages of the Wa twenty-four hours a day via ingenious bamboo aqueducts. Before long the bathroom taps started to make promising gurgling noises, but by then I was far too tired to move.

Dodgy plumbing was the least of Scott's problems when he first visited Kengtung in 1890. He almost died there.

Kengtung was a large and influential state about the size of Belgium, and traditionally paid an annual tribute to the king of Burma. This tribute consisted of a ragbag of goodies: gold, silver, musical instruments, weapons, elephants, ponies and – you'll have to trust me on this one – dried squirrels. Then, during King Thibaw's chaotic reign, the saopha spectacularly renounced his loyalty by murdering the Burmese royal resident in Kengtung and thirty of his guards, a piece of treachery that Thibaw was too feeble to avenge. Kengtung later began a cordial correspondence with Burma's new British overlords, but the state's formal submission to colonial rule had yet to be received. Distance was the main obstacle. From the nearest British outpost Kengtung was a month's hard slog through unknown terrain. 'Only twelve or fifteen thousand tigers and as many people inhabit it,' warned an article in the *Pall Mall Gazette*, 'and the latter are nearly all hill-tribesmen of the most primitive sort . . . living on the scanty spoils of their bow and spears.'

Scott had been itching to go to Kengtung for some time. In 1890 he set out with eighteen Sikh soldiers led by a Captain Pink – possibly not the best commander for this sensitive mission, since he was prone to declaring often and loudly that all natives were 'Dogs, and sons of '. There were also a dozen or so untrained recruits, including by one account 'rough spear-men to give a touch of romance to the cortege', as well as Burmese clerks and servants, and a few lumbering elephants. Supplies were carried on mules driven by Panthays, a group of Chinese Muslims who claimed Kublai Khan's ferocious horsemen as their ancestors, and were now famed for ferrying goods on tracks through the hills. As a colleague of Scott's later observed, it was hardly the most impressive procession to represent the imperial majesty of England.

Kengtung was a fortified town with a moat and wall built by King Alaungpaya in the eighteenth century. Scott marched into town and struck camp outside the palace gates, where Kengtung's ruler paid him a formal visit. The saopha was dressed in a shimmering satin coat, gold-bespangled trousers, and fancy slippers with upturned toes. He wore diamond rings on his fingers and solid-gold cylinders through his ear lobes. He rode a caparisoned pony shaded by followers clutching numerous gold umbrellas in the style of the great Burmese kings. A well-armed bodyguard of several hundred men accompanied him. None of this, however, could hide the fact that the fearsome ruler of mighty Kengtung State was only sixteen years old.

Even so, Scott could not afford to let his guard down for a moment. His small party was invited to pitch its tents in the compound where the Burmese resident and his guard had been massacred, and the camp was immediately surrounded by two or three thousand curious townsfolk. The young ruler of Kengtung, Scott knew, was also a bit of a loose cannon: 'It was reported that the Sawbwa had often shot men merely for his own pleasure or

Scott with Capt. Pink (*centre*) and a camp doctor *en route* to Kengtung
in 1890. Scott holds a pocket watch to time this self-portrait. (British Library)

to test a new rifle; he was, as the Clerk remarked, "unacquainted
with the Penal Code".' Many of the British party fully expected to
be butchered in their beds.

The fear and suspicion were mutual. Scott reported how the
saopha had been 'very nervous' during their first meeting. From
his camp outside the palace gates he could hear the ominous boom
of a Shan long-drum, which was struck three times whenever
the edgy saopha wanted to summon his guards. 'We heard three
strokes on this drum a good many times during the next few days,'
noted Scott.

But he himself was not a man to be easily unsettled. While
the rest of the camp attended a noisy festival inside the palace
compound, Scott was experimenting with his new hobby of
photography, which a British colonel had introduced him to during
one long rainy season at Fort Stedman. Photography had become
a simpler art to master since the recent introduction of dry plates,
which required shorter exposure times and no messy chemical
preparation. This breakthrough coincided with the voracious
appetite in Victorian Britain for exotic images from far-flung

corners of the Empire. But nineteenth-century photographers still battled daily with technical limitations, especially those like Scott who eschewed studios for rare documentary work in remote places. Even dry plates were made of glass and were easily spoiled by moisture, and transporting them safely along bumpy tracks through the Burmese jungle required immense care. The large-plate camera itself was about as portable as a microwave oven. Roving photographers also had to bring their own darkrooms. Scott used a converted field latrine. Inside he would develop images that would be reproduced in magazines in Britain and America, including *National Geographic*, compiling over the years a mammoth portfolio that is today a priceless ethnographic record of Burma and its myriad tribes. One memorable self-portrait shows a grinning Scott on his way to Kengtung, with a sombre Captain Pink standing stiffly beside him. Scott holds his swagger stick and pith helmet in one hand, and in the other a pocket watch to time the exposure.

Scott was in his rudimentary darkroom developing another plate when he heard a commotion outside. He emerged to find a breathless clerk. The Panthay muleteers had gone to the festival in search of liquor, the clerk said, and had got into a fight with the saopha's men. Shots had been fired. One Panthay lay dead, riddled with bullets drilled into his back. A second Panthay had limped back to camp with a shoulder wound, and was now being nursed with pipes of opium.

The fate of the entire mission rested upon what Scott did next. Noting that, rather worryingly, the festival music had stopped, Scott dispatched a letter to the palace, explaining that the Panthays were British subjects, and that he would expect the saopha to identify the guilty men and hand them over for punishment. By morning it was clear to him that this would not happen, for it had emerged by then that the man who had shot the Panthay repeatedly in the back as he lay in the dirt was the young saopha himself.

Scott's situation was now extremely perilous. His tiny party was vastly outnumbered. He was 300 miles from the nearest British outpost. The local chief was a hot-headed young autocrat with a fondness for random violence who could order his men to attack at any moment. Retreat was not an option. 'The only thing it seemed to me was to carry off the situation with a high hand,' reasoned Scott. 'Prestige was everything. The slightest hint of nervousness would be fatal.'

The next day saw a visit from the saopha's chief minister, 'a white-haired old gentleman with a soapy manner'. Scott demanded that the minister produce the missing Panthay, dead or alive, or pay 1,500 rupees in compensation to the bereaved family. While shocked at the sum, the minister jumped on this face-saving solution, and promised to ask the guardian nat of the town where the Panthay could be hiding. Meanwhile, word came that the saopha had heard much about British military displays, and asked if Scott could arrange one in the palace grounds. It sounded like a trap, but again Scott had no option but to agree.

He took no weapon, but was accompanied by his orderly, a fearsome Pathan tribesman from the Afghan frontier, who had a revolver hidden beneath his flowing robes. 'There were thousands of people all round the open space of green when we arrived. I went up on to the veranda and sat beside the Sawbwa, and my Pathan stood straight up behind me ready to put a bullet through the chief's head at the first sign of treachery.'

While Captain Pink's men charged up and down the parade ground with fixed bayonets, Scott told the saopha of the other wonders of modern British warfare – of cannon big enough for a man to crawl inside; of machine guns that could cut down crowds 'as a reaper cut paddy'. He meant all this as a veiled threat, but the saopha was too excited to register it. Instead, he expressed a keen desire to acquire such powerful weapons and try them out. 'He said it wouldn't matter at all so long as the right people were killed,' reported Scott. 'Apparently there were plenty he could spare.'

The display went off without a hitch. With rations running short, Scott was under pressure to leave Kengtung as soon as possible. The chief never did produce the missing Panthay mule man, despite elaborate consultations with the town's guardian nat, and the compensation Scott demanded was duly paid. A tense situation now defused, Scott finally raised the question of the saopha's allegiance to the British Crown – his whole purpose for coming to Kengtung. The teenage chief treated the notion with 'imperturbable nonchalance', wrote Scott. 'He had nothing to say against it, and saw no particular advantages in it. I had to argue in every way I knew until, at last, out of sheer boredom, he agreed that a covenant should be drawn up.'

And so, in this fraught and then rather diffident manner, Scott added another 12,000 square miles of territory to the British Empire. The whole process had taken just over two weeks.

Some years later, when the Kengtung saopha had grown up and learned some manners, he was passing around cakes at a garden party in Maymyo when he casually mentioned how he had fully intended to massacre Scott and his men in their sleep. But his wives had complained, and so he didn't. On the whole, he said, knowing what he now knew, 'the ladies had been right'.

Early the next morning I went out for a pre-breakfast stroll. The sky was cartoon blue, the air crisper than anything I'd breathed for months. Kengtung seemed a green, sleepy, friendly place; even the barbed-wire fence around the police station was entwined with fairy lights. The town centre was occupied by a sun-baked congregation of monasteries and temples emitting a mesmeric drone of prayers. Radiating out from there were narrow, winding streets flanked by old shop-houses of ochre brick with dark, wooden balconies and tiled roofs spotted with (and possibly held together by) rioting clumps of lichen. Many street corners were guarded by knee-high stone griffins, which grimaced across T-junctions or down dead-end alleys – a kind of Shan feng shui I had never seen before. I passed through the city's old eastern gate, now whitewashed and featureless like a child's playing block. Just beyond it was the local office of the National League for Democracy; a female party member stood in the doorway, observing a neighbourhood which seemed studiously to ignore her presence.

Also near the gate was a small compound containing the tombs of the saophas. These were a row of monuments, some grandly baroque – an onion-shaped dome, a seven-tiered roof – but mostly simple pimples of whitewashed stone. The last in the row belonged to the last ruler of Kengtung, an Australian-educated saopha called Sao Sai Long – 'Shorty' to his friends. The gate was padlocked, but I could see that the tombs were freshly painted and the compound scrupulously swept. There were gnarled candles and handfuls of votive rice on a ledge outside. No saopha had reigned in Kengtung for forty years, but the townsfolk evidently still honoured the memory of their feudal rulers.

From my hotel room I could see a monstrous building called the Kyaing Tong New Hotel – 'Kyaing Tong' being the military's needless Burmanisation of 'Kengtung' I had been specifically warned not to stay there. 'It's full of Burmese spooks,' a friend in Mae Sai had told me. It seemed like an interesting venue for breakfast.

There were two military policemen at the hotel doorway. I sensed that their every instinct was to bar my way, but I swept forward and they missed their chance. There were more soldiers in the ill-lit foyer, where a low table had been precision-laid with cups and saucers. Slumped despondently in a chair nearby was an official photographer hugging his camera. Some top brass were obviously expected at any minute. There was a glass cabinet adrift in the foyer's centre containing souvenirs which were, sadly, crappy rather than tacky – faded postcards, factory-woven 'ethnic fabrics', and so on. I was hoping for a boxed set of miniature Burmese generals, or at the very least an I LOVE MYANMAR fridge magnet. Or perhaps a length of barbed wire, tastefully mounted, to commemorate the recent news, publicised without irony in the state press, that Burma now produced so much of the stuff it had begun exporting it.

The dining room was a huge, soul-sucking hangar with geckos clucking behind its thick net curtains. I sat at the only table not piled high with soiled crockery. The waiting staff were clustered around a television in a far corner. It showed a presenter sitting with abnormal rigidity, as if she had a cocked gun jammed into the small of her back. 'And here are the headlines,' she said (for some reason there were two English bulletins every day). 'Today Secretary One of the State Peace and Development Council, Lieutenant General Khin Nyunt, addressed the third bi-monthly coordination meeting of the Ministry of Transport in Yangon . . .'

And there was Khin Nyunt, Burma's Poo Bah and Big Brother, basking in the camera lights like a lizard in the sun. He was lecturing a roomful of unsmiling Burmese who sat as if they had cocked guns jammed into the smalls of their backs too. When they were not on it, and therefore not obliged to behave like scolded schoolchildren, the Burmese regarded television as a big joke. The country's most famous comedian was a man called Zarganar. In 1990 he joked that he'd just bought a new colour television, but when he got it home and turned it on it only had two colours: green and orange. Zarganar, whose name means 'tweezers', was poking fun at the endless airtime devoted to showing generals in uniform making meritorious donations to orange-robed monks. He was arrested after the show, and spent the next five years in the notorious Insein Prison in Rangoon's northern suburbs. (And yes, Insein is pronounced 'Insane'.) Two more comedians, Pa Pa Lay and Lu Zaw, were arrested in 1996 for satirising the military at a show for opposition politicians at Aung San Suu Kyi's house. The junta sentenced them to seven years' hard labour -- which British comedian Mark Thomas remarked darkly was 'one fuck of a heckle'.

Over breakfast at the Kyaing Tong New Hotel I settled down to write up my notes. Tucked into the back of my journal was a photograph which a tour guide back in Tachilek had given me. He had produced it furtively, his eyes flickering left and right, as if selling me a fake Rolex or kiddie porn. The photo showed only a building, but a building with a remarkable history.

The Indian-inspired palace at Kengtung, built after the chief's visit to Delhi.

It was the old Kengtung Palace, built in 1905 by Sao Kawng Kiao Intaleng, the fifty-third great saopha of Kengtung. (His predecessor was the trigger-happy teenager Scott had met.) I had a picture of Intaleng too. He was a sombre trout of a man, with bushy eyebrows, a ploughshare jaw, and waist-length hair wound into a topknot inside his turban. Pious and enlightened, Intaleng was a popular ruler who was knighted by the British for abolishing domestic slavery. He was also a devotee of martial arts, and famous for his ability to leap from the back of one elephant to another. Intaleng needed his athleticism: he had six wives, who took it in turns to visit his chambers each night, carrying a herbal aphrodisiac on a gold tray.

My photo showed Intaleng's palace to be a monumental structure, imperial in scale and distinctly Indian in style, suited more to the grand boulevards of Lutyens's Delhi than to the remote mountain fiefdom of Kengtung. Nobody knew for sure why Intaleng had taken such a fancy to the architecture of India, but it seemed clear enough to me. It was because Scott had taken him there – along with a large party of Shan aristocrats – to celebrate the coronation of King Edward VII at the Delhi Durbar of 1903.

Scott had had a flurry of last-minute arrangements to make

for the durbar. Had Intaleng ensured that his elephants were 'gaily caparisoned with trappings of Shan or Burmese design', as headquarters had instructed? Did the Yawnghwe saopha have any footwear other than the carpet slippers he habitually wore to public events? And what to do about all the wives? The saopha of South Hsenwi, in a rare fit of moderation, would bring only five of his fifty consorts. The Mongpawn saopha brought none at all; Scott compared him to 'the Irishman who did not take his wife on his honeymoon because he could not afford it'. As for Intaleng, he took only his mahadevi to Delhi, and she would be outshone by his remarkable half-sister, the Princess Tip Htila.

Scott was a great admirer of Tip Htila. She was his kind of woman. A shrewd trader, she rode armed at the head of a train of pack mules, which were once impounded after she had grazed them on the governor's lawn in Rangoon. She sold elephants and, as the times advanced, motor cars, then made a fortune in teak extraction and British road-building contracts. She divorced her first husband, the ruler of the Shan state of Keng Hkam, and outlived a second. 'In her day she must have been rash, magnificent, as bold as a lion,' wrote Maurice Collis, who met her in Kengtung when she was a sprightly old woman who had happily gambled away her fortune and lived on a monthly pension of seven pounds and ten shillings in an apartment behind the palace throne hall. Scott took a wonderful photograph of the princess in her prime. She was an impish beauty with a Mona Lisa smile, and wore an enormous turban at a jaunty angle. She stood with one hand propped on her hip, the other holding a cheroot, while four male retainers squatted abjectly at her tiny feet. 'Tip Htila, sister of the Kengtung sawbwa,' read Scott's caption dreamily, 'a very clever lady.'

Escorting Tip Htila, the saophas of Kengtung and five other states, and their hundreds-strong retinues to the Delhi Durbar was no picnic, Scott discovered. A special train took them down to Rangoon, where they boarded a steamer across the Bay of Bengal. They arrived in Calcutta on Christmas Eve, 1902, to a minor disaster: a butter-fingered maid dropped Tip Htila's jewellery basket into the Hooghly River. Then tempers frayed on the packed train from Howrah station, and some brave soul punched Scott's Pathan orderly on the nose. 'Kengtung looking very dissipated,' wrote Scott when the party had finally reached the immense camp ground at Delhi. 'Tip Htila very down about her jewellery.' Scott also had to scotch rumours that the durbar was part of a dastardly British plot to kidnap the saophas – King Thibaw's forced exile to India was still fresh in many memories.

Scott's portrait of Princess Tip Htila, the Kengtung chief's sister. (British Library)

But the pomp and splendour of the next few days lifted everyone's spirits. The 1903 durbar was a glittering panorama of Asian pageantry attended by over 100 rulers of states under British sovereignty. Delhi was transformed into an Indian Empire in miniature, as lavishly appointed pavilions were erected across the city to accommodate the varied and fabled rulers of India – among them the maharaja of Jammu and Kashmir, the rajas of Rajgarh and Rutlam, the Gaekwar of Baroda, the Rao of Cutch, the Mir of Khairpur, the nawab of Tonk and, viewing the proceedings through a gold-embroidered curtain from her silken palanquin, the reclusive begum of Bhopal.

The Shan chiefs were a brilliant thread in this great imperial tapestry. During the state entry into Delhi, the saophas of Mongnai and Kengtung, along with Princess Tip Htila, rode in a spectacular procession of elephants led by the maharaja of Mysore and the Nizam of Hyderabad. Each elephant was equipped with a howdah of silver and gold trimmed with crocodile skin or peacock feathers, and bore a native ruler dripping with jewels. Scott rode with the Kengtung party as their elephant waddled solemnly past the Mutiny-scarred walls of the Red Fort, around the soaring minarets of the Jama Masjid, and through the cheering crowds of Chandni Chouk. 'All along the route we were snapped by hundreds of cameras,' he recorded, 'and in several places the populace clapped us. At the Jumna Masjid two elephants ran away, and several people had narrow escapes.' The saophas wore blazing golden robes with multiple folds like pagoda roofs, and solid-gold sandals. The Yawnghwe mahadevi's dress had such spectacular wings and tails that at a later garden party there was talk of sawing the back off a chair to accommodate it. 'The weight of Monè's [Mongnai's] dress is tremendous,' marvelled Scott. 'These stiff gold dresses are unlike anything else. Tip Htila wore gold bracelets notwithstanding her loss. Each weighed 10 lbs. pure gold. Altogether,' he concluded with immense pride in his diary that night, reaching for a footballing metaphor, 'I think Burma scored today.'

On the way home the saophas stopped in Calcutta to buy souvenirs. The saopha of Mongnai bought a dozen perambulators (he had no children) and a bulldog.

Lord Curzon, the viceroy of India, had asked Scott what had most impressed the saophas at the durbar. 'One of them had said it was the number of white women,' replied Scott. 'He had had no idea there were so many white women in the world.' But it was Sao Kawng Kiao Intaleng, the saopha of Kengtung, who was most profoundly affected by the gathering. The wealth and grandeur of India's native rulers, the immense areas they controlled, the respect they were apparently accorded by the British – all this made him see the Shan chiefs in a new light. 'We thought we were great men,' Intaleng was heard to remark, 'but now we see that we are only monkeys from the jungle.'

But Intaleng was also inspired, and back in Kengtung he levied a special tax from each household and employed an Indian architect to design a palace to rival the buildings of Delhi. The result was mammoth, extravagant and (some would say) ugly. Two muscular turrets with fluted cupolas squatted next to elegantly arched windows framed with delicate relief work. Rising incongruously above this Moghul-inspired facade was a dark teak roof topped by a third dome with a traditional royal spire. The walls were several feet thick. Intaleng's throne sat in a cavernous teak-beamed hall where daylight barely penetrated, and one of the saopha's nineteen children would recall being so terrified by its shadowy expanse that she always hitched up her sarong and sprinted across it. The only room equipped with chairs was used to receive British officials.

Sao Kawng Kiao Intaleng lived there until his death in 1935. His palace survived the war – it was built to last – but the country was disintegrating around it. In the 1950s Burmese troops advanced into the Shan hills to repel Nationalist Chinese forces retreating from Mao's China, and were in turn attacked by increasingly well-organised Shan guerrilla units. Ethnic insurgencies were igniting in other regions. In 1959, at a grand ceremony in Taunggyi, the thirty-four Shan saophas formally relinquished their feudal powers, and the Shan states became Shan State. However, the saophas kept their palaces and royal titles, and by this time many were influential politicians – notably, the saopha of Yawnghwe, who was Burma's first president, and the popular ruler of Hsipaw, Sao Kya Seng. Within four years, both men were dead – victims of Ne Win's military coup. The last occupant of Kengtung Palace, Sao Sai Long – a.k.a. Shorty – was incarcerated at Insein Prison, and the palace his legendary ancestor had built was seized by the military.

Like the rest of Burma, it fell into terminal decline. The original teak roof rotted and was replaced by tin. By the 1990s the military had declared the building unsafe and slated it for demolition. These were the dark, dangerous days following the bloody crushing of the 1988 democracy uprising, yet still the locals found the courage to protest. Opposition was focused through a venerable abbot, who went to Rangoon to plead for a stay of execution for the palace.

It was ripped down anyway. In 1992, while soldiers held back the townsfolk, the plump Moghul turrets were girdled with thick chains and then pulled by armoured personnel carriers. Twice the chains snapped. People said this was proof of how strong the old palace was. Burmese workers and prisoners from Kengtung jail did the rest – no Shan would take part. The immense teak rafters were salvaged to build a school for army children; pulverised stone from the walls was used to lay a road around Kengtung's military base. The demolition took a whole month.

Meanwhile, in Mandalay, the Burmese regime began to spend millions of kyat on constructing a replica of Thibaw's palace, an irony not lost on one Shan resistance newspaper, which accused the generals of 'swallowing our history and resurrecting theirs'. The demolition of Kengtung Palace was part of an assault on Shan culture. It included the Burmanisation of place names – 'Nyaungshwe' not 'Yawnghwe'; 'Kyaing Tong' not 'Kengtung' – and the destruction of signs bearing village names in the Shan language. Monks must still ask for permission from local authorities to teach in Shan. The upshot of all this was that many young Shan did not understand their mother tongue. An exiled Shan journalist estimated that 40 per cent of Shans could not read the newsletter he produced.

With the razing of the palace, the Shan lost forever a unique part of their history. But the building remained a cherished symbol of nationhood. I would notice photographs of it all over Kengtung, defiantly pinned up in discreet corners of shops or market stalls. The land where it had stood lay empty for years. Then the vegetation was cleared and work began on a new building. The authorities promised that this new structure would serve the Shan people; the Shan people would be proud of it, they said. The workers were mainly men and women from the Akha hill tribe. At least a dozen of them perished during the construction, not just from work-site accidents, but also, it was believed, from a mysterious illness that made them simply lay down and die. The new building, when it was finished, had many ghosts.

After breakfast I went to see it. I carefully put the photo of the old palace back into my journal and walked out through the hotel garden. It was overgrown in places, bare in others. There was some knackered plastic furniture, and a swimming pool with crumbling steps leading down to two inches of snot-green water. I stood at the poolside and looked up at the peeling walls of the hotel. I looked at it for a while, trying to think it out of existence. Because this was what they'd ripped down the wonderful old palace for. This was what they'd built in its place. The Kyaing Tong New Hotel: a shabby concrete box for official photo-ops and military breakfast meetings. It was absolutely heartbreaking.

*

For every misery inflicted by the Burmese government there was a tonic, and for me, in Kengtung, it was Sai Lek.

He had been recommended to me as a guide, and I found him in a suitably cloak-and-dagger fashion, by leaving a message with a certain person at a particular address in town. Thirty minutes later Sai Lek roared up on a borrowed motorbike. He was a dashing, laid-back Shan in his twenties, and, I quickly discovered, ferociously bright. His political savvy was due in part to the military's merciless harassment of his family for their democratic views. But while his loathing of the Burmese military was profound – as a teenager he had stood at the gates of Kengtung Palace, watching the bulldozers with impotent rage – it was not consuming. He refused to be bitter about what the regime had denied him (a university education, for starters), and was instead concentrating on his next move, which was landing a job in Thailand – Thai being one of half a dozen languages he had taught himself.

I was counting on Sai Lek to tell me about the 'outer palaces'. Sao Kawng Kiao Intaleng had built not only a palace, but also a villa for each of his six wives. Sai Lek knew of two that had survived. One had been converted into a government guest house. The other was the private home of a Shan royal who lived abroad.

'We can go and have a look around it if you want,' said Sai Lek.

'That's possible?'

Sai Lek smiled and said, 'Why not?' which was his way of saying, 'Of course!'

The villa was not far from the Kyaing Tong New Hotel and was surrounded by a wall which in recent times had been heightened, as if for defence against a formidable enemy – bulldozers, possibly. The building had an almost Mediterranean feel, with whitewashed walls, wooden shutters, and a muddle of plant pots in the front porch, and the garden was bursting with a profusion of rose bushes and mango trees. This idyllic property was looked after by an aged family caretaker. The villa had been built for Sao Nang Woon Yong, the saopha's fifth wife, and was still owned by one of her descendants. The owner rarely visited, said the caretaker as he led us through the gloomy ground floor. There was nothing much to see – just a few curling photos of minor Shan royals, some worm-nibbled books, and an ancient leather whip which Sai Lek immediately picked up and began slashing the dusty air with.

'For a horse,' explained the caretaker.

'For the saopha to whip his people with,' grinned Sai Lek.

Afterwards Sai Lek took me on a high-speed tour of the town on his motorbike. We shot out through the south gate – where, under the saophas of old, public executions took place – and followed the town wall on its meandering path through the countryside. In a nineteenth-century siege of the town, giant rockets were launched from these ramparts to stampede the Siamese war elephants. The fortifications have been crumbling away ever since; Scott found them 'picturesque rather than formidable'.

We ended up on 'One-Tree Hill', named after a dipterocarpous monster that soared 218 feet into the sky. The tree had been planted in 1751, and even in Scott's time it was tall enough to be spotted for miles around, indicating to weary travellers that Kengtung was near. Now, wouldn't you know it, Burmese soldiers ran the tree, and we had to pay them an entrance fee. Bizarrely, they also tried to sell us hand-made greetings cards. A few years back each section of Burma's military was ordered to find ways of generating extra cash, and Kengtung's soldiers had obviously branched out into fancy stationery. I later heard that Military Intelligence ran a prawn farm.

The spectacular view from One-Tree Hill was dominated by one colossal building – some sort of resort reserved for military personnel, said Sai Lek. Similar buildings were scattered all over Burma like Monopoly pieces; I had seen an almost identical complex under construction in Kalaw. While Burma's schools, hospitals and universities had been shut down or robbed of equipment and funds, the nation's scant resources had been diverted to create military schools, military hospitals, military universities – in effect, a parallel society for members of the armed forces. Membership of this provided certain privileges, and a good incentive to preserve the status quo. It was one reason why the Burmese army had held power for so long. That and the fact that they had all the guns.

'You see those football pitches down there?' asked Sai Lek, pointing into the valley. 'They used to be paddy fields. The military ordered two villages to move away, and took all the land. Now the people have nothing.' There was a match in progress, and we watched it in silence. 'The soldiers play football very well,' said Sai Lek drily.

We sat there and discussed our plan for the next day. I wanted to visit Mongla, a boom town near the Chinese border which I had heard a lot about, none of it good. It was an autonomous region of Burma run by a Shan-Chinese drug trafficker and his ethnic-Wa allies, and had an unsavoury reputation as a freewheeling centre for gambling and prostitution. 'There are no Burmese soldiers there,' said Sai Lek. 'There it is like –' he struggled to find a word to describe a place without Burmese soldiers: 'There it is like democracy.'

Shan chiefs at the Delhi Durbar. The Kengtung chief is second from left. (British Library)

The currency most widely accepted in Mongla was the Chinese yuan, and Sai Lek suggested we go to Kengtung market to convert some of my fine American dollars. The market was a crowded grid of wooden stalls, but the money-changers were easy to find: I just listened for the soft percussion of large silver coins jangling in their hands. The coins were antique Indian rupees as big as milk-bottle tops, some bearing the profile of a young Queen Victoria and dating back to 1840. Local farmers still bought livestock with Indian rupees, although only the newer ones were used – 'the ones with the guy on them', as Sai Lek put it, meaning Edward VII, King and Emperor. Many ethnic groups incorporated old coins into their costume. Kayan women hung chains of rupees from their neck rings, although this was rarely seen among refugees, who were often forced to sell the coins to buy safe passage into Thailand.

I bought a handful of rupees to add to the now bewildering mix of currencies in my pocket, all of them accepted in the Kengtung area: Thai baht, Chinese yuan, Burmese kyat, US dollars, and Foreign Exchange Certificates – the regime's funny money, a kind of faux-dollar for tourists.

The market was thronging with ethnic minorities. At every corner I was bowled over by the sight of a woman in magnificent tribal finery. A ruddy-faced Lisu woman browsed at a cosmetics stall in an embroidered blue smock and maroon leggings with delicate peppermint-green hems, a sprig of herbs threaded deftly through her ear lobe for safe keeping. There was an Akha woman with a stunning triangular headdress protected from the noon sun by a black wimple and festooned with coins and baubles, and a Silver Palaung woman wearing a cummerbund of beaten silver and black rattan hoops stacked around her buttocks. In marked contrast, I spotted a dark-skinned woman wearing nothing but a skimpy sarong. I thought at the time that she was the town lunatic, but learned later that Shan women in nearby villages still walk around – as Scott said of the Wa – 'all unabashed, unhaberdashed, unheeding'.

Sai Lek was an expert at identifying the different ethnic groups. That made one of us.

'That woman over there,' I'd say – 'she's an Akha, right?'

'No,' Sai Lek would patiently reply. 'She is not an Akha. She is a Lahu.'

'Right. But *that* woman is Tai Loi.'

'No. Not Loi. Lisu.' And so on.

Only a few weeks before there had been a near-riot at the market. The wholly improbable cause? Ten foxy Russian dancers from a Mongla nightclub shopping for souvenirs. Like most of Kengtung's males, and a large proportion of its females, Sai Lek had raced down to the market to watch these strikingly pale creatures strut in fluorescent hot pants among the Akha and the Palaung, the Lisu and the Loi. He was still visibly affected by the memory. 'Their clothes were so *tight*,' he said.

A troupe of Slavic beauties marooned in a Burmese border town – the Mongla trip was sounding less like work by the minute. 'These Russian girls,' I asked Sai Lek. 'Do you think we might bump into them tomorrow?'

Sai Lek's eyes lit up. 'Why not?'

10

The following morning Sai Lek and I rented a car and set off for Mongla. It was only about two hours away, but our driver decided to honour us by making a bid for a new Kengtung-Mongla land-speed record. Puffing casually on a filthy great cheroot, he flung the car along steep, winding, unsurfaced mountain roads while a wide-eyed Tweetie Pie toy attached to the dashboard headbanged its approval. He was your classic Buddhist driver: one foot on the accelerator, the other in the afterlife. He lived in a world without brakes. Twice we nearly skidded off the road and down the mountain. Sai Lek, who was your classic Buddhist passenger, laughed heartily both times, which meant he was either very happy or, like me, crapping himself. It was impossible to tell.

Fortunately the scenery provided ample distractions. The Shan villages had houses with crumbling tiled roofs shaped like axe heads. These were glimpsed through thick groves of trees, which in turn were surrounded by electric-green rice fields patrolled by squadrons of low-flying storks. I saw ancient monasteries, all in a similar state of picturesque dishevelment, as if they had been raised twenty feet off the ground and then dropped. Spying on us from a distance through a curtain of mist was Loi Sam Dao, or 'Three Times Bigger Mountain', where fields of opium poppies still flourished.

George Scott criss-crossed Shan State for over two decades, but I could find no mention of Mongla in his diaries. This wasn't really surprising. Mongla was an insignificant village in a sparsely populated area. Only recently had it earned its notoriety as one of the most important drug-running centres in Burma.

Mongla owed its remarkable transformation to a Shan-Chinese warlord called Lin Mingxian. Lin had been a field commander in the Communist Party of Burma, or CPB, a formidable insurgent group which once occupied a large swathe of northeastern Shan state. The CPB had huge stocks of arms and ammunition, and most of its 15,000-plus soldiers were Wa hill-tribesmen, whose ferocity in battle earned them favourable comparisons with the Gurkhas. In 1989, however, the Wa rebelled, storming the CPB's headquarters on the China-Burma frontier and shattering the group into numerous factions. One of these factions would become the United Wa State Army, now one of the largest armed drug-trafficking organisations on the planet. (I'd be meeting it later.) Another faction was led by Lin Mingxian, who with over 3,500 soldiers took control of an opium-rich wilderness bordering China, Laos and Thailand.

What happened next was extraordinary. Rather than take on Lin and his well-equipped private army, the Burmese regime cut a deal with him. The terms were extremely generous. In return for keeping the peace, Lin was granted immunity from prosecution and full autonomy in the Mongla region. The regime also gave him lucrative business concessions in gold, timber and gems, as well as – crucially – tacit permission to trade in opium.

This Faustian deal, which was sweetened by Lin's regular 'contributions' to high-ranking Burmese officers, was one of several the junta made with the opium warlords within its borders. They have helped Burma become the world's largest opium producer after Afghanistan. Soon Lin Mingxian was opening new heroin-smuggling routes in Southeast Asia to get his product to the USA and Australia. The US State Department identified Lin and his Wa allies as key players in the heroin and methamphetamine trade.

Drugs made Lin a very rich man, but were still only one source of his enormous income. Mongla was a trans-shipment area for smuggling Chinese labourers through Thailand and into America. For this service the labourers paid up to $40,000 each; some paid again with their lives. Three hundred Chinese hailing from Lin's territory were aboard a ship which ran aground off New Jersey in 1993. Scores of them drowned trying to swim ashore through heavy seas.

Meanwhile, Mongla grew. Casinos were built, and soon thousands of Chinese tourists from neighbouring Yunnan Province were pouring over the border to visit them. Later I picked up an official tourism leaflet, written in Chinese, which described Mongla as 'a beautiful and prosperous region [with] unique natural scenery and curious local customs'. One of those curious customs was public executions. Lin governed his private fiefdom with medieval brutality. On one occasion three men suspected of plotting to assassinate him were dragged into the busy market and machine-gunned to death by his teenage bodyguards.

Mongla's smack-fuelled prosperity grew evident as our journey progressed. The road got busier, and we saw many expensive cars with Mongla licence plates.

'Nobody dares to touch these cars,' remarked Sai Lek. 'The people inside are powerful.'

'What do you mean?' I asked.

'They have guns.'

'Ah.'

To reach Mongla you must negotiate a bewildering variety of checkpoints. At the Nam Loi River we showed our documents at a Burmese immigration office. On the other side of the bridge we were stopped again, this time by Burmese troops. We continued, and were soon waved through two fortified checkpoints manned by conspicuously armed soldiers. This was the first indication that we had entered Lin Mingxian's territory: the soldiers were not Burmese, but belonged to the National Democratic Alliance Army, a fancy name for Lin's private militia. A few miles further on our entry was officially recorded at a small roadside booth. Inside sat a grumpy, half-naked man playing Tetris. We gave him our documents and paid him an 'entrance fee' of eighty Chinese yuan, or about six pounds, plus the usual compulsory gratuity for his attentive service and for being such an all-round nice chap.

We drove on through lush countryside. Tai Loi women with beaded sporrans trudged in single file past teetering stacks of hay; water buffalo wallowed in a stream which followed the road; and then – bam! – there was a vast wasteland stripped of vegetation where a golf course and entertainment complex were under construction. The last few miles of road were the smoothest in Burma. After a morning of rattling along a stony route, I could actually hear what Sai Lek was saying in the front seat; I could hear birds singing. Construction companies from Thailand built many of the roads in the parts of Burma run by drug traffickers. The Wa were particularly cherished clients, because they paid the construction companies on the spot after each mile was completed – in cash.

Mongla sprawled across a spacious valley bounded by dark hills. We drove along the high street, where many old buildings had been demolished and replaced by the standard-issue shop-houses. It was hot – Mandalay hot – and most residents had retreated to the cool interiors of their shops, where I could hear the click and slap of mahjong tiles. The streets were empty apart from a grimy Akha woman sifting through the trash cans. Near the market I spotted a nightclub whose sign had been translated into English in that wonderfully literal way of the Chinese. It read, 'FOREIGN AMOROUS FEELING PLACE' – which you have to admit was a pretty good name for a feeling place.

We didn't linger for long, since Sai Lek was worried we'd miss the transvestite show – the first attraction on our whistle-stop tour of Mongla. The venue was to be found on a hill to the south of town, at the end of a road leading past the crocodile show and through landscaped hills. At the top of the hill was a large car park packed with Chinese minibuses. The show was taking place in a long hall. It was dark inside, and packed with people, the air moist

A Burmese ladyboy in the border town of Mongla.

and overbreathed and circulated by several ineffectual ceiling fans. A low stage festooned with cheap flashing lights ran the length of the room. One transvestite gyrated upon it in a translucent top and high heels. Another sat on the stage edge, panties around the knees, masturbating. A third transvestite lay nearby, legs akimbo, doing something unspeakable with a cigarette. I couldn't quite see what: there were so many heads craning into my line of vision. A song was playing, scratchily amplified:

Ladyboy, ladyboy,
I wanna be a ladyboy.

And what was amazing about all this was the audience: they were all elderly Chinese couples on day trips from Yunnan Province. About 10,000 Chinese tourists visit Mongla every day, and for what? To watch pre-op trannies twiddling with themselves. Grandmothers with blue-rinsed hair sat unflinching as a trannie waltzed on in a see-through flamenco dress with pompoms on the hems and danced lewdly to the ladyboy song. Then the stage lights went off and the audience filed out in near darkness, although a crowd of men stayed behind to taunt the performers and squeeze and prod their breasts. One ladyboy gave it back too, grabbing the men's cocks through their baggy polyester trousers and tugging them vigorously. I saw several elderly Chinese men emerge from the lugubrious hall looking confused but happy.

The scene outside was scarcely believable. Five or six trannies in see-through tops stood beneath the noonday sun and invited Chinese tourists to pose with them. One of the Chinese was a wizened old lady, who stood sandwiched between two sets of surgically perfect breasts, valiantly flashing a V-sign. I was the only white face in the crowd, and soon a slinky creature in a spectacular red dress zeroed in. Much more boy than lady, she flounced over and fluttered her fake eyelashes at me. Then she whispered to Sai Lek.

'She says you must come with her to that building over there,' he translated. 'She wants to see your cock. She says it will only take five minutes.'

'Can't you get rid of her?' I hissed.

Sai Lek nodded, and spoke at length with the ladyboy. They seemed to be . . . negotiating.

'She said she wants to give you a blow for free,' said Sai Lek finally. He was trying not to smile. 'I think she loves you.'

The ladyboy pouted and smouldered. I grinned and sprinted for the car.

By now, Chinese minibuses were squealing out of the parking lot in convoys. Sai Lek told our driver to follow. The minibuses wound back down the hill and parked before a temple with a giant sculpture of a reclining Buddha. The temple didn't have much in the way of meditative calm. Before the Buddha stood two pretty girls in candy-floss dresses who for ten yuan posed for photos with their pet python. It was curled up miserably in a basin with its mouth taped shut. Next to them were two more girls with a peacock. Downstairs, at the entrance, shops offered a narrow but highly popular selection of souvenirs: jade bracelets, packets of ginseng, and hard-core pornographic CDs with covers explicitly previewing their penetrative delights. There were also sets of postcards featuring Mongla's ladyboys in nipple-revealing evening wear.

They starred in the official Mongla calendar too. January showed a dazzling ladyboy swinging in the crook of an elephant's trunk; December had two ladyboys badly superimposed against a New Hampshire autumn. It was by far the cheapest, shoddiest, tackiest souvenir I had ever seen. I bought two.

Our next stop was the National Races Museum, a modest version of the 'ethnic village' I had seen under construction on a Rangoon swamp. Chinese tourists streamed in boisterous high spirits through a decorative wooden gateway flanked by two lookout posts, each occupied by a man in faux-tribal dress blowing wearily on a conch shell. All the exhibits in this museum were alive, of course, although Sai Lek and I found there was a lot of cheating. The young woman in Akha tribal costume standing at the gate – the one playing the Game Boy – was a local Shan. So was the Lahu girl sitting on the motorbike next to her.

We were swept up on a wave of Chinese tourists and carried along a winding path which led past wooden huts occupied by representatives of various ethnic groups. There were two old Shan women flogging herbal medicines, as well as a large contingent of Kayan 'long-necks'. We crowded into a round hut to watch them perform a traditional dance, which involved the flicking of colourful hankies. It was a lot like Morris dancing, except not so silly.

The next show was clearly anticipated by the Chinese tourists. While the wives dutifully hung back, the men crowded along a low wooden fence. Beyond it was an artificial grove of ferns and waterfalls. Five women wearing wet sarongs appeared, and began to pour water slowly over themselves. Occasionally a woman would let a sarong slip to show a glistening brown breast. The Chinese men craned forward; two guards blew whistles and shooed them back. The women splashed about in desultory fashion for another five minutes and then, upon some hidden cue, picked up their buckets and tossed water over the leching spectators. The men scampered back to their wives. There was much hilarity.

Afterwards one of the girls sat on the grass combing her wet hair. I got Sai Lek to ask her what aspect of tribal culture her display was meant to illustrate.

'We are Burman ladies washing and playing with water,' she explained sweetly.

And was she Burman?

'Oh no. I'm Shan. All of us are from Mongla.'

Waiting in a thatched shelter on the next slope were four Kayaw women – *real* Kayaw women. The Kayaw were a little-studied ethnic group known among tour guides in Thailand as the 'big knees', for their spiralling knee coils. These women wore matching brass ankle rings, splendid garlands of Indian rupees worth a small fortune, and short, pink-checked skirts like abbreviated kilts. Their ear lobes were distended by silver cylinders as fat as rolling pins. Probably to avoid slave raiders, the Kayaw lived on 'absurdly steep hills', wrote Scott, and this explained why the women I saw had thighs like East German shot-putters – which in turn might help explain why Kayaw societies are strictly matriarchal. Scott (who was very fussy about hygiene) recorded how a Kayaw mother washed her child every morning and evening for a year after birth, and then never again, that first year being considered 'enough washing to last a lifetime'.

Another deluge of Chinese caught up with us, and we escaped to browse the souvenir stalls. They all sold cigarettes, Burmese stamps and coins, and one-yuan packets of contraceptive pills from Europe and America. A vendor told Sai Lek the pills were very popular among Chinese women; they preferred them to the high-dose horrors prescribed back home. At the gate, I noticed that the management had thoughtfully provided a special room for Chinese tourists who considered even exotic foreign holidays an unwanted distraction from the addiction of mah-jong, and a po-faced quartet sat inside slapping tiles on a table.

On our way back into town we stopped to check out a stone amphitheatre, Mongla's only impressive building. It was a circus. We had missed the show, thankfully, and instead made an unofficial tour of the cages. A lioness watched us pass with searing alertness; the tiger and the lion were asleep, dreaming of jungle and savannah. Next door to the amphitheatre was a domed structure so shoddily built it looked half-finished. It had in fact been completed months before, and housed a rival transvestite cabaret from Thailand.

Our next stop was the opium museum. This was opened in 1997 by the big cheese himself, Lieutenant General Khin Nyunt, to commemorate the supposed eradication of drugs in the Mongla region. Like other museums built during the dictatorship, this one resembled a temple, with a seven-tiered spire, gold-painted finials, and lots of architectural twiddly bits. Inside were all the exhibits one would expect: photos of dead junkies; photos of generals wagging their chins over packets of heroin; photos of the same heroin (one assumed) going up in flames at various drug-burning ceremonies. I was drawn to a display about rehabilitation, lavishly captioned 'The Demonstration on Drug Abuse Treatment and Education Activities and Finally Came to the Normal Stream of Life'. It consisted of four tableaux incorporating life-size mannequins. The first tableau showed two youngsters shooting up; they had long hair, faded jeans, and T-shirts bearing the legend 'Bad to the Bone'. The next showed one junkie in handcuffs, and the second lying dead with a syringe sticking from his arm. Then we saw the survivor in a hospital bed, surrounded by caring medical staff.

Finally we witnessed the junkie's glorious rebirth. He now had short hair and wore a crisp green longyi and a white waistcoat.

This uniform, and the badge pinned to his waistcoat, identified him as a member of the Union Solidarity Development Association. What was the USDA? I once asked a learned Burmese friend that very question. 'I can explain it to you in one word,' he replied. 'Bullshit.' Dangerous bullshit, too. The USDA was a nationalist organisation which acted as the regime's Rottweiler; Aung San Suu Kyi has compared it to the Hitler Youth. At one USDA rally a Burmese general urged the audience to kill Aung San Suu Kyi; her car was later stoned by a mob in a well-planned and terrifying attack in 1996. The USDA also had other uses. I once went to a Rangoon football match where a meagre crowd of regulars – mainly mouthy youths and diehard gamblers – was suddenly swollen by thousands of people in USDA uniforms, trucked in to impress a gaggle of generals in attendance. The organisation claimed to have over 7 million members, although this was a hollow boast: joining the USDA was compulsory for government officials, and access to education, housing and health care often depended on being a member. (By contrast, members of Aung San Suu Kyi's National League for Democracy were often denied medical treatment.) Rangoon prostitutes carried USDA membership cards so that the police didn't arrest them.

The mannequin display at the museum illustrated not just a junkie's noble path to rehabilitation, but also – and perhaps more importantly for the regime's propagandists – his glorious transformation from soap-dodging Westernised reprobate into clean-cut Burman patriot. The Burmese military liked to characterise its war on drugs as part of a wider campaign against colonialism and all its nefarious agents. This was spelled out by Khin Nyunt in a speech at Mongla in 1999. He blamed Burma's drug scourge on the 'pernicious legacy' of British colonialists – a legacy exacerbated by what he called 'the unscrupulous actions of the politically motivated neo-colonialist clandestine organisations'. This hardly explained or excused the regime's abysmal record in drug control. Since 1988 – when Khin Nyunt and his clique rose to power – opium production in Burma had more than doubled. This startling increase was due largely to the generous concessions the regime had granted Mongla's ruler Lin Mingxian and other ethnic drug lords.

Nor could colonialists (or even neo-colonialists) be blamed for the staggering quantities of methamphetamine produced in Burma's lawless border areas. In 1999 an estimated half a billion pills poured into Thailand, where the highly addictive drug was called *ya ba* or 'insanity medicine'. *Ya ba* was much easier to make and distribute than heroin. Using a relatively simple chemical procedure, two men in a jungle hut could manufacture about 10,000 pills every day. Along the Thai-Burma border there were reportedly dozens of such labs, which, unlike fields of swaying opium poppies, could not be detected by spy satellites. Each pill cost less than ten cents to produce. At the border it sold for about seventy cents. By the time a pill reached Bangkok it was worth anything up to three dollars. Cheap and readily available, *ya ba* ripped through Thailand's slums, factories, universities and nightclubs, leaving over a quarter of a million addicts in its wake. The lucrative trade corrupted hundreds of police and other officials who, under normal circumstances, were duty-bound to stop it. The only substance more addictive than *ya ba* was the money made from peddling it.

Narcotics were Burma's only growth industry, and the military regime depended heavily on drug money to keep the nation's economy afloat. By one estimate, 60 per cent of all private investment in Rangoon was drug-related; Mandalay's economic boom was fuelled by narcotics. Drug money also provided most of Burma's hard-currency reserves. This analysis, if true – and I've learned much of it from Bertil Lintner, a leading Burma expert – reveals how utterly Burma's economy depends on drugs. The biggest junkies of all are the generals themselves.

A Chinese tour group arrived at the museum with a flag-waving guide and embarked upon a high-speed tour. I pursued them upstairs. They paused before a glass cabinet containing toilet-roll covers – these had been crocheted by heroin rehab patients – then did a record-breaking lap of a room dedicated to the brief but glorious history of Mongla. This was a room worth dallying in. Among the photos on display was one of Khin Nyunt cutting the museum's ribbon. Standing beside him was a tall, chinless man with piggy eyes dressed in Shan national costume. According to the caption, his name was Sai Leun. He appeared in many photos, although none of the captions explained who he was. I had Burmese press reports which described Sai Leun as 'the leader of national races in the Mongla region'. Another photo showed Khin Nyunt presenting him with a 'medal of honour' for his 'outstanding performance' in eradicating drugs in Mongla. Sai Leun was clearly a man with a strong reputation as an anti-narcotics crusader.

The hell he was. What the museum's captions didn't explain was that Sai Leun was the Shan alias for Lin Mingxian, the heroin kingpin who ran Mongla. There were many more buddy photos of Khin Nyunt and Lin Mingxian, a.k.a. Sai Leun. One showed them at the consecration of Mongla's main Buddhist temple, a concrete grotesquerie perched on the next hilltop like a stranded UFO. Both men sat beside the monks, as if they were equals, rather than in positions of reverence at the monks' feet. Sai Lek, a devout Buddhist, found this deeply offensive.

I was fascinated by another photo. It showed Sai Leun, a.k.a. Lin Mingxian, presenting a brightly wrapped gift to a man identified as 'J. Dennis Hastert'. Could this be Denny Hastert, Illinois congressman and Speaker of the US House of Representatives? Yes it could: Hastert visited Burma with a delegation of Republican congressmen in 1996, ostensibly to inspect drug-eradication methods. The delegation was wined and dined by the generals before visiting Lin Mingxian in Mongla. It was unclear what Hastert achieved by meeting Lin, beyond providing a priceless photo opportunity for a known heroin trafficker anxious to whitewash his recent past and recast himself as an anti-drugs tsar. In the museum photo Hastert looked distinctly uncomfortable in Lin's company, as well he might. Later I looked up Hastert's web page, and found a photograph of him holding a T-shirt which read, 'Drugs Kill.' I wonder if he gave one to Lin Mingxian. After all, Lin was the chairman of something called the Mongla Action Committee on Narcotics – a committee reduced in numbers when another of its less-than-distinguished members was arrested in a sting operation by Thai police and the US Drug Enforcement Administration and extradited to New York on narcotics charges. This was three months after Hastert's visit.

Did Denny Hastert know he was pressing palms with a man whose refineries produced heroin sold on US streets? Maybe someone should ask him. Then again, why pick on Hastert? He was not the first American politician to pay his respects to Mongla's drug lord, and probably won't be the last. In 1993 New York congressman Charles Rangel – former chairman of the House Committee on Narcotics – took a delegation to meet Lin Mingxian. Three months after Rangel's visit, the bullet-strewn corpses of Lin's three would-be assassins lay bleeding in the market.

It seemed to me that Lin Mingxian understood something his distinguished visitors did not, and it was this: if you shake the hands of enough prominent Americans, the blood on yours will eventually rub off.

The museum had one last display. Outside was a small plot with a few miserable poppies where, for one yuan each, tourists could watch two Wa soldiers score the bulbs with knives and demonstrate the opium resin oozing out. Sai Lek and I got there late, and the Wa soldiers were already counting up their takings. They were small men with very dark, unsmiling faces. When Sai Lek tried to start a conversation, they threw the money in the box and walked off. We were invisible to them.

We retired to the hotel for a few hours. Sai Lek took a nap, while I ransacked an ill-refrigerated minibar in a vain search for a beer cooler than cow spit. Our driver went to one of the many cheap whorehouses lining Mongla's streets, where a 'short time' with a Chinese peasant girl cost him sixty yuan, or about a fiver. Sai Lek believed that Mongla's booming sex industry, with its limitless supplies of Chinese women and girls just across the porous border, was fuelling the spread of HIV in the region. A few years before, he said, people were so terrified of contracting the disease from a sexual partner that there were no weddings in Kengtung for eight months.

In the evening we cruised one of Mongla's biggest casinos, looking for the infamous Russian dancers. The casino was a shabby concrete ziggurat with two brutally illuminated floors of baccarat tables. They were thronged by ruddy-faced Yunnanese folk placing low-value bets, although vast sums of drug money were said to be laundered through the private gaming rooms. On the top floor was a hall where the Russian dancers performed – but not tonight. To our great disappointment, we had arrived on their day off.

We left the casino and traipsed through puddles of reflected neon to a nearby nightclub. And there our luck returned: two gorgeous Russian dancers stood outside.

We struck up a conversation in fractured English. They were from Siberia, they said, and had met their current Chinese boss on a cross-border trip to Manchuria. They were called Natasha and Julietta.

'So when's your next show?' I asked Natasha, gesturing towards the casino.

'That is not our show,' she bristled.

'But it says the girls are from Russia.'

'They are from Belorussia,' corrected Natasha – adding with a little sneer, '*Minsk* girls.'

Not to be confused with Natasha and her Siberian troupe, who danced at a hall near my hotel. The other dancers were inside the club. It was mobbed. One lithe Russian beauty effortlessly threaded her way around the dance floor, past cartwheeling Chinese drunks and arrhythmically jerking local girls. A solitary Thai ladyboy jigged about before a full-length mirror, appraising her muscly arms between hungry glances around the room.

Sai Lek and I sat at the edge of the dance floor drinking beer. Waiters wheeled past trolleys of snacks, as if we were at a dim-sum parlour or an English tea shop. Sai Lek spent the next hour dreamily admiring a stunning Russian brunette over his beer glass. He desperately wanted to ask her to dance, but was terrified she would spurn him. She was an extremely good dancer.

Discos were very different affairs in Kengtung. Sai Lek had taken me to one. It was a rough shack with a dusty wooden floor and a slowly spinning disco light. If you were flush, you could pay to dance with one of the house dancers. I watched how it worked. A young guy bought a booklet of tickets for 100 kyat from a matron wedged behind a desk at the edge of the dance floor. Then he chose one of several dancers sitting primly along the far wall. She wore a miniskirt and – because it was rainy and cold that night – an anorak over her dimpled knees. The girl stood up, folded away her anorak, took the guy's ticket book, and they began dancing. Every thirty seconds a very loud fire bell rang, and the girl, as unthinking as a Pavlovian dog, would rip a ticket from the book. This went on until the book was empty and the floor confettied with shredded tickets. Then the girl sat down again and laid the anorak over her legs. All in all it was a pretty soulless exchange, but it still held one advantage over the Mongla club we now sat in: the chances of rejection were virtually nil. The chances of being rejected by a beautiful Russian dancer who had been shrugging off local boys all night were perilously high, and Sai Lek knew it.

'OK,' he suddenly announced. 'Now I am going to dance with the beautiful Russian girl,' and he strode out and danced with her, winding and unwinding his hands in the hypnotic style of Shan dancing. And she loved it.

I was drunkenly admiring all this – thinking how these Shan lads really have a handle on boundless youthful optimism – when I felt a tap on my shoulder.

'Would you dance with me?'

It was another Russian dancer. She was not the lithe beauty, but a statuesque woman in heavy make-up, probably in her early thirties. She took my hand and pulled me to the dance floor, and as soon as we got there the music slowed – the universal signal to entwine yourself around a woman and stick your tongue in her ear.

But that didn't happen. First we introduced ourselves; her name was Nastya – short for Anastasia. Then she put a hand on my shoulder, I put a hand round her chunky waist, and we swayed about on the spot. It was like waltzing on rat glue. It was all incredibly formal.

'How old are you?' asked Nastya.

'Thirty-two,' I replied. 'You?'

'Sixteen.'

What? I was gobsmacked. She had looked much older. Only sixteen – and in a hellhole like Mongla! My heart pitter-pattered in empathic terror. Nastya said most of the Russian girls were the same age, although one was all of twenty-two. 'Ah, a babushka,' I joked feebly, and she tittered like the schoolgirl she should have been.

Knowing she was sixteen made all the difference. I was now holding her at arm's length, like a Ming vase. While couples around us snogged and fondled, we rocked gently back and forth, a still pool of propriety in a wildly writhing universe.

'Where are you from?' she asked at last.

'London,' I said.

'London,' she sighed. 'I too would like to go to London.'

'Perhaps you will one day.'

We swayed around for a little bit.

'I have been to Paris,' she said.

'Did you like Paris?' I asked.

'Yes, I liked Paris. I liked Paris very much.'

I decided to say something bold. 'They say it is a city for lovers.'

'Yes,' she said.

I walked back to the hotel with a drunk and triumphant Sai Lek. 'Do you think she liked me?' he babbled. 'Do you *really* think she liked me?' Flashes of lightning silhouetted the surrounding hills, and soon it was raining hard again. Mongla's streets had something you rarely see in Burma's provincial centres, and never see in such remote areas: functioning street lights. The town had a twenty-four-hour power supply, thanks to a hydroelectric dam built by the United Nations, whose global remit apparently now included spending vast sums of money bringing light to a gambling town run by an obscenely wealthy heroin trafficker.

Back in my room I lay on the bed and reflected upon what had been the strangest of days. How did a place as bizarre as Mongla ever get built? A missionary in Thailand later provided a fairly convincing explanation. 'You have to understand how these guys' minds work,' he told me. 'They're drug lords. They can't travel the world. They're on every wanted list there is – DEA, FBI, CIA, Interpol, you name it. So instead they stay put and buy a satellite TV with hundreds of channels, and this is how they see the world. But of course this gives them an incredibly warped view of it.' As a result of this warped view, he continued, you first build the bars, casinos and whorehouses; then the ladyboy cabaret, Russian girlie shows, and a circus arena to pester rare and magnificent animals in. You toy with plans for a school and a hospital, but forget about the court and the jailhouse, since justice is summary and executions are carried out in the market place. Then you throw up a temple and a museum to dignify it all, and get the UN to light everything.

Maybe this was how all towns like Mongla got built. I wouldn't know, because I'd never been anywhere remotely like Mongla. I later learned that the Burmese regime regarded the place as a model of development and wise government – a tourist paradise risen from the ashes of all those drug-burning ceremonies. But I wondered whether the Chinese visitors whose money sustained Mongla agreed. A friend in Yunnan who knew of Mongla by reputation said the town was known in Chinese as *zhongguo de gangmen*, a phrase which trips off the tongue and means 'the anus of China'.

I went out to the balcony to watch the rain. I couldn't remember the last time I had seen such a violent storm. People were running helter-skelter for cover, as if an air raid were in progress, and the lone palm in the hotel forecourt seemed close to snapping under the force of the wind. Just when I thought it had peaked, the storm increased in fury, lightning blasted across the sky, and every single light in Mongla blinked out. Car headlights scanned the dark streets like searchlights, briefly illuminating bedraggled groups of people huddling beneath violently flapping shop awnings. I stood on the balcony for a while, and could hear nothing but the white noise of the pounding rain.

Then, defiantly, the lights of Mongla flickered on again.

A funny thing happened on the way back from Mongla. We were bucketing through the mountains when the driver slowed down to throw a few notes in a silver collection bowl sitting at the roadside. At that moment I spotted out of the corner of my eye a curious figure scuttling down the hillside from a small stupa. He was grinning madly and waving a wad of banknotes. It was a *yathe*, or traditional Burmese hermit, instantly recognisable by his peculiar hat, which looked something like a water bottle pulled over the head. We stopped to say hello. He seemed overjoyed to see us, and the feeling was mutual. I had wanted to meet a *yathe* for a long time – they were as rare as tigers in Burma these days – and here I was face to face with one.

And an expressive face, too. The *yathe* had wild dark eyes with red-misted corneas, a wispy beard, and hyperactive eyebrows that wriggled along his forehead as he spoke. His teeth were jagged with decay from the corrosive lime used in betel quids, which monks often chew in the belief that it aids meditation. His smile was none the less dazzling. Up close I could see in the peak of his hat the outline of an object about the size and shape of a pack of cards. As I understood it, this contained some kind of sacred Buddhist relic which *yathe* use to seed the countryside with stupas like this one. He invited us to see the stupa, and Sai Lek and I followed his flowing robes up the hillside.

The *yathe* was a lesser-spotted creature even in Scott's time. Back then, he noted, an unknown number of hermits lived in cells burrowed in cliffs along the Irrawaddy River – 'as anyone who has gone out to shoot the rock pigeons which abound there will very speedily find out'. Scott also recorded a small community living on Mandalay Hill: 'Visitors to the sacred spot occasionally came across one of the hermits striding along, wrapped in thought, grasping an iron staff hung about with rings, the rattle of which warns the people to get out of the way and not to disturb the holy man's meditations.' *Yathe* were famous for practising the art of alchemy. They believed that by discovering the Burmese equivalent of the philosopher's stone they could gain superhuman powers to resist disease, breathe underwater and fly through the air.

Our *yathe* was much more down to earth. I had expected him to live in a cave insulated with damp Pali manuscripts, but he bedded down in a building site next to the stupa. He spoke twenty to the dozen, as if he hadn't talked for a hundred years, although there were plenty of workmen around for company. 'There are very few *yathe* left in Burma,' he said, and then explained why in a very pleasing way: 'With a quid of betel nut it is easy to block out the sun. It is easy to lose the world. But it is very, very hard to become a *yathe*. Your mind must be like the earth. If a man stands upon you, you must do nothing. If a man stamps upon you, you must do nothing.'

'When he speaks his face looks like a crazy man,' whispered Sai Lek, 'but the words he speaks are very wonderful.'

The *yathe* said he had lived at the stupa for three years. I asked where he came from before that, and he waved absently to the next hill, past an Akha village on the ridge below. I sensed there was some friction between the *yathe* and the Akha, who were all Christians. 'The children are not so polite,' he sniffed, 'and many people there smoke opium.' Then his eyebrows did a Mexican wave across his forehead. 'Next time you come,' he beamed, 'we will have very good facilities.' He shook his fistful of banknotes at the building site. 'Toilets!' he announced. 'And a cafeteria.'

I gave him a donation, and in return the *yathe* grinned and coughed up another pearl of wisdom. 'Remember,' he said, 'it is very easy to find a rock, but not so a precious stone.' And with that we said goodbye and drove flat out for Kengtung.

'It is very easy to find a rock, but not so a precious stone.' I would never forget the wisdom of the *yathe*. But, to be honest, I got some much more memorable advice from another holy man I met in Thailand. He was an American missionary who, like George Scott, had spent time among the former headhunters of the Wa tribe. The Wa lived in remote hilltop villages along Burma's lawless frontier and were traditionally hostile to outsiders, but I had long been determined to visit them. I asked the missionary how. 'If I were you,' he told me, 'I'd pray a whole bunch before I went up there. But if you're not afraid to die, then give it a shot.'

Then he blessed me – always a bad sign. 'Dear Lord,' he drawled, bowing his head, 'please watch over Andrew as he makes his way among our Wa brothers. Give him your strength and your wisdom so that he may achieve his noble mission, and protect him from all danger. Amen.' It was a thoughtful gesture, I now realise, but at the time it felt like the last rites for a dying man.

11

My fascination with the Wa had begun on a sweltering afternoon in Rangoon a year or two before. I had had an idle hour to kill and, to be frank, was desperate for some air conditioning. It was time to visit the National Museum.

As it turned out, Rangoon's power was down and the whole museum was dark and stifling. Armed with a torch, I picked my way up darkened stairways to the top floor, to where the Burmese regime had assembled a loveless tribute to the ethnic minorities in its thrall. It was a huge, unvisited room milling with mannequins in various tribal costumes. I walked around the room until I came across the Wa exhibit. It wasn't up to much. It showed two dummies dressed in shabby black pyjamas, with a sign beneath in Burmese and English. The Burmese for 'Wa', I noted, was the single-syllable character 'O': a nothing, a cipher, a mystery. As I trained my torchlight on the sign, it struck me that the Wa were perhaps the most misunderstood and seldom-met tribe in all Burma.

Now there were over a million Wa, a quarter of them in China, but in Victorian times the tribe was a tenth of the size and almost nothing was known about it. That began to change only in 1893, when George Scott undertook the first of several dangerous missions into Wa territory. The Wa lived in large fortified villages in the Burmese highlands and, despite their tiny numbers, were so isolated even from each other that they spoke dozens of dialects. Their chief notoriety was as headhunters, although an odd system of classification acknowledged that one Wa village was not necessarily as barbaric as the next. For example, the 'Tame Wa' did not chop human heads at all, but instead worshipped the skulls of bears, panthers and other wild animals. The 'Intermediate Wa' indulged in what Scott called 'fits of head-hunting', or only took the heads of criminals, or bought their heads pre-cut from fiercer tribesmen. Most terrifying of all were the 'Wild Wa'. Given half a chance, they would decapitate just about anyone.

Not surprisingly, the Wa were much feared by Burma's other ethnic minorities. They were also despised for their backwardness. The Wa, it was said, produced no handicrafts other than whittled-bamboo utensils and some laughably rudimentary weaving. They walked around in loincloths, and regarded betel-blackened teeth as a mark of beauty. They ate from the same troughs as their livestock, and on special occasions enjoyed a beef stew sprinkled with ox droppings. They had no traditional medicine to speak of, relying instead on futile ceremonies to placate the malevolent ghosts

Wild Wa headhunters.

they held responsible for the horrific diseases that devastated their communities. They had just one musical instrument, made from the tip of a buffalo horn, but only used it to play (as Scott put it) 'rather grotesque little airs'. They were illiterate, of course, but less forgivably they were innumerate too: one observer noted that a Wa selling bananas at so much for six could not price fifteen of them, and if three were left over he would simply eat them. Their natural aggression was fuelled by the all-day consumption of immense quantities of rice liquor. 'Among the Wa,' wrote an American journalist working in post-war China, 'it is traditional that you cannot settle anything without a drink and you cannot settle anything when you are drunk. This leaves a remarkably small margin of time when anything can be settled.' And, as if all this were not enough to earn the undying scorn of their hill-tribe neighbours, the Wa never washed. Ever.

Traditionally, nobody loathed the Wa more than the Shan. The coronation of Sao Kawng Kiao Intaleng, the last great saopha of Kengtung, featured the ritual expulsion of two elderly Wa men from the throne room, a re-enactment of a past Shan conquest over the Wa hordes. Many Shan were convinced that the Wa were cannibals. A 1932 British account mentioned 'fourth-hand reports' of Wa tribesmen 'killing and roasting and eating Shan children'. Even now the Wa remained a kind of universal bogeyman. When a Shan mother wanted to quieten her restless child, she might whisper, 'Shh! A Wa is coming!'

A much less hysterical description of Wa customs was to be found in the *Gazetteer*. Scott was fascinated by these rare and fearsome people, and particularly by their creation myth, which offered an elaborate explanation for the origins of headhunting. 'The Wa claim tadpoles for their rude fore-fathers,' explained Scott. 'As tadpoles they spent their first years in Nawng Hkeo, a mysterious lake on the top of a hill range, seven thousand feet high, in the centre of head-cutting country.' These tadpoles became frogs, and the frogs evolved into hungry, cave-dwelling ogres with red eyes who cast no shadow when they moved. They hunted deer, pigs and other wild animals, but as long as these were their only diet they had no offspring. Then, one day, the ogres ventured into a country inhabited by men. They captured one and ate him, and carried off his skull. 'After this they had many young ogrelets, all of whom, however, appeared in human form,' continued Scott.

The parents therefore placed the human skull on a post and worshipped it. There were nine sons, who established themselves in the nine Wa glens, mostly in the west, and they bred and mustered rapidly. The ten daughters settled on the fells and were even more prolific. Their descendants are the most thorough in head-hunting and the skulls are always men's. The language the new race spoke was at first that of the frog, a sort of Brekkekkekkexkoax, but this was elaborated in time into modern Wa.

One thing leaped out at me from this colourful description in the *Gazetteer*. What was this 'mysterious lake' called Nawng Hkeo at the heart of head-cutting country in which, according to folklore, the Wa began life as tadpoles? Did it even exist outside Wa mythology? For a long time I couldn't find out. Then I was directed to an old account by V. C. Pitchford, a British surveyor who set out in 1937 to solve what he called 'the age long riddle of the fairy lake in the remotest part of the wild Wa country'. Apparently the lake did exist, but few outsiders had ever seen it – thus its almost mythical status. 'The fairy lake lies on a cloud-capped mountain,' ran one description in Pitchford's account,

in the middle of a silent forest where mortals dare not dwell. Its waters are so deep, so cold, that no fish can live. At its four corners four cliffs rise sheer from the water into high rocky peaks. From its waters flow the rivers of the world. From its primaeval waters sprang the forebears of the Wa race, and when they became men they lived in the cavern of Pakkatei and there learnt the mystery of headhunting, whereby they waxed fruitful and multiplied exceedingly.

Pitchford faced all sorts of difficulties with locating the lake, not least of which was its name. Scott referred to it as 'Nawng Hkeo', which simply meant 'Green Lake' in Shan. According to Pitchford, the Shan also called it 'Namtongling', while the Wa name was 'Kaing Kret'. Nevertheless, though delayed by an epidemic of smallpox, Pitchford's column hacked through the jungle to discover the lake nestling in a depression on a 7,300-foot ridge. The lake was tiny – only 600 yards long and half as wide – and was hidden in a dense forest of fern, cane, bamboo and giant padauk trees. It was, wrote Pitchford, a 'mysterious and beautiful spot'.

As far as I was aware, V. C. Pitchford was the first and only white man to see Nawng Hkeo. George Scott's books and journals mentioned the lake several times, but it was unclear whether Scott himself had been there. Then I came across an old British map which showed the lake, as well as Scott's expeditions in Wa country in 1893 and 1897. Both times his party had explored regions south of Nawng Hkeo, on one occasion passing as close to the lake as ten miles but then veering away, as if repelled by the giant ridge on which it sat. Scott, it seemed, never went there.

This was when I decided to hike into the Wa hills and see the fabled Wa lake of Nawng Hkeo for myself. Following in Scott's footsteps was all well and good. But to reach a remote area he had written about but never visited – to out-Scott Scott – now there was a challenge.

It wouldn't be easy. The Wa weren't headhunters any more – they harvested the last crop of skulls in the 1970s – but their modern reincarnation was just as frightening. Now the opium-rich Wa hills were controlled by one of the world's largest drug-trafficking organisations, the United Wa State Army. And at the very heart of this criminal empire lay the lake of Nawng Hkeo – patrolled no longer by headhunting tribesmen, but by the heavily armed troops of the UWSA.

It was impossible to live in Thailand, as I did, and not know about the UWSA. In many ways the 'Red Wa', as Thais also called them, were public enemy number one. The UWSA was another breakaway faction of the defunct Communist Party of Burma, and in 1989 it had struck a ceasefire agreement with the Burmese government which was not dissimilar to Lin Mingxian's in Mongla. This peace deal effectively gave the UWSA control of large areas along Burma's border with Thailand and China, and allowed the Wa to concentrate on what they did best: refining raw opium into heroin for the world's markets.

Then, in 1993, the UWSA also began to produce methamphetamine or *ya ba* – the poor man's Ecstasy. Millions of pills poured out of the UWSA's jungle laboratories and into neighbouring Thailand, which was soon convulsed with an unprecedented pandemic of drug abuse. Every day, it seemed, my morning paper carried another horrific picture – a man crazed on *ya ba* leaping to his death from an apartment roof; a bleary-eyed addict holding a knife to a toddler's throat, and then slicing it as the police lunged to arrest him. The statistics were just as frightening: it was estimated, for example, that two-thirds of all crime in Bangkok was now drug-related.

Desperate Thai addicts were not the UWSA's only customers. If you have been on holiday in Thailand and have bought a bootleg CD from a street vendor, then you have unwittingly made the tycoon drug lords of the UWSA a little bit richer: these CDs are believed to be manufactured in Wa-occupied areas of Burma. And if you have bought Ecstasy at a Bangkok club, or at the famous full-moon party on the island of Koh Phangan, then you have probably just sampled the latest addition to the UWSA's bulging pharmacy. Thai police now believed that high-tech Wa laboratories were producing the designer drug for half the price of their Dutch rivals. There were also reports of Wa methamphetamine and Ecstasy reaching markets in both Europe and Australia.

Like Lin Mingxian, the UWSA was invited by the Burmese regime to reinvest its drug profits in legitimate businesses. Through its main company, Myanmar Kyone Yeom Group – one of Burma's largest – the UWSA had interests in real estate, finance, mining, tourism and transport, and offices in several Asian cities and in the USA. But, while obscenely wealthy, the United Wa State Army was not, as its name suggested, united. It was actually split in two. The southern command controlled large areas along the Thai-Burma border, while the northern command, led by an ethnic Chinese warlord called Pao Yuqiang, held sway along Burma's north-east border with China, the traditional Wa heartland where the lake was located. Pao Yuqiang – often known simply as 'the General' – ran his narco-empire from Panghsang, a lawless Wa frontier town which served as headquarters for the UWSA's northern command. He was rumoured to be so rich that he needed two trucks to ferry all his money around. He was also vicious and paranoid. On one occasion in Panghsang four young UWSA officers were arrested on suspicion of conspiring against the General. Justice – if that's the word – was swift and brutal: all four were pistol-whipped to death on the spot.

Like Lin Mingxian, Pao had a cosy relationship with Burma's military leaders. I had a number of photos, obtained from a highly disreputable source, which recorded a visit to the Wa hills by Lieutenant General Khin Nyunt. It was easy to spot Pao: he was, as someone had once told me, 'a typical rich Wa – short, fat and dark'. In one photo, Pao and Khin Nyunt stood side by side, grinning at some just-told joke. Strangely, they were also holding hands. Cosy, as I said.

The Burmese government extended similar courtesies to General Pao's men. Flush with drug money, the Wa had a reputation in Burma's cities as thugs and rabble-rousers, and wherever I travelled I heard horror stories about them. The previous year a Mandalay liquor-store owner had been shot dead by a drunken Wa man. In another notorious incident in Mandalay, some Wa revellers who had never driven before bought a Mercedes, got drunk, and slammed the car into a crowded bus stop. Several people were killed, but the Wa involved were released by the Burmese authorities 'in the national interest'. Burma's generals had no intention of jeopardising their fragile ceasefire with bellicose, well-armed Wa drug lords for the sake of a few dead bystanders in Mandalay.

While their leaders whooped it up in urban nightspots, the majority of Wa were condemned to rural lives of wretched poverty. Most Wa peasants produced barely enough food to feed their families. In the Wa hills, water was scarce, disease rampant. The immense profits of the drug trade did not trickle down to the village level, and the Wa remained among the most disadvantaged of Burma's ethnic minorities.

Hiking into UWSA-held areas would be risky, I knew, but just how risky was hard to fathom. V. C. Pitchford had paid tribute to Scott's courage during his travels in Wa territory in the 1890s. Scott's modest column of troops had no reinforcements within 100 miles, and for communication relied entirely upon the heliograph, which was useless in bad weather. Pitchford, on the other hand, had three other columns within a radius of fifty miles, and was equipped with wireless. 'Moreover,' continued Pitchford in 1937, 'Wa armament has advanced very little, if anything, since Scott's time.'

Since Pitchford's time, however, Wa armament had advanced

very greatly, thanks largely to the invention of the AK-47 assault rifle, which, in a region awash with small arms, cost less to buy than a decent pair of hiking boots. The UWSA had been described as the best-equipped insurgent force in Asia outside Afghanistan. Its armoury included assault rifles, night-vision goggles, rocket-propelled grenades, heavy machine guns, 120-mm mortars, and SAM-7 missiles – not to mention thousands of battle-hardened soldiers with a well-deserved reputation for ferocity.

Then there were the plagues. As I prepared for my trip, reports were filtering down from the hills of an epidemic of malaria, typhoid and anthrax sweeping Wa-controlled areas. By one estimate, as many as 10,000 people had died in one border town in less than three months. Thousands more were thought to be infected, and the Thai border police had turned away truckloads of Wa refugees dying of malaria and anthrax. These epidemics, and their medieval scale, were the direct result of another massive but seldom reported relocation programme in Burma. In recent years, over 100,000 Wa people had been forcibly moved from their homes in the north to settle along Burma's border with Thailand. They arrived by the truckload at makeshift camps with little food and no sanitation, and were prey to every disease. This forced migration, directed by the UWSA, was cynically heralded by the Burmese junta as part of an ambitious campaign to make Wa territory 'drug free' by the year 2005 – the idea being to shift hill people away from the poppy-growing highlands into lower-lying regions where alternative crops could be grown. The whole campaign was a big lie. Western analysts belatedly realised that, rather than eradicating opium poppies, the UWSA was using Wa refugees to cultivate new poppy fields in the south. It was feared that Burma's next opium harvest would be the biggest in years.

Still, in true Orwellian style, the Burmese junta was keen to convince the world that these new areas were poppy-free. A group of foreign reporters were helicoptered into a UWSA-controlled area near Tachilek to tour orchards, pig farms and other agricultural projects. Accompanying them was the chief Burmese government spokesman, Hla Min, a humourless lieutenant colonel nicknamed by reporters 'Hlaugh-a-Minute'. The trip's telegenic finale was the destruction of a nearby poppy field by UWSA soldiers armed with sticks. On closer inspection, the more perceptive reporters noticed that the bulbs of these poppies bore tell-tale scores: they had already been bled of opium resin. As the Wa soldiers fanned out across the field, the assembled journalists realised that they were witnessing not the permanent destruction of an opium crop, but merely the process by which old plants were chopped down in preparation for planting the next season's poppies.

These media junkets were derisively termed 'poppy-whacking tours' by the Bangkok press. Nevertheless, joining such a tour would have provided me with a safe, official route into Wa-controlled areas. But of course I would have seen only what the junta wanted me to see. And, anyway, the regime wasn't running poppy-whacking tours to the northern Wa hills, home to the main opium fields of the UWSA – and to the lake of Nawng Hkeo. No, I would have to plot my own route into the wilderness. I began to plan.

I had read that there were only two modern sources of topographical information on this remote area of Burma. The first was satellite mapping; the second – incredibly – was the information gathered by George Scott on his forays into the Wa hills over a century before. Possibly the very first map of Wa country was kept at Cambridge University Library, part of a collection begun by Scott when his brother, Forsyth, was master of St John's College. Created by a local expert during Scott's 1893 mission, it was a schematic drawing of the Wa hills, a picturesque jumble of roughly drawn peaks labeled in cursive Burmese script, and showed Nawng Hkeo as an imperfect circle surrounded by jagged peaks. It was practically useless for navigation, but I would carry a copy of it as a talisman into the Wa hills anyway.

At the other end of the cartographical scale was a 1979 US satellite map, published by the impressive-sounding Defense Mapping Agency Aerospace Center at St Louis Air Force Station in Missouri. It was an immense, cumbersome thing – almost as big as my writing desk – and depicted the rugged Wa terrain with contours of bewildering detail. It bore a number of mysterious and rather ominous warnings, such as 'Aircraft infringing upon Non-Free Flying Territory may be fired on without warning' and 'Night Flying over BURMA is PROHIBITED.' In places the US cartographers had been defeated, and the map had patches of dazzling white, along with the legend RELIEF DATA INCOMPLETE – which I liked to think was the US Air Force's way of saying, 'HERE BE DRAGONS'.

It was a map made for adventure. I spent so many hours poring over it that I sometimes felt that I could almost redraw it from memory alone. Nawng Hkeo was marked as a speck of blue the size of a pinhead. A small river trailed from its north-west corner, making the lake look – fittingly enough – like a tadpole wriggling through the hills. The dense cluster of contours that surrounded it would, on the ground, translate into a gruelling trek to over 7,000 feet.

The USAF map would be invaluable for determining the best

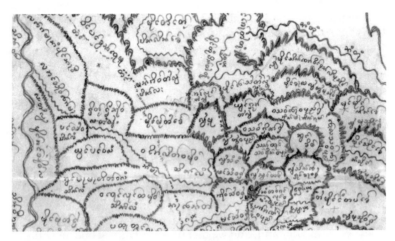

A sketch map made for Scott by a local guide for the 1893 Wild Wa Expedition. The lake, Nawng Hkeo is marked on the right as a circle surrounded by jagged peaks.

place to attempt the illegal crossing into Burmese territory. I planned to cross from China, ideally at a remote point unpatrolled by border guards, and as far away from the lawless UWSA base at Panghsang as possible. The map had two serious drawbacks. Composed of snapshots from geostationary orbit, it was primarily a relief map designed to prevent American pilots from slamming their expensive aircraft into the sides of mountains. This meant that on-the-ground details – names of villages, for example – were sketchy. More worryingly was what would happen if the Wa, Chinese or Burmese authorities caught me in possession of the map. This was a part of the world where all Westerners were assumed to be American spies, and it would be hard to convince a suspicious official that I was just an innocent writer while carrying a high-tech map produced by the US military. The best way to deal with this problem, I decided, was not to think about it.

And, anyway, I had a bigger problem. Nobody would come with me. My attempts to find a travelling companion had failed dismally. What seemed to me like a once-in-a-lifetime invitation – 'Do you want to rediscover a semi-mythical mountain lake not seen by white man since 1937 and now protected by one of South-East Asia's largest drug-trafficking organisations? – elicited only teeth-sucking excuses and suddenly remembered appointments at Thai beach resorts. Then, just as I was getting desperate, I met David.

I was on a fact-finding mission to Kunming, the capital of China's Yunnan Province. Kunming was the frenetic eastern terminus of the Burma Road, and the source of many goods carried by convoys to Mandalay. Nearly all the city's ancient buildings were being ripped down in an orgy of development, and only rare glimpses of old China survived in a rapidly growing complex of glass and steel. But Kunming was still proud of its ethnic heritage: many of Burma's tribes, including the Wa, could be found in Yunnan Province too. The city was also home to the Yunnan Minorities Village, the mother of all human zoos and the model for all the 'ethnic villages' springing up across Burma.

This ethnic diversity was part of what had attracted David to Kunming. Born in Arizona, he was a student of Chinese who had made many trips to Wa villages in Yunnan and was sincerely passionate about their plight. I had been given his name by a missionary in Thailand, and we met up for breakfast one morning at a hotel in downtown Kunming. Cheerful and gangly, with a shock of peroxide hair, he was in his early twenties, and looked and sounded as American as apple pie. But in fact years of study in China had left him culturally remote from his homeland. 'If you asked me now where my true home was,' he told me, pouring maple syrup on to a teetering stack of pancakes, 'I'd have to answer, "With the Lord".' David was a devout Christian. He was also a natural comedian, as well as a talented guitarist and songwriter. (Later he would play me his classic tribute to the ropy English-language skills of many Chinese, an anthem entitled 'Hello OK I Love You Bye-Bye'.) But most of all, David was completely and utterly fearless.

'So,' I asked him, 'do you want to come and look for a semi-mythical Wa lake on a –'

'Sure,' said David. 'I'll come.'

12

Two months later David and I were sipping complimentary cans of mango juice on a noon flight to the southern Yunnanese city of Simao, while an infinite vista of green mountains unfurled beneath us.

'It's beautiful,' I said.

'Sure it is,' agreed David breezily. 'But remember what the Wa say: "Nothing is as beautiful as a three-pronged fork."' The fork, he reminded me, was what the Wa once displayed their freshly chopped human heads on. I had given David a stack of reading material on the Wa, including extracts from Scott's jungle diaries, and he had obviously done his homework. I was also pleased to see he was carrying only a small backpack: we would have no porters to lug our stuff into the hills. Only later did I discover that David's backpack was stuffed to the brim with Snickers bars, Pringles and other high-calorie snacks – 'Survival rations,' he beamed.

The plane dropped through a hole in the clouds and banked sharply to land at Simao airport. As we stepped on to the tarmac, the hot tropical sun came as a shock after the Aberdonian chill of Kunming. David stripped off his jersey to reveal a T-shirt which said, 'WHEN YOU FLEE TEMPTATION DON'T LEAVE A FORWARDING ADDRESS.'

Simao, like Kunming, was a work in progress, its wide, palm-lined streets boiling with dust thrown off by construction sites. This boom-town atmosphere was due in part to Wa drug money, which was being invested in hotels and casinos in Chinese towns all along the border with Burma. It was hard to believe that, fifty years before, bubonic plague had brought Simao to the brink of extinction: by 1950 only 3,000 people survived out of an original population of 70,000, and most of them had malaria. 'Marry off your wife if you mean to cross the Simao basin,' went a hill-tribe saying from those days. But the land around here was also tremendously fertile, and in the past farmers sometimes burned rice for fuel while other parts of China were stricken by famine.

At Simao we hired a car and driver for the seven-hour journey through the hills to Ximeng. This remote town near the Burmese border would be the jumping-off point for our expedition into the Wa hills. After lunch we set out through rolling hills planted with tea and sugar cane, and fringed with explosions of bamboo. The road was blessedly empty of traffic, apart from herds of sleepy water buffalo and the ubiquitous *tuolaji* or 'hand-driven tractor', a kind of gargantuan, smoke-puking lawnmower used to ferry tribespeople to and from the fields.

In the late afternoon we crossed the Mekong River, still muddied by the last of the monsoon rains, then headed west along a road featured on none of my maps. Our car slalomed gently through lush, secluded valleys, the soothing fragrance of wood smoke and buffalo dung pouring through the open windows. Before long we stopped to show our passports at a police checkpoint, a reminder that until recently areas of Yunnan bordering Burma were off-limits to foreigners. A year before, even this part of our trip would have been illegal.

The busy market town of Lancang lay in the valley below, obscured by the smoke from its many brick kilns. Lancang was the largest town close to the northern Wa hills, and the UWSA had an ambiguous presence here. Local men were regularly recruited by the UWSA to work on the poppy fields over the border, and senior Wa soldiers were rowdy patrons of the town's brothels and bars. Only a month before, the UWSA leader Pao Yuqiang had reportedly strangled a twenty-year-old prostitute to death after an argument in a Lancang massage parlour. The murder was hushed up with the judicious distribution of 200,000 yuan among local officials.

Beyond Lancang a narrow cobbled road spiralled up into Wa country. Somewhere on this last stretch we would cross the old 'Scott Line'. This provisional boundary between China and the British Empire had been established by Scott at the turn of the century after a series of colourful jungle negotiations with his Chinese counterparts. The Chinese delegation was led by a general called Liu, whom Scott would remember as 'a delightful old chucklehead'. Liu's chief aide, who was named Chen, better fitted the cliché of Chinese inscrutability. His famously emotionless demeanour had given rise to a local proverb: 'He is neither dead nor alive. He is Chen.'

The work was potentially dangerous – Scott noted that giant boa constrictors had abducted several Chinese soldiers – but chiefly involved the prosaic task of erecting stone cairns to mark the border. More hazardous, perhaps, was a forty-course Chinese banquet thrown to honour the British party. For Scott, always a small eater, the honour was a torture. After dinner a British officer performed on his banjo; a Chinese mandarin responded by dancing a Scottish reel and singing 'Auld Lang Syne'. Meanwhile, a British medical officer who dispensed medicines to sick members of the Chinese party 'received as fee a very large bear, with a temper of a most pronounced character', recalled Scott. 'After trying every known sedative, he abandoned his fee among the pine trees.' Amid all the fun and games, Scott still found time for, well, more games:

'The thud of the football may be heard in the camp the greater part of the day.'

David and I barrelled onward. The road we were driving along owed its tortuous route to disagreements between various Wa clans, forging a path through now defunct chiefdoms which had once agreed to its construction, and skirting those which hadn't. It was the loneliest of roads, and showed signs of hasty repairs where the rains had swept whole sections into adjacent gorges. We had now left behind the rolling, fertile hills and entered a barren moonscape littered with craggy rocks spewed up by some volcanic convulsion millennia before. There were no people; the only villages I could see were forlorn settlements clinging to increasingly steep slopes far from the road.

As the sun set, I noticed for the first time that the storm-bruised bolsters of cloud massed along the horizon were punctured by dark, sawtooth peaks. I felt a familiar jolt of nervous excitement. Months before, I had sat in the back of a speeding pick-up truck full of Shan guerrillas, approaching a different section of these same formidable natural fortifications which cut Burma off from its north-eastern neighbours. Beyond them lay the border badlands, which foreigners entered at their own peril.

Night fell, and I lay back in my seat to watch the stars wheeling above us. I was just dozing off when the driver braked suddenly and I was thrown forward in my seat.

'What's going on?' I asked David.

'Dunno,' he said. 'I think there's something blocking the road.'

It was a large bush weighted with stones and placed in the dead centre of the road. The driver did not get out to move it, but instead squeezed the car past and then floored the accelerator. Banditry was not unknown in this area, and the obstruction seemed purpose-built for an ambush. As we sped away, David and I scanned the darkness for signs of life. Suddenly the hills didn't seem so empty any more.

We tunnelled upward through a dense grove of bamboo, and emerged to our first glimpse of Ximeng, dimly apparent on the hilltop beneath a dense congregation of stars. It was dismally undeserving of its heavenly backdrop. The town was an abomination of concrete squatting in a cleft in the mountains. Its streets were dark and deserted, and illuminated only by a few forgotten streetlights and the red glow bleeding from the doorways of brothels and karaoke joints. As we spun round the town square, a piece of heroic Communist statuary reared briefly from the gloom. Many houses were in the process of being demolished.

We checked into the only hotel with official permission to receive foreigners. The receptionist was a feisty, ruddy-faced Dai woman, an ethnic cousin of the Shans and Thais. When David asked her why the town was so deserted, she replied that half of Ximeng's population had already been moved to a new town being constructed some twenty-five miles away. She didn't really know why. Not everyone had moved, she said, only those ordered to by their *danwei* or work unit.

'So what will happen to Ximeng when everyone has gone?' asked David.

The Dai receptionist shrugged. 'It'll become a ghost town,' she said, as if the sudden and unexplained abandonment of Chinese towns was the most natural thing in the world.

A second woman appeared to show us to our room. Hugging herself miserably against the cold, she led us past the hotel brothel, where a dozen or so teenage hookers lounged and giggled on massage couches. Our room had seen better days, and held better odours. The woman watched us appraise our desolate surroundings, then asked dolefully, 'I don't suppose you want any prostitutes?'

The door had no deadlock, so David propped a large metal tray against it as an early-warning device should any of the bellowing drunkards now milling outside the brothel decide to burst in for a late-night English lesson.

It had taken David and me only a single day to reach Ximeng. George Scott took rather longer. The Wild Wa Expedition of 1893 set off for Ximeng – then known as Monghka – from the east, from British Burma, and endured two months of hard slog before it arrived.

The expedition started badly, and proceeded in an atmosphere of near mutiny. Scott's mission depended upon scores of recalcitrant porters, who were understandably petrified at the prospect of carrying heavy loads into headhunting territory. There was also a column of unruly Punjabi troops, whose reputation for heavy-handedness went before them, causing villagers to flee as Scott approached. Many of the party fell sick and had to be sent back to headquarters at Lashio. Scott himself had a fever and an alarmingly swollen foot ('insect bite or something'), and for one humiliating day he had to be carried on a chair slung between bamboo poles. Even his inquisitive dog, Pan, got a jungle leech lodged painfully in his nostril.

Also joining this dangerous mission was Scott's beloved wife, Dora. She went on all his marching tours into the wilderness, yet very little is known about this most adventurous of expat wives. Scott is partly to blame. He never mentioned Dora in his official diaries, and there are only a few lines about her in his surviving private journals – for example, when he noted her skill at billiards after a victorious game against the advocate general, or praised her gifts as a gardener. '18th Oct. Dora's French beans ready for the table,' he wrote in a rainswept Lashio while compiling the *Gazetteer*. 'Best French beans ever known.'

Scott was especially proud of his wife's capacity to 'do good marching' during the most gruelling of jungle tours. On one occasion the Scotts were separated from their party, and for three days lived in a village hut on a diet of coarse rice – 'eaten', as one reporter winced, 'with a bamboo spoon'. White women were an unimagined rarity in remotest Burma, and Dora – dressed as always in a riding habit – was mobbed by curious hillfolk wherever she travelled. As *Black and White* recorded, the doughty Mrs Scott 'bore the hardships bravely, as became the wife of a courageous pioneer, [and] endured the daily and nightly scrutiny and inquisitive examinations of literally thousands of squatting savages – "I regarded it as very good fun," to quote her own words'. Unlike her husband, Dora appeared to be in good health as they set off into the Wa hills, although her spirits plummeted when two porters lost her paintbox in the fast-flowing Salween River. 'Frightfully hard luck,' scribbled Scott in his diary. 'Dora's one pleasure gone & just when we are getting to an interesting new country.'

The expedition followed an old mule traders' path through undulating forests of oak and chestnut, pausing to take potshots at porcupines and silver pheasants, before climbing into the uncharted hills, where dense mist blotted out the sun and a vicious wind roared through the trees at night. In his diary, Scott scrupulously recorded the rising altitude (measured by boiling water) and the plunging temperature, as well as other noteworthy events: 'Shortly after breakfast an inundation of mules tore down our tent and it required the rest of the day to mend it.' Before long he came across an unmistakable sign that he had entered Wild Wa country: three human skulls leering from a dim grove of trees.

The Wa were not the only headhunters in the British Empire: the Naga of northern Burma and the Dyak of Borneo both collected human skulls. However, unlike the Dyak, who saw these gruesome trophies as proof of warrior prowess, the Wa believed that human skulls propitiated the evil spirits which caused pestilence, famine and drought. For a Wa tribesman, argued Scott, a grinning human skull was merely the equivalent of holy water, or the sign of the

Cross, or 'hallelujahs at a Salvation Army service'. 'Without a skull his crops would fail; without a skull his kine might die; without a skull the father and mother spirits would be shamed and might be enraged; if there were no protecting skull the other spirits, who are all malignant, might gain entrance and kill the inhabitants, or drink all the liquor.'

The Wa headhunting season began in March or April, when the new fields were being planted. Parties of fearsome Wa warriors armed with long knives patrolled the jungle to ambush passers-by or raid other villages. These villages often retaliated in kind, sparking bloody vendettas that lasted for centuries. The victim's freshly severed head was tied by the hair to a bamboo pole and carried back to the village, where it was kept in a spirit house until the flesh and sinews had rotted away and the bone had blanched to the proper colour. Then it was mounted on a wooden post in a dark, secluded grove near the village. Little was known about the lengthy celebrations that accompanied this ritual. 'There seems, however, to be much slaughtering of buffaloes, pigs, and fowls,' wrote Scott, 'much chanting of spells by the village wise men, but above all much drinking of spirits by everybody. This last item no doubt accounts for the meagreness of the information on the subject.'

The headhunting season had not quite begun, but Scott had every reason to be on his guard. The Wa coveted the heads of foreigners, believing that foreign ghosts did not know their way out of the hills and so could not stray far from the rice fields they were meant to safeguard. 'An unprotected stranger is therefore pretty sure to lose his head if he wanders among the Wild Was, no matter what the time of the year may be.'

Scott's first run-in with the Wa came near the village of Motwo. Three Wa men were captured and sent ahead to warn others not to fight. Then, leaving Dora behind, Scott and an advance guard marched into the village. Like many Wa settlements, Motwo had over 100 houses – a remarkable size compared to the villages of Burma's other tribes, and clearly meant for self-protection. 'Met by about 20 half-drunk villagers with a bunch of green plantains and a sugar cane,' wrote Scott. 'The great bulk fled. Handed over to us for an hour or two five guns as a proof of confidence and yelled about in a state of excitement for some time.' He sent word for Dora, who galloped down to join him, and before long the chief of Motwo appeared too. The chief ordered a great feast to be prepared for his unexpected foreign guests, and soon the village rang with the terrified squeals of pigs, abruptly silenced by gunfire and then butchered for the table.

Encouraged by the friendly reception at Motwo, the party marched further east to Mot Hsamo, a dilapidated Wa settlement overrun with rats and permeated by the stench of dried pigs hanging from the rafters of every house. A meeting with the chief proved futile – 'turned out to be a child of six who would not leave his mother' – so Scott struck camp outside the village. Nearby lay a large wooden coffin occupied by a fresh corpse. All night long drunken villagers celebrated by firing guns into the air, which did not reduce Scott's growing sense of unease. Nor did the lack of discipline in his own ranks. Gambling was a problem, and after one brawl Scott confiscated money and had the perpetrators flogged. Supplies had begun to go missing too, including 'a dozen cases of whisky (alas)' and Scott's bath. Despite these trials and deprivations – and despite the excruciating pain in his feet, which had been badly skinned during the trek – Scott found time to develop 'a few Kodak views' in his field darkroom. His mood was not improved by the discovery that many photographic plates had been ruined by the damp.

Hilltops which would in Shan country have been covered with jungle were, in Wa territory, treeless and sown with rice and opium poppies, the result of centuries of industrious cultivation. This meant that most Wa villages were visible for miles – and, correspondingly, anyone approaching was easily spotted. While the tribe's blood-thirsty reputation was usually more than enough to discourage casual visitors, Wa settlements were also protected by a formidable stockade of reinforced earthworks densely covered in thorn bushes and surrounded by a cleverly concealed ditch lined with bamboo spikes. The only entrance was a long, low, narrow tunnel made of earth or rough slabs of wood, which curved slightly to prevent bullets or arrows from being shot up it. Anyone lucky enough to penetrate this far would be met by Wa warriors armed with spears, swords, poisoned arrows and the occasional musket. 'A Wa village is a very formidable place,' said Scott. 'Against all the arms which any of their neighbours possess it is impregnable, and it could not be carried by direct attack except by a very determined enemy, prepared to suffer very considerable loss.'

It was with great caution, then, that Scott approached the fortified village of Loilem, which was already in a state of siege. He had been instructed to receive the formal submission of its Wa chief who had asked for British help in facing down attacks by bellicose Wa rivals. The expedition arrived at Loilem through fields tended by hostile Wa farmers: 'Inhabitants much the wildest we have seen yet. The bulk of them out with drawn dhas [curved swords], spears and crossbows & jabbering away.' Ominously, the tunnel entrance to the village was barred by a pile of coffins. Moving these aside, Scott carefully negotiated the tunnel to find twenty Wa warriors waiting at the other end; everyone else had scarpered, including the chief. Scott – who as usual was unarmed – 'soothed them without much trouble', then explored the chief's dim and dirty house, its roof 'stuck full of chicken bones tied in couples, many of them black & glistening with the smoke of years'. There was a fire still burning, attended by the chief's pet parrot, suggesting that the man had only recently fled.

It was the next day before Loilem's chief found the courage to return, along with hundreds of 'wild-looking savages with matted hair'. Vastly outnumbered, Scott unveiled his secret weapon: a nice spot of tea. He and Dora, armed with a pot of jam, retired to the chief's house for that most English of rituals; Scott even photographed Dora spreading a jam sandwich for the Wa leader. Outside, meanwhile, 'the whole hillside swarmed with armed men. The discussion was very long and noisy, and was conducted almost entirely in Wa . . . There was at the end a great chanting of ritual by the elders, a passing backwards and forwards of fowls' legs and pigs' hams, and finally the slaughtering of a gigantic buffalo which the meeting ate'.

This gathering gave Scott the opportunity to study the Wa at close quarters. While 'not altogether attractive' as a people, he observed, 'many of the men are models of athletic build, and the women, like most of the women of the hill tribes, have very substantial charms and marvellously developed legs'. Basic hygiene, however, was unheard of: 'The state of dirt of both men and women is absolutely beyond belief and is only limited by the point beyond which extraneous matter refuses to adhere to human flesh.'

Despite their impressive physiques, the Wa were not generally known as great sportsmen. Before Scott's arrival, the closest they got to competitive sport was an occasional stone-throwing contest 'in which many are permanently injured'. Nevertheless, Scott did arrange a sports day. It was an astonishing success, with over 1,000 Wa men taking part. Anyone straying into the village of Loilem in February 1893 would have been greeted by the bewildering sight of the most feared tribesmen in all Burma taking part in piggyback and sack races under Scott's direction. However, it appears that he made no attempt to introduce football to the Wa, owing perhaps to what one British academic would later describe to me as 'the risk of overenthusiasm and resulting massacres'. Most Wa men were not only heavily armed but also profoundly intoxicated on

Wa women photographed by Scott (*top*, British Library) and by the author a century later (*left*). Their appearance has hardly changed.

opium and rice liquor, conditions which were hardly conducive to explaining the offside rule.

Monghka was still five days' trek away, and getting there took Scott past the skull groves of the semi-naked Wa Pwi tribe – 'big powerful men, some very dark, with shaven heads and thick necks, rather like the statues of Roman emperors'. Until 1893 it was generally believed that 'primitive' sub-tribes like the Wa Pwi were cannibals, but Scott's research helped scotch this myth: 'They say that they do not eat human flesh. Lots of head cutting however goes on all over the place and one gentleman present announced that he had accumulated three heads quite lately, though he admitted that his village had lost four or five.' News that the Wa did not eat their victims, only hacked their heads off, could not have reassured the rest of the expedition's nervous members.

In mid-February the expedition finally reached Monghka – modern-day Ximeng. By Scott's calculations it stood at a height of 7,000 feet on a massive ridge, at the northern end of which was Nawng Hkeo – 'the mountain lake concerning which has been invented such an extraordinary amount of fable'. He had arrived in Monghka on the eve of Chinese New Year, and its devout inhabitants were lighting candles and joss sticks at rustic shrines throughout the village. Scott was possibly the only Westerner ever to see Monghka at its zenith. There was a plethora of temples, chief among them the *Fu-Fang* or 'Buddha House', a baroque structure built (Scott ventured) by a Tibetan architect. Monghka was an isolated outpost of Buddhism which owed its existence to pilgrims stopping off on their way to Bodhgaya, the holy site in India where the Buddha was said to have achieved enlightenment beneath a banyan tree. Scott would describe Monghka as 'a centre of comparative civilization in the midst of a wilderness of unmitigated savages'. Many villagers dared not stray more than five miles away for fear of running foul of a Wa headhunting party.

The ruler of this tiny hilltop theocracy was a jittery ecclesiastic known in Chinese as the *Ta fu yé*, or 'Great Duty Teacher'. Swathed in white robes, he came out to greet Scott with gifts of fruit and votive candles. 'He spoke in Chinese,' recalled Scott, 'and kow-towed, though he is a sort of Grand Lama, then he condescended to shake hands.' The *Ta fu yé*, himself an object of local veneration, was anxious to impress his British guest. Monghka had long paid an annual tribute of livestock, opium and liquor to Sung Ramang, a much feared Wa chief who lived to the west. Now the Chinese had begun to demand tribute too. The *Ta fu yé* 'lives in a state of terror', wrote Scott. 'He confided to me his hatred of the Chinese, his terror of the Was, and his desire to become a British subject' – a status which, on this occasion, Scott had no authority to confer.

The next day there were parades and native bands to usher in the Year of the Snake. There was also evidence in Monghka that the head-cutting season was well under way. Scott spotted two human heads under a village tree, being prepared for exhibition; two more sat on platters beneath some carved wooden posts. Since mostly Tame Wa lived in Monghka's immediate vicinity, these skulls had probably been bought rather than butchered. Scott made efforts to evaluate this macabre currency:

> Heads of the Lem Shans are . . . very lightly esteemed among the professed head-hunters; two rupees will buy a good grinning Lem skull, whereas a Chinaman's will fetch 30 rupees, a Burman's – they are very scarce now – 50, while a novelty in the shape of an entire stranger's, such as an Englishman's, would imply a free fight in all the hills for its possession.

Monghka was as far east as Scott's orders permitted him to go. Here the expedition turned around and headed in a westerly direction towards the village of the Wa chieftain Sung Ramang. If Scott had followed the ridge northward, however, he would soon have reached Nawng Hkeo. But, as he explained later, 'It was no use going on to Nawnghkeo. It was a jungly road, rising all the way, and there was nothing around the lake except jungle.' There were other considerations. Scott's supply route was already stretched to breaking point, while his porters seemed on the brink of revolt. 'Greater difficulty than ever in getting rice,' he wrote with palpable weariness before leaving Monghka. 'Not even a day's supply came in today. A general inclination to make out that it is my fault.'

The expedition ploughed on nevertheless, passing through poppy fields and villages where piles of human heads sat ripening in the sun. At one settlement – it is not recorded which one – angry villagers massed on the stockade to warn the British against entering. Scott then performed an extraordinary act of jungle diplomacy. 'Other officers would have either retreated, abandoning the expedition, or fought their way through, leaving a legacy of hate,' recounted the historian G. E. Harvey. 'Scott made his men halt while he went forward unarmed, almost within bow shot, and although he could only speak through four successive interpreters, as the language was at five removes, in a few minutes he had those angry savages on the walls laughing at his jokes.' He was then invited into the village.

But Scott's legendary powers of persuasion failed him at the village of the powerful Sung Ramang. It was 'a huge big place' sitting in a cleft on a saddleback ridge, and surrounded by a very deep ditch bridged with planks of wood. The British column was met outside by a Wa tribesman with 'some nasty holes on his left temple' – apparently the great Sung Ramang himself. Scott presented this curiously perforated man with a knife and a pipe, before discovering he was not the chief at all. To Scott's frustration,

five more impostors, some with chicken bones threaded through
their ear lobes, would also introduce themselves as Sung Ramang:

> We sat for some time in the Chief's house, and almost certainly
> spoke with him without a knowledge of which in the crowd he
> was. Sung Ramang is said to have derived his good fortune from
> the possession of a nine-tailed dog. When even an allusion to
> this notable animal failed to arouse the pride and disclose the
> person of its owner, I gave up the attempt in despair.

But Scott was not disappointed by the 'fresh grinning horrors'
of Sung Ramang's skull groves. While most villages counted their
heads in the tens or twenties, the jungly avenue linking Sung
Ramang's village with the next boasted 200 or more. 'The skulls
are in all stages of preservation,' enthused Scott, 'some of them
glistening white and perfect in every detail, some discoloured with
the green mould of one or more rains, some patched over with
lichens, or shaggy with moss, some falling to pieces, the teeth gone,
the jaws crumbling away, the sutures yawning wide.' As Scott
climbed a ridge to the next village, he stumbled across two corpses,
decapitated and with their hands and feet cut off – 'evidence
without question that the head-hunting was in full swing'. Two
more headless bodies lay in the undergrowth nearby.

Plotting a route into Wa country had proved easy enough. Finding
a safe way out of terrain crawling with headhunting parties was
another matter entirely. The expedition was now passing through
increasingly hostile territory. At one settlement Scott paused to
photograph a crescent of skull posts while a group of surly villagers
looked on. 'Shortly after a great row in the village, beating of drums,
flourishing of bamboo spears and fantastic dancing by men, mostly
drunk . . . All passed off well but the villagers swarmed about like
wasps, demonstrated with bamboo javelins & effervesced with
their drums for the rest of the night.' One day the Scotts marched
fourteen miles over boulders and swamps, only to be welcomed by
agitated Wa villagers who pelted them with stones. 'Trying rather,'
noted Scott, 'but Dora never complains.'

Scott relied heavily on local tribesmen to find him a safe path
out of the Wa hills. They were often recruited at gunpoint, and
were generally too drunk or terrified (usually both) to be of much
use. 'Endless bother with guides,' fumed Scott in his diary. 'Had
no sooner started than the guide refused to go beyond the upper
villages. He solemnly unfastened a piece of rag, and taking out the
two-anna bits that had been given him, handed them back, and

then just legged it.' At the next village Scott conscripted another Wa man, who seemed 'more reasonable and less drunk'. But, as guides went, he was

> a most unwilling one, and the very dirtiest man I ever saw, caked with greasy black filth . . . He evidently thought he was to be sacrificed for a [skull] post. So his astonishment was great when we arrived in camp and I set him free, paid him and told him to go. For a few seconds he stood stupefied, looking at the money; then he sprang up, embraced a nearby Muso, and would have embraced me had I not warned him with the toe of my boot against such a procedure.

The 1893 Wild Wa Expedition finally limped into Lashio on 24 May – just in time for Mr and Mrs Scott to wash and change for an afternoon parade to celebrate Queen Victoria's birthday. Scott's exhausted porters – whom he had cajoled, cursed, threatened and thrashed for the previous 172 days – got the last laugh: his camera, and many of his rare photos of the Wild Wa, never arrived at Lashio.

While fraught with difficulties, the expedition had been a success. It had provided a wealth of startling new information on a previously unexplored territory, occupied by a tribe long demonised by outsiders. 'The Wa are not nearly so ferocious as they have for years had the credit of being,' Scott concluded.

> Heads are not lopped off for mere wantonness, but as a sort of *auto da fé*, or at any rate on mistaken agricultural theories. Apart from this foible, the Wa are admitted to be not bad neighbours. They are not thieves like the Kachin and the Kwi, and they do not make raids and burn villages. The cutting off of heads inevitably tempers esteem, and the amount they drink and the extent to which they neglect to wash, tend to create dislike, but otherwise their qualities command approval. They are brave, independent, energetic, ingenious, and industrious.

In summary, wrote Scott, 'The Wa are very extraordinary people.'
But Scott was wildly wrong about two things. First, he predicted that headhunting would die out by the end of the nineteenth century. But, even as the century turned, there occurred a 'ghastly incident which was to leave a stain on the frontier' (as one colonial writer characterised it). During another excursion into Wa territory, in 1900, two inquisitive Englishmen in Scott's party sneaked into a village in the hopes of seeing the famous skull posts. The

villagers, who were drunk, rewarded the men's curiosity by stoning them into a light coma and then decapitating them. Disobeying direct orders to ignore the incident and return quietly at all costs, Scott instructed his troops to burn a number of Wa villages as punishment, so that 'even the Wa would know in the future that it does not pay to meddle with white men'. In the fighting that followed, a bullet passed through his sleeve, bruising his arm. Scott hoped that the heads of his colleagues had perished in the fire. But, according to one Shan historian, the skulls had been spirited away by the Wa long before the British assault began, and were still 'cherished with affection and reverence' twenty-five years later. The Wa would not stop chopping heads until the 1970s.

The second thing that Scott was wrong about was Nawng Hkeo: the lake, he predicted, 'may yet become a show-place' for tourists. As David and I were about to discover, nothing could have been further from the truth.

13

I awoke in our Ximeng hotel room to find David sitting stock-still on his bed reading underlined passages in a heavy black Bible. I left the room quietly, and stood outside to watch the sun struggle over a distant ridge. A squealing sow trotted past at double speed, leisurely pursued by three men with dirt-encrusted aprons and large knives.

'Do you know how they kill pigs in China?' asked David, who had appeared holding a steaming glass of instant cappuccino.

'Tell me.'

'I saw it once. They stick a huge spike up its butt and bleed it to death. Apparently the meat tastes better that way.' He sipped his cappuccino philosophically. 'You do *not* want to see it, believe me.'

As far as I could establish, Monghka officially became Ximeng ('Western Union') in 1960, when China and Burma finally settled a series of long-running border disputes. The negotiations dismantled what was left of the 'Scott Line' and granted China a chunk of Wa territory which had nominally belonged to British Burma. This territory included Monghka, but not the fabled lake of Nawng Hkeo, which lay at the northern end of the same immense mountain ridge that was now bisected by the Sino-Burmese border.

Our plan was simple. David and I would catch a local bus heading up the ridge to a point where, according to my US Air Force map, there was an old bridge situated less than a mile from the border. There were no villages near there, or at least none were marked on my map; hopefully there were no Chinese border posts either. Here we would get off the bus and walk into Burma.

But first we set out for the market, to buy last-minute supplies. Daylight did not improve Ximeng; it was an irredeemably ugly place. Nothing of old Monghka remained, although it was said that local farmers occasionally unearthed a section of the original walls. The buffalo head was the symbol of the Wa, and you saw it everywhere: on shop signs, on roof eaves, beneath the heroic statue in the town square. It made Ximeng seem like a stricken outpost of Chicago Bulls supporters.

The market was small and hectic with trade. A billboard at its entrance exhorted citizens not to shoot endangered wildlife, although nearby I came across a Chinese apothecary squatting beside a display of animal parts, most prominently a tiger's paw still bearing a patch of gorgeous fur. He was also selling a tiger penis with its terrifying retrobarbs, a slab of tiger gall bladder, and the incomplete skull of a barking deer.

We wandered the market's cramped aisles for supplies – cartons of Honghe-brand cigarettes to smooth our dealings with the Wa, more high-calorie snacks to replenish David's stores. When Scott visited Monghka in 1893 he found the villagers 'clothed in a way which suggested that even less would have been more decent' – particularly the strapping and minimally clad Wa women. Seventy years later, when the Chinese Communists arrived, most Monghka citizens still wore only ragged loincloths in even the coldest weather. I spotted a few old women in thigh-length sarongs, black vests and turbans, with rattan rings wrapped around their calves – the traditional costume of what Scott would have recognised as the 'Tame Wa.' But most Wa women were now dressed in bright synthetic fabrics, while their menfolk wore faded military fatigues, often with a peeling UWSA patch, and sat around smoking cigarettes through enormous bamboo bongs. These covered the entire bottom half of their faces, and looked a bit like truncated didgeridoos.

Ximeng was the 'capital' of something called the Wa Ximeng Autonomous County. But, as far as I could see, the Wa had only the autonomy to be poor. The Chinese ran most of the shops and drove all the cars, while the Wa perched on the kerbs like placid birds, their handsome faces stoic and expressionless. It was hard to judge how they felt about this disparity in wealth. Wa hatred of the Chinese was said to be deep-seated and rooted in folklore. According to one story, the Wa hunted heads not because of their blood-thirsty ogre ancestors, but because the Chinese had tricked them into it. A third-century warrior called Chu Ko-liang gave the Wa some rice to sow. When it did not grow – the crafty Chu Ko-liang had boiled it first – the Wa were persuaded that only by offering human heads would their crops prosper. Only then did Chu Ko-liang give them proper rice to sow, thus ensuring that the Wa would always be too busy cutting each other's heads off to prevent the advance into their hills of the wily Chinese.

The myth seemed to me a popular articulation of the traditional Wa hatred of the Chinese. But then the Wa, shut away in their fortified hilltop villages, were fearful and suspicious of all outsiders, whatever their race. As Scott once wrote, 'Nobody in the Wa country really wants us.' Isolation condemned the Wa to poverty and backwardness – there was not a single school or hospital in the Wa hills until after the Second World War – but it also gave them an independence not enjoyed by other ethnic minorities. Just how much they cherished their isolation was starkly illustrated during the Frontier Areas Committee of Inquiry in Maymyo in 1947 – an attempt by the departing British to find out what shape post-independence Burma might take. A transcript of the proceedings recorded this sullen exchange between members of the committee and a representative of the Wa chief of Mongkong:

COMMITTEE: Do you know anything about the object of this Committee?

WA: I do not know anything.

COMMITTEE: The object of this Committee is to find out what the peoples of the Frontier Areas want as regards their political future.

WA: As for the future, we would like to remain as in the past, that is to be independent of other people.

COMMITTEE: Do you want any sort of association with other people? What about the Shans? Do you want to be joined up with them?

WA: We do not want to join with anybody because in the past we have been very independent.

COMMITTEE: Don't you want education, clothing, good food, good houses, hospitals, etc.?

WA: We are very wild people and we do not appreciate all these things.

COMMITTEE: Do you have any communication with other people, for example with the Shans and the Chinese? Or do you live entirely by yourselves?

WA: We live entirely by ourselves.

The committee chairman, clearly exasperated by these answers, then quizzed a second Wa representative. 'Have you got any ideas as to how you would like the Wa States to be administered in the future?' he asked. The reply was a blank 'No.' It was inevitable, then, that so many others would try to administer the hills for the Wa – the British, then the Burmese, then the Chinese, and now the millionaire drug lords of the UWSA.

It was still a mystery to us why Ximeng was being abandoned by government dictate. An even bigger mystery, perhaps, was why a hilltop market town at the end of a bad road to nowhere had been so built up in the first place: it boasted a bank, a post office, a hospital, and a number of half-vacated apartment and office blocks. At the bus-ticket office we met a local policeman, who finally solved the first mystery. 'Landslides,' he said authoritatively. 'Everyone's got to leave because the town is slipping off the mountain.'

There was a karmic logic to Ximeng's final demise. The bustling theocracy of Monghka that Scott had known was now a spiritless place. There was supposed to be a small temple left in Ximeng, although I could never find it. None of the shops had household shrines, a familiar feature of Chinese-run businesses the world over. Years of Communist rule had successfully expunged Ximeng's religious past and replaced it with *fazhan* or 'development', the dominant creed of modern China. In the market, David had asked a stallholder what religion the locals followed. 'The old people are still animists,' she replied. 'But the younger people' – and here she plucked a ten-yuan note from a ragged wad of money – 'they believe only in this.'

And now, in a grand biblical finale, the mountain was shrugging this godless eyesore from its flanks and the exodus had begun.

We left at noon on a disintegrating minibus, bucketing northward along a cratered road while a clutch of evil-looking rat traps rattled unnervingly on the luggage rack above my head. The passengers were mainly chattering Wa women returning from Ximeng market. I liked the sound of the Wa language. With its glottal stops and rolling Rs, it sounded a bit like a Scottish accent played backwards – a joyous, gurgling noise, like water rushing over stones. The women often began sentences with a long exclamatory hoot which David, to their great delight, was an expert at mimicking. A number of Wa words supposedly owed their origins to the British. The Wa word for 'peas', for example, was *apees*; 'jacket' was *ja*, and 'trousers' was *cloh* (from 'cloth'). I tried out a few words from a Wa vocabulary copied from Scott's *Gazetteer*, and was gratified to find that the women understood me.

We passed through a handful of villages, most of them grim settlements catering to nearby silver mines. There was rumoured to be gold in the Wa hills, though no one had ever discovered it. Scott's explorations around Monghka came up with nothing, and when the Burmese sent an army of 300 men to search for Wa gold they found none and were massacred down to the last man. There was plenty of silver and other valuable minerals, however, and in places the valleys echoed with the clatter of heavy machinery at Chinese-run mines.

Less than an hour from Ximeng the road plunged into a deep, wooded gorge chiselled by a fast-flowing river, and there was the bridge marked on my map. Much to the driver's bemusement, we asked to get off and sat at the roadside until the bus had puttered over the next hill. David ate a bar of chocolate, and then said, 'Let's go to Burma.'

Near the bridge was a cattle path leading up off the road in a

A view of the Wa hills today.

UWSA soldiers playing ball at Lugula village in the Wa hills.

westerly direction. We trekked along it through head-high elephant grass, staying within earshot of the river, until the path dropped steeply to meet a bubbling tributary. We waded across, and there on the riverbank was a lonely concrete post carved with Chinese and Burmese characters. We had reached the border.

David kissed the post – diplomatically, on both sides – and then we discovered another path, which burrowed through thick forest and emerged in a secluded valley ridged with dead rice terraces. There were no people, only a few water buffalo that froze in mid-munch to watch us go by. A huge mountain now reared up before us, and high on its flank we could make out a scattering of roofs. I had no idea what this village was called – it wasn't on the map – but calculated it was well inside Burma. Hopefully we would get a friendly reception there, and would find someone who could direct us to the lake. I took a compass reading, and then we battled on through tangled undergrowth, the hot sun beating down.

An hour or so later we came across an elderly Wa couple hacking away at a dry field. The old woman wore a headband of beaten silver, and held a slender pipe in her rotting teeth. In a nearby grove three Wa men were chopping trees. All of them, I noticed, wore caps with UWSA insignia. We stopped to chat – they spoke rudimentary Chinese – and to pass out cigarettes. They were friendly and inquisitive, and happily unbothered that we had entered Burma illegally; it was a border they barely recognised.

'What are you selling?' asked one man, pointing to our backpacks. He obviously thought we were traders of some kind. For the first time since leaving the bridge, I started to relax.

We hiked out of the bamboo grove and climbed higher into a haunting landscape of barren fields sectioned off with drystone walls. It bore a disorienting resemblance to the Highlands of Scotland, the country I'd grown up in, and I wondered if George Scott had made the same observation. Then it began to rain. Fearing that the village would be lost in the clouds, we took another compass reading and forged on.

The last hour was a slog up a steep path slippery with mud and dung. Exhausted, we finally reached the Wa village in the late afternoon, entering it through a raised stockade of sharpened bamboo. There were about fifty houses, most with tin roofs covered in sodden hay, on a bare hillside scraped clear of all vegetation. Adjoining each house was a platform raised on stilts, occupied by a scrofulous dog which, like the pigs below, was destined for the family cooking pot. As we walked by, the dogs sprang to life and bounded down to snap at our heels. The village was otherwise deserted – most people were out in the fields – and David and I blundered around until we found a woman feeding her pigs. She spoke no Chinese, however, which meant it was time for me to deploy the only full sentence of Wa I knew.

'*Mom peh bekam yam peh,*' I said. This, I had been told, meant 'Take me to your leader.'

The effect was startling. The woman hooted extravagantly, said something in rapid-fire Wa, then ducked back into her house, shaking her head and chuckling maniacally.

David raised one eyebrow. 'Nice one,' he said.

We climbed further up into the village. It was centred around a basketball court with vintage hoops, flanked by a ramshackle wooden schoolhouse where, judging by the noise, a class was in progress. Nearby was a small shop run by a handsome woman with a face creased with laugh lines.

'What is this place?' David asked her in Chinese.

The woman stared at him. 'This', she replied, 'is a foreign country' – and she might have added, 'you dummy'.

The woman cheerfully served us beer and pot noodles from her surprisingly well-stocked shelves, while someone was dispatched to fetch the village teacher. While we ate, she told us that her brother had emigrated to America – 'Very far away,' she added, because we were obviously a bit dim.

Mist boiled up the hillside, obliterating China. Huge clouds made mysterious migrations towards the setting sun. A school bell clanged, and children in grubby tracksuits spilled out on to the basketball court. The teacher soon arrived – in a Tommy Hilfiger shirt, yellow shorts and jungle boots. Although he was Wa, he went by the Chinese name 'Wei Long'. He was a thin, taciturn man with a sleepy expression. When he invited us to stay the night with his family, we gratefully accepted. As I heaved my backpack on to my shoulders, Wei Long pointed and said, 'That bag looks heavy.'

'Yeah,' said David, 'but I bet it's not so heavy for a Wa.'

'It is as heavy as it is,' said the teacher blankly. 'It doesn't get lighter just because someone else carries it.'

'Er, right,' said David. Such exchanges, we would find, were typical with the Wa. Was the teacher joking, or being wise; or was he just plain stupid? It was hard to tell. Ask a Wa a question and the answer would always take on unpredictable trajectories. It was like throwing porridge at a ceiling fan.

Wei Long's one-room house was made of brick, and was therefore luxurious by Wa standards. A single lantern illuminated walls plastered with posters of classical heroes from Chinese movies.

This tiny space was home to the teacher, his wife, her mother and sister, and Wei Long's infant son – a sickly, mewling thing, whose bottom peeked between the folds of Chinese split pants.

Wei Long's wife, also a teacher, was a strikingly beautiful Wa woman with large, dark eyes and a Whitney Houston smile. 'Do you want to wash your face?' she asked.

'Why?' asked David, trying a bit of Wa humour himself. 'Do our faces look dirty?'

'Yes,' she said, then blushed. 'I mean, no.' Everyone in the room laughed – even Wei Long.

The village, which was called Lugula, had not existed a year before. On UWSA orders, its inhabitants had recently moved from another village closer to the Chinese border. 'Everyone's been so busy building their own houses they can't help others build theirs,' said Wei Long. When we asked him why the villagers had been relocated, he replied, 'It's more convenient.' By now, such cryptic explanations sounded almost reasonable to me. Everywhere in Burma people were on the move, usually against their will and for reasons they barely understood. Wei Long added that David and I were not the first foreigners to come to Lugula. A delegation of Burmese generals had visited a few months before, accompanied by a group of white people – probably representatives of the United Nations, whose drug-eradication activities in Wa country were both secretive and dubious. It seemed likely that Lugula had been built as some kind of showpiece Wa village. Why else would outsiders be invited to see it?

Classes at the school were taught not in Wa or Burmese, but entirely in Chinese – 'Because they tell us to,' explained Wei Long. 'They' were the UWSA leaders in Panghsang. The fact that many Wa children would not learn their mother tongue didn't seem to bother Wei Long unduly. Indeed, while he and his wife communicated with each other in Wa, both parents spoke to their baby in a Yunnan dialect of Chinese.

I told David to ask the teachers if they felt the Burmese or the Chinese looked down on the Wa in any way. 'Sometimes we feel that,' Wei Long's wife replied. 'But it is only the ignorant who think ill of us.' I told her about an eminent Burmese historian I had met in Rangoon – an enlightened and well-travelled man – who had said to me, in all seriousness, that Wa women consider it unlucky to give birth to twins, and allow the children to be taken away and smothered to death.

The teachers ignored this. 'If people took the trouble to visit us,' said Wei Long, 'then perhaps they'd find that the Wa are not so bad after all.' He stared at the candle for a while, obviously choosing his words carefully. 'In some cases,' he said, 'the Wa leaders themselves – people with money and status – look down on their own people too.'

Wei Long said he would show us to where we were sleeping. Outside it was almost pitch-dark, the gloom punctuated here and there by tribesmen carrying dim torches or a cupped, flickering candle. We were led into an adjoining barn reeking of rice liquor fermenting in earthen pots. The floor was packed mud, and there was a low fire burning. We were to sleep in a narrow bed wedged into a corner. It was usually occupied by three wide-eyed teenage boys, who now lay on a mat on the floor, chins in hands, watching us intently.

David took one look at the bed and decided that the floor would be much more comfortable. 'Move over, guys,' he said to the boys. 'I'm sleeping next to you.'

'But why?' asked one of them. 'It's cold and hard down here.'

'But it's cold and hard for you too,' said David.

'I know,' said the boy brightly, 'but we're peasants.'

I lay on the bed and tried to write up my journal by the light of a guttering candle. It was hopeless. Rain pounded on the roof and began leaking on to the bed. Then David and the boys started a burping contest, eventually won by hilarious default when David lavishly broke wind.

'Isn't it incredible?' David told them. 'You're Wa and thirteen years old. I'm American and twenty-two. He's English and thirty-three. And yet we all find farts so funny?'

The boys nodded vigorously in agreement, then decided it was time to entrust us with an important piece of information. It was a soft monosyllable, whispered like a secret password: *'pum'*. It was, the boys gravely explained, the Wa word for 'fart'.

Neither Wei Long nor his wife had heard of Nawng Hkeo, so, early the next morning, we decided to trek deeper into the hills and ask at villages along the way. The teachers made us noodles for breakfast, fortified by strips of mystery meat strung up to dry above the fire. As we set off, a thick, drenching mist descended once again. Good, I thought: the mist will hide us.

An old woman watched us march out of Lugula. Her jaw drooped with astonishment, sending a delicate silver pipe tumbling into the mud. But most Wa seemed unfazed by our presence. The mist cleared briefly to reveal a long valley of rice terraces, and not for the first time I marvelled at the sheer human industry required to clear, sow and reap such a vast area. We soon came to a small village, and were quickly encircled by a pack of snarling dogs. Tottering behind them came an old Wa man in a Mao cap. In broken Chinese, he said his wife was very ill. Would we come and look at her? Fearing the worst, we agreed to visit his house.

Wa houses, it must be said, do not look particularly welcoming. They sit in a pen of mud and animal dung and food leftovers picked at by chickens and pigs. The roof is usually straw, with its eaves reaching down to about three feet off the ground – a design that Scott believed protected the home against harsh sun and high winds. Smoke from the hearth seeps out of the roof lending the house the appearance of a steaming woolly mammoth. Ducking under the eaves, unsuspecting visitors usually find themselves nose to nose with a cow.

Climbing a short ladder up to the doorway, David and I followed the old man inside. The interior was dark and smoky – Wa houses have no windows – and more cramped than the huge roof suggested. A few battered enamel bowls and bamboo utensils were scattered around a hearth set into the floor, which was constructed from roughly hewn planks of wood with strategic cracks where rubbish could be swept down to the chickens below. Right at the back, sitting on a bed, was an elderly woman.

She held herself upright by grasping a rope hanging over her. Her eyes were shut and she was breathing heavily; she was utterly lost in pain. The covers were pulled aside and, by torchlight, we could see that her belly was obscenely swollen. If she had been younger I would have assumed she was in her final weeks of pregnancy. She probably had some sort of massive tumour or haemorrhage. The nearest hospital was in Ximeng, but moving her, David and I agreed, would probably be fatal. I was reluctant to give her any of the heavy-duty painkillers in my meagre first-aid kit; there was no knowing how her fragile body might react.

We handed her husband some Boots multivitamins – bright, colourful pills, all the way from England, we told him. He was delighted. Then we gave his grandchildren balloons and Polaroid photos of themselves. Then we walked on in silence, feeling useless and shabby.

The path joined a cobbled road leading to Yawngbre, a large village I was relieved to find on my map. According to my calculations, the lake was less than six miles away. Surely someone in the village could tell us how to get there.

Wei Long had suggested we contact a local Wa teacher called

Li Ping, but Yawngbre's tiny schoolhouse was empty. On the blackboard were a few words of Burmese script – the first indication, really, that we were in Burma. Someone had scrawled a Chinese four-character slogan on a nearby doorpost. 'People are small,' it warned, 'ghosts are big.'

We found the teacher in the shack next door, strumming a badly tuned guitar. He was a slick twenty-four-year-old Wa in a neat Hawaiian shirt, snow-white trousers and spotless sneakers. It was an impractical form of dress for the country, but calculated to signal that Li Ping, who was trained in Ximeng, did not have to till fields for a living any more. Over a mid-morning beer we asked about Nawng Hkeo. At first Li Ping didn't seem to know it, so I prompted him with a few fables I had heard. It was said, for example, that if you fired an arrow across the lake it would halt abruptly in mid-air then plummet directly downward into the water. Chinese soldiers had once fired AK-47s across it, and were amazed to see the bullets do the same. Afterwards four of the soldiers were ordered to dive into the lake to investigate. They never resurfaced.

Li Ping dragged thoughtfully on his cigarette. 'I think you mean Dragon Pool,' he said. 'It's about an hour from here. You can take a bus if you like.' He looked at his watch. 'There should be one along around noon.'

David and I were sceptical. Was 'Dragon Pool' – Li Ping had named it in Chinese – the same lake as Nawng Hkeo? Could it really be that easy? According to my research, which admittedly relied on Pitchford's 1937 account, there were no Wa settlements near the lake, never mind a road plied by a daily bus.

Just to make sure, we went to quiz some older men squatting outside, grinning up at us through diabolic dentistry. The conversation, translated from English to Chinese by David, then from Chinese to Wa by Li Ping, went something like this:

'Is there a lake near here?'

'Yes.'

'Where is it?'

'Where is what?'

'The lake.'

'What lake?'

'The lake you said was near here.'

'Oh, there's no lake around here.'

Either they didn't know the lake or they didn't want us to go there. Perhaps, as in Scott's time, the Wa still had only the dimmest grasp of the geography of their own hills. 'It is difficult to find a man who can guide you correctly on even a ten mile march, so little do they travel on their own account,' Scott had bemoaned. 'Hundreds of them never leave the range on which they were born.' But our Wa informants did seem eager to please. As with any remote people who have had little contact with the outside world, for them the safest answer to most questions posed by a stranger was 'Yes'.

Instead of waiting for a bus that might never come, David and I decided to find the driver of a truck that was parked in the village and cadge a lift. We could hear voices coming from a small concrete building nearby, so David rapped boldly on the door. It flew open and, to my alarm, a platoon of surly-looking UWSA soldiers poured out and swarmed around us. This, I thought, was not good.

David was soon enmeshed in another classic Wa conversation. ('Where is the driver of the truck?' 'What truck?' 'The truck you're leaning against.' 'What about it?') Then I saw that one UWSA soldier – thuggish, neat uniform, possibly an officer – had broken away from the pack. He now squatted nearby, spat between his feet, and began to prod experimentally at a walkie-talkie. Who was he trying to contact? My mind raced: he was conferring with the UWSA high command in Panghsang; he would be ordered to detain the foreigners; this would be the end of the road for us.

'David,' I muttered, 'I don't like the look of this.'

He had already seen the walkie-talkie Wa. 'Me neither,' he said. We pulled on our backpacks and made a sharp exit.

Ten minutes later we were walking a lonely road carved from the mist-swept hills. Yawngbre was now behind us, but our brush with the UWSA had been unsettling. Although the prospect of being detained in Panghsang alarmed me, I was fairly confident that David and I could talk our way out of UWSA custody; the worst that would happen was that we would be kicked back over the border into China. What worried me much more was a run-in with the Burmese authorities. While this was unlikely – the UWSA controlled these hills, after all – it was not inconceivable. The Burmese regime took a dim view of intruders into what it still regarded as sovereign territory.

At that moment my thoughts were interrupted by the sound of gunfire – six or seven measured retorts, probably from a high-powered rifle, which cracked up the valley from Yawngbre's direction. It sounded like a signal. David was unbothered, but afterwards I found myself walking a little faster.

There were a surprising number of cars on the road, mostly plush four-wheel-drive Toyotas with UWSA licence plates. We had already decided it would be best to avoid being spotted, so every time a car approached we scrambled into the bushes to hide. David quickly got tired of this. He sat down at the roadside and pulled a tube of Pringles from his backpack.

'What exactly is it that we're supposed to be scared of?' he asked. 'I mean, what's the *worst* that could happen?'

'Well,' I said, 'they could arrest us and take us to Panghsang.'

'What's so bad about Panghsang?'

And so I told him about the Panghsang murders – the four Wa officers bludgeoned to death with rifle butts – and about the whore-strangling general, and about the brutal justice that prevailed among the UWSA.

David looked at me incredulously. 'And you wait until *now* to tell me this?'

Suddenly we heard a crunch of gears. There was a truck approaching. We flagged it down, and David talked to the driver, a Wa man from Lancang, who was taking bags of cement to a place further up the road. We clambered gratefully aboard, and were soon grinding uphill through thick cloud into the heart of Wa country. The driver swung the truck around sharp corners with the usual nonchalance, even though the visibility was less than five yards at times. The treacherous conditions had already claimed one victim. Through a hole in the clouds we saw a small truck sitting in its own debris on the hillside far below, crushed like a Coke can.

The driver confirmed what I had suspected: that the road was relatively new. 'Two years ago you couldn't get through,' he said. Climbing ever higher, we soon passed fields fenced off with bamboo stakes. It looked as if carrots were being grown there, but these were opium poppies in their early stages. The fields belonged to the UWSA, the driver explained, not local farmers. 'You should come back here in March or April,' he said. 'Then the whole hills are in flower.'

An hour later the driver dropped us by the roadside, then manoeuvred the truck into a turn-off where it was swallowed by the mist. We had arrived at a settlement of some kind – but what, exactly? It was one of the most desolate I had ever seen. There were a few abandoned shacks with wattled bamboo walls and roofs of tattered tarpaulin. Beyond them I could make out a series of substantial two-storey buildings. I hadn't expected to find any settlement up here, and at first I assumed that the buildings were some kind of mine or factory. Then the mist parted and I saw the flag. It was red and blue, and featured a red star rising over a range of mountains. We were standing outside a large UWSA barracks.

'Great,' said David when I told him. 'Just super.'

Peering down the road, I could see a dark patch forming in the mist. It grew bigger and took shape, and suddenly an elderly Wa man was standing before us. David asked him about Dragon Pool. He pointed mutely back the way he had come, then dematerialised into the mist again. We walked briskly past the entrance to the barracks, then followed a path which seemed to skirt the compound and head in the general direction the old man had indicated. Soon the path turned into a channel of ankle-deep mud and then ended abruptly before a pile of gravel. By now we were utterly disoriented; I couldn't see more than ten yards in any direction. Then we heard voices, muffled by the dense blanket of fog, and decided to walk towards them. We laboured up a bank of soft earth, walked between two dimly outlined buildings – and found ourselves smack in the middle of the garrison's parade ground. From all directions indistinct figures approached with the slow stealth of zombies.

'Are you feeling a bit nervous now?' asked David.

'Yes,' I said.

'Me too.'

But I was actually feeling strangely serene. We had spent a nerve-racking day trying to dodge the attentions of UWSA soldiers. Now we were standing in the middle of a compound crawling with them. Whatever happens next is completely out of our control, I told myself, and found the thought oddly comforting.

But it turned out that we had the upper hand. Imagine the soldiers' surprise when two white men loomed from the murk to ask politely, 'Excuse me, we're looking for a lake . . .' We had soon attracted a crowd of UWSA men. While I passed out cigarettes – lots of cigarettes – David struck up a conversation with a Wa soldier called Aiga. He was a sad, soft-spoken man who barely came up to David's shoulder. Yes, Aiga said: he knew the lake. It was less than an hour's walk away. And, yes, he was happy to take us there. 'But first,' he said – and here our spirits sagged – 'I have to get permission from my commander.'

We were led into a room in the nearest barrack house and told to wait. The room was bare apart from a few tiny stools and a low fire. A mangy puppy sat in the warm ashes, crunching on a chicken bone. I heard the room's heavy iron door scrape shut behind me, and wondered briefly whether David and I were, after all, now under arrest.

The commander arrived ten minutes later. He was a squat, humourless man with fat, sulky lips and the dead eyes of a shark. It was, I reflected, the last face you see before your head is chopped off. He asked us where we were from and how old we were, but never asked what was, to our minds, the most obvious question of all, which was, *What the hell are you doing here?*

David told him about the lake, but he seemed unconvinced by our interest. Dimly recalling what was expected of officialdom, he asked to see our passports. There was a tense silence as he studied each page minutely. Then he said, 'Where are your visas?'

My heart sank, This was it. Our quest for the lake was about to end in a grim room in a Wa army barracks. But I hadn't reckoned on my companion. David's father sold insurance for a living, and if his patter was as good as David's then he must have sold an awful lot of it.

'Visas?' repeated David blithely, as if he'd never heard of such a thing. 'No, no. I think you'll find that foreigners have a totally different system of doing things. Now about this lake...'

Finally the Wa commander said we could go to the lake if we left our passports with him.

'Listen,' said David, who was still in flimflam mode, 'I don't know your first name. I don't know your last name. I don't know your mother's name. *I don't know who you are.* And you expect me to leave my passport with you?'

The Wa commander looked at David blankly. The puppy in the ashes began to retch, and he prodded it absent-mindedly with his lit cigarette. He was getting dangerously bored. 'If you don't leave your passports with me,' he said firmly, 'you don't go to the lake.'

So we left our passports with him.

Minutes later we were back outside, the mist swirling around us, while Aiga raised an honour guard. Just visible at one end of the parade ground was a large two-storey mansion with tiled walls and Chinese-style roofs curling into Wa buffalo horns; parked outside was a fleet of brand-new, top-of-the-range LandCruisers. Aiga told us that the house and cars belonged to Pao Yidao, a name I recognised. He was the brother of UWSA commander Pao Yuqiang, who had appointed him as the 'governor' of the northern Wa hills. We also learned from Aiga that this remote garrison was some kind of UWSA treasury, which set me wondering what kind of ill-gotten wealth was stored in Pao Yidao's house. Bricks of US dollars and bank-fresh Chinese yuan under the beds? A poolroom stacked with gold ingots? Aiga was reluctant to say any more, and David and I thought it unwise to go and investigate.

We were now encircled by soldiers again. They were a pretty sorry-looking bunch. Most were dressed in mismatched uniforms and wore flip-flops or laceless jungle boots on their feet. Many were just boys, and one was obviously illiterate: he had sewn his badge on back to front – ASWU.

David looked a bit bewildered. 'I feel like I'm in a war zone,' he said. 'Well, am I?'

'Not any more,' I replied confidently. 'I'm sure there was fighting here in the past, but that's all over now. Look around you. I think you'll find that none of the soldiers have guns' – which, of course, was the cue for two soldiers to appear with assault rifles and crisp new UWSA fatigues. One of them led the way, grasping his M-22 in one hand and an umbrella in the other. We picked our way through a muddy wasteland behind the barracks to where an unpaved mining road led off into the forest.

The two Wa guides who led V. C. Pitchford to the lake in 1937 had been scared of being spotted by other Wa tribesmen while taking foreigners to what was regarded as a sacred site, and had insisted upon wearing disguises before proceeding. Two of Pitchford's men offered their blue flannel blazers, and the Wa stretched these over their muscular frames. 'Their only other clothing was the abbreviated bathing drawers of the wild Wa,' remarked Pitchford. Even then the guides refused to walk at the head of the party.

By comparison, our Wa guides were a quietly obliging bunch who seemed glad of the outing. There wasn't much else to do around there. We heard later that, the day before, someone in the garrison had accidentally blown himself up with industrial dynamite – an event which, judging by its enthusiastic retelling, was the closest thing to entertainment in those parts.

David nodded at our escort. 'So why do we need all these guys with guns?' he asked Aiga.

'To protect you from big animals,' Aiga replied.

'What sort of big animals do you get around here?'

'Tigers,' said Aiga.

'What about bears?' asked David.

'No,' replied Aiga. 'We don't get any bears.' He thought for a while. 'Actually,' he said, 'We don't get any tigers either.'

David turned to me and grinned. 'Are these guys goobers, or what?'

Aiga hailed originally from Ximeng, and had joined the UWSA less than two years ago. 'I joined because I heard there was a lot of development up here,' he explained. 'I thought I could make some money. But I've been here for over a year now and I've still got nothing.' The UWSA gave new recruits work and lodgings, he said, but no food – and no pay. So how on earth did Aiga live? He just shrugged. 'I'm going to go back to Ximeng soon,' he said quietly. Until the 1960s slavery was not uncommon among the Wa. Slaves were usually taken in lieu of unpaid debts, and laboured for subsistence under the mercy of all-powerful masters. They could be bought or sold – an adult was worth three buffalo; a child one ox or a muzzle-loader – and could be killed if they were disobedient or if they stole food or opium. The stark existence that Aiga was describing sounded like a modern form of bonded labour, in this case under the unquestionable authority of the UWSA.

The mining road curved sharply to the left, and our Wa guides ducked through an invisible opening in the undergrowth. Soon we were scrambling down a narrow, muddy path which plunged through a gloomy forest of skeletal trees and dripping bamboo. 'I suppose this is where these Wa guys take us aside and bludgeon us to death with their rifle butts,' said David cheerfully. Labouring under the weight of my sodden backpack, I was too breathless to tell David just how unfunny this was.

After half an hour the path abruptly levelled off, and I could see through the trees a strip of swamp fronded by bulrushes – and, beyond, a grey nothingness like the edge of the world. Now breathless with excitement, I threw off my backpack and pushed through the reedy banks until the earth went soft beneath me.

And then I just stood there, grinning like an idiot, my Adidas trainers slowly filling up with the same primeval sludge the Wa had crawled from all those aeons ago. We had arrived on the sacred shores of Nawng Hkeo.

As Pitchford had promised, it was a bewitching place. The ancient, moss-covered trees along the banks threw gnarled branches over the lake's silvery surface, which was smooth and undisturbed by any marine life. Diaphanous curtains of mist obscured our view, but also lent the scene an eerie, monochromatic perfection. The bulrushes looked like brush strokes on a minimalist Japanese painting. There was no sound – not a single bird to be heard – until the soldiers began squelching restlessly in the shallows.

The fog cleared to offer a tantalising glimpse of the dense forests on the far shore, then closed in once again. Aiga said a huge mountain rose from the other side – he pointed almost directly upward to give us an idea of its size – and then went on to offer a description of the lake's surroundings which exactly matched Pitchford's account. 'What met our gaze', wrote Pitchford in 1937, 'was a rough oblong of still clear water with a range of thickly forested hills on the west; a high, three-sided, thickly forested rocky peak of conical shape standing back from the north-west corner; and at the north end, a grass-covered morass beyond which, on higher ground, was more dense forest.' The conical peak Pitchford described – and which Aiga had pointed towards – was home to

Hpyi Mut, the lake's guardian spirit, who according to local legend descended each night to sweep the shores clean with an enormous broom.

We asked to take some photos, and the soldiers were happy to pose for them. They straightened their uniforms, rehoisted their rifles, and, once they had assumed suitably grave expressions, stood stiffly to attention beside us. Then, grabbing my water bottle, I ventured into the shallows to get a souvenir: a sample of the lake.

'No,' said one of the soldiers sharply.

When David asked why, the soldiers replied that they had orders not to let the foreigners take any water from the lake. Was it because the lake was sacred? The question was met with expressions of unfathomable blankness. Nobody would say.

Aiga announced it was time to go. I put the offending water bottle away, and began to hike back to the UWSA base – smiling from the secret knowledge that a generous sample of the fabled Wa lake of Nawng Hkeo was sloshing around in my trainers.

An hour later we were standing with Aiga outside a roadside shop near the army base. The shop owner had a car, and after some brisk, Chinese-style bargaining by David ('Four hundred yuan? You're farting so much I can hardly breathe!'), agreed to drive us back to Yawngbre for a fair price.

At that moment a covered truck pulled up. A tarpaulin flap was flung aside, and seven UWSA soldiers jumped out carrying assault rifles with fixed bayonets. Some orders were barked, and a dozen or so men in handcuffs and rattling leg irons climbed out of the truck. A soldier with a yard-long stick beat them into a ragged line. Then they were roped together and began to shuffle abjectly past us, stooped from the weight of their chains.

Suddenly one prisoner broke line and began to clank awkwardly towards us. Two soldiers raised their rifles and aimed at him – aimed at us. I could feel David stiffen beside me. But then the man with the big stick appeared and the prisoner stopped in his tracks and shrank, bracing for the blow. Aiga seemed hardly to notice all this, so I assumed that chain gangs were a regular sight. Some of the prisoners had carried shovels; they were off to slave in the poppy fields. But what were they guilty of? 'They probably stole some opium or something,' Aiga replied absently.

A few minutes passed, and then, by marked contrast, six or seven Mitsubishi Pajeros with darkened windows roared out of the gloom, sped past us, then disappeared into the garrison post. They had taken only seconds to pass, but I observed that two of the trucks were pick-ups crammed with alert soldiers toting Kalashnikovs and grenade launchers. A convoy so heavily armed could have been carrying only one man: the commander of the northern UWSA, General Pao Yuqiang himself.

It was definitely time to go. We climbed into the shop owner's car and he drove us back down the mountain, descending through the clouds and into clear weather like an aircraft on its final approach. He dropped us not far from Yawngbre, and for a while we sat in dazed silence at the roadside. The afternoon sun illuminated a peaceful valley of rice terraces cut with breathtaking precision. The whole scene back on the hill – the desolate garrison post, the eerily placid lake, the chain gang clanking nightmarishly from the fog – began to seem like a dream.

So I sat there until I had convinced myself that the dream was real; that the mythical Wa lake of Nawng Hkeo really did exist; and that I had been there. And then we began to walk to China.

Epilogue

George Scott was among the last of the guilt-free imperialists. He was a devout believer in the civilising power of colonial rule, and was convinced that the slow march of British values across the globe was both inevitable and righteous. But the age of imperial overreach was dawning, and Britain's zest for conquest was diminishing. Partly as a result, Scott's career climaxed in a series of professional and personal disasters from which he would never really recover.

First came his posting in 1893 to Bangkok as chargé d'affaires, potentially the springboard to a distinguished diplomatic career. Scott threw himself into the work, quickly gaining notoriety in London for ordering, at some expense, a grand new flagstaff for the British legation. The flagstaff (which stood for decades outside the British Embassy in Bangkok) collapsed during the raising ceremony. 'Very bad luck,' observed Scott privately, and he was right. He was underfunded, poorly briefed and buffeted by political changes at home – not least the election as prime minister of Lord Salisbury, whose famous maxim on foreign affairs ('Whatever happens will be for the worse, and therefore it is in our interest that as little should happen as possible') hardly fitted with Scott's muscular brand of empire-building.

Dora Scott was his greatest asset in Bangkok. She was a favourite at the court of King Chulalongkorn, who is still revered today as the father of modern Thailand. But the city's unforgiving climate quickly told on her health, and she was frequently unwell there. Even so, when Scott was instructed to travel to a wild region of the Upper Mekhong, and there negotiate the border between British Burma and French Laos, the fragile Dora opted to join him. Scott almost certainly tried to persuade her to sail to Rangoon instead and wait for him there, but Dora would have none of it. It was a fateful decision.

In October 1894 the Scotts left Bangkok amid great pomp on a steam launch provided by a Thai prince, and continued overland on a battalion of elephants. Scott met his French counterparts at the remote town of Monghsing in modern-day Laos, and soon found himself entangled in lengthy and fruitless negotiations. 'For four or five months,' reported the *Pall Mall Gazette*, 'the parties wandered around in a purposeless way, arguing and taking stock of the land – and each other; half the time they were in the swamps, whose exhalations resembled nothing but a "London particular", with the smoke of great jungle fires superadded, making surveying impossible.' Despite Scott's best efforts, the mission was a spectacular failure, and he and Dora journeyed onward to Mandalay. At one point a mysterious disease killed all their ponies, forcing the Scotts to walk over fifty miles through thick jungle before they could buy new animals. They finally arrived in Mandalay in June 1895, after an epic and gruelling journey of nearly 2,000 miles.

By now Dora was suffering from malaria; Scott possibly was too. After a short home leave in Britain, and with his diplomatic ambitions effectively dashed, in August 1896 he returned to Burma to be met by the news that his mother was dead. He was apparently too distracted by grief to recognise that Dora, who had returned to Burma with him, was dying too. They moved into a new home, which leaked badly (as all but the best-built houses still do) during Rangoon's relentless monsoon season and was 'extraordinarily stifling' in the rare moments when the rain abated. For a month Scott laboured on the *Gazetteer* until the colonial authorities confirmed his next posting in Burma. Then, with Dora's health in rapid decline, the Scotts boarded a steamer for Mandalay in the desperate hope that the dry climate of Upper Burma would help. It did, but only briefly. 'Dora horribly weak,' wrote Scott on 7 October 1896. 'Cannot do much better than stand' Then, a week later:

> Dora has to be carried now. Can't stand even [with] assistance. Thought it was simple weakness and was glad because she took a good deal of fruit & milk. A little after one however she began to breathe heavily. Her head burning hot and extremities cold. Tried chafing & rubbing her feet & hands with camphor & whisky, but in vain. She had great difficulty in hearing & understanding & gradually lost all consciousness. Sent all over the town for the doctor. He came just in time to see her die.

Scott was devastated. His wife of only six years was dead, and he knew there was only one person to blame: himself. 'My poor Dora,' he wrote, 'if had only had courage enough to refuse to bring you out this last time . . . Oh it is cruel.'

Dora was buried beneath a simple plaster cross in a Mandalay graveyard. An entire week passed before Scott found the strength to put pen to paper again. 'Dora looked peacefully asleep to the end,' he began.

Seemed hard to believe that I had lost her for ever and I went back time and time again with the desperate hope that she might wake up again. I think & hope she died without pain, but she, as well as I, had no idea death was so near and we did not say goodbye to one another. It was the first time she ever left me no matter for how short a time without doing so.

Back in Rangoon, in the house they had so recently moved into together, Scott set about the heartbreaking task of sorting through Dora's unemptied boxes. 'But in the very first I came upon a present brought from home, which she evidently intended to give me at Christmas. My poor lost darling.'

A vital part of Scott died with Dora. Afterwards he seemed to abandon any hope of promotion in the colonial service. Instead, he set off once more for the rugged Shan hills, the scene of his earliest adventures, and would not emerge again until his retirement in 1910. 'Of course, if you order me to come down I shall have to come,' he once told his superiors. 'But I warn you I shall be as incompetent and insubordinate in the plains as I have been in the hills.'

And so, less than three months after Dora's death, Scott was back in the wilderness on another doomed mission – this time to 'pacify' the Wa. In a letter to rebellious Wa chiefs, Scott warned, 'The whole of the Wa States cannot resist British troops for even one week' – a highly dubious assertion, as it turned out. Scott's column was met by furious resistance from the Wa, and his mission soon took on a punitive character resembling the 'butcher and bolt' campaign he had witnessed in Perak as a young war correspondent. This time, however, it was Scott who ordered troops to plunder and burn the villages.

It is hard to recognise him in this campaign; harder still to like him. He certainly seemed to have lost that 'gift for winning over untutored peoples' for which so many of his charmed contemporaries would praise him – those skills as a jungle diplomat that had once had the Wild Wa laughing at his jokes. His appointment five years later as superintendent of the Shan states further removed him from the tribespeople among whom he had spent the most eventful years of his life. Installed at the residency in Taunggyi, and flush with the award of a long-awaited knighthood, Scott was no longer a man of action but an aloof figure of colonial power – a status only reinforced by the publication in 1900 of the first volume of his sweeping and authoritative *Gazetteer*.

Five years later he married again, to Eleanor McCarthy, the

An adventure yarn co-authored by Scott and his third wife Geraldine Mitton; a cartoon of Scott drawn by a Savage Club colleague, 11 May 1918. (British Library)

only daughter of a county-court judge, and together they had a daughter, Padmina. (She died in her eighties, just months before I tracked her down.) It was an unhappy marriage: Eleanor had no taste for frontier life. Scott later wrote a novel in which, rather cruelly, Eleanor appeared in thinly fictionalised form as a placid, dumpy, unliterary woman called Barbara – 'one of those matches that cut a man off from his friends'. The marriage was dissolved in 1918.

By this time Scott had already met the remarkable woman who would be his third wife and the last Lady Scott. And, oddly, it was the Wa who brought them together. Scott had already retired to London when in 1912 he was visited by a flamboyant author called Geraldine Mitton. The daughter of a Durham vicar, Mitton had written a book called *A Bachelor Girl in Burma*, and was deeply influenced by her time in Rangoon. Scott already knew her by reputation, noting in his diary that she 'wore Burmese dress and smoked Burmese cheroots all the way. She is about six foot and must have looked somewhat singular.' He was clearly intrigued.

Mitton wanted to pick Scott's brains for a children's story about the Wa. They ended up writing it together: *In the Grip of the Wild Wa* was published a year later. (A typical line: 'There was a close, musty smell, indescribably revolting. "My hat!" said Luiz. "This is one of their famous skull avenues." ') But it is hard to like Mitton too. After Scott's death, she transcribed many of his diaries, ruthlessly excising all mention of his previous wives – a rehashing of history worthy of Burma's propagandists today. Neither wife was mentioned in Mitton's 1936 hagiography, *Scott of the Shan Hills*, an unforgivable omission in Dora's case. Later I looked through Scott's entire photo collection and couldn't find a single image of Dora. Mitton must have excised those as well.

But Scott had found happiness again. He married Mitton in 1920, and they moved to the tiny village of Graffham in Sussex. Scott wrote prolifically, churning out more books on Burma and essays for various academic journals. He also began to write fiction, apparently in an attempt to supplement his meagre government pension. But he was a desperately unsuccessful novelist. Much of his fiction – *Under an Eastern Sky*, *A Frontier Man*, *The Green Moth* – was set in Burma and co-written by Mitton. A solo effort about a Burmese jewel heist entitled *Why Not?* was particularly dull, although Mitton loyally noted that 'the club scenes are life-like'.

And then Scott's life dissolves into fragments. He was a diehard fan of Graffham FC. He talked to his dog. He hated strawberries. In the morning he wrote in his upstairs study; in the afternoon he put on a floppy hat his wife hated, and gardened. On Sundays he read the lessons in Graffham's church, and would be remembered as a tiny man with a booming voice. And in the evenings he read aloud to Mitton. 'He had all a Scot's horror of demonstration,' she would recollect, 'but with it a curious sensibility. It was a trouble to him to the day of his death that if he came across any sentiment he could not control his voice . . . If he ran across any pathos, there was a sudden break in the deep voice, throat-clearing, an elaborate pretence of cleaning his glasses, and sometimes: "What a fool I am!"'

George Scott, the explorer, sportsman, photographer, linguist, journalist and scholar – one man born with the energy of ten – died on 4 April 1935 at the age of eighty-four. He was buried beneath a granite sarcophagus in Graffham graveyard. 'MORS JANUA VITAE,' read the inscription: 'Death is the gateway to life.'

And what an extraordinarily long and eventful life it had been. 'Once,' recalled Mitton, 'when he had lain silent but not asleep for a long time, I asked him of what he was thinking, and he answered with quiet emphasis: "Of many, many things."'

Scott once called Burma 'a sort of recess, a blind alley, a back reach'. It is a description that still rings true a century later. The same country which, in the heady years after independence, was tipped to become one of South-East Asia's success stories is today a recluse in a region of breakneck change. The 1962 military coup plunged Burma into an isolation not known since King Thibaw's time, and transformed a fledgling democracy rich in natural resources into a land of poverty and fear. The generals who run the country still rage against the evils of colonialism, yet they share at least one thing with the imperialists of old: a blind conviction that they alone know what is best for the country. Most people living in Burma today have never known true peace or true freedom.

It is tempting to speculate how Scott might have viewed modern Burma. How would he react to a report which describes how Burmese soldiers in Chin State tortured a group of church leaders by ordering them to lie on their backs and stare at the sun? Or to the ongoing relocations in Shan State, where the regime is now depopulating an area to build an environmentally disastrous dam on the Salween River? Or to a government that spends over half its budget on defence while malnutrition rates among the under-threes compare in severity with those of Burundi and Sudan? Or to the generals themselves, who pose self-righteously as sworn enemies of the narcotics trade while selling their country to ethnic-Chinese drug lords?

He would react as the rest of the world does (when it's listening): with anger and with horror.

As I write this, a much-thumbed volume of the *Gazetteer* sits on the bookshelf before me. I have only one other book that is bulkier, and it is the *Burma Human Rights Yearbook*. This is the modern equivalent of Scott's magnum opus, a gazetteer of the misery perpetrated by a corrupt and power-crazed regime bent on denying its people the right to forge their own destinies. After nearly four decades of military rule, it is hard to imagine the frustrations of Burma's embattled populace. Aung San Suu Kyi, the torch-bearer for the second struggle for independence, is still proving, in her courageous stand against the generals, Scott's observation that 'a Burmese woman really in earnest about her business is more than a match for any man'. Over 1,800 political prisoners languish in jail, among them students, doctors, teachers, lawyers, writers, farmers and housewives. Meanwhile, bloated by drug money and propped up by other despotic Asian regimes, the Burmese military seems more powerful than ever.

But miracles happen – just ask Philip the Miracle Monk. I got to know Philip better as the months passed. I would wait for him, aptly enough, at the Democracy Monument in Bangkok, getting high on the city's rush-hour head-rush of roasting wok oil, strangled jasmine and carbon monoxide. He would appear from nowhere, robes billowing, hopelessly late, and lead me through Bangkok back alleys clogged with sleeping dogs to his monastery. It was beautiful, and startlingly quiet, a pond of tranquillity in the city's ocean of chaos, with low whitewashed bungalows framed by bougainvillea. Inside one bungalow two novices were watching a noisy Jackie Chan movie on HBO. Here Philip felt he could speak freely.

'What is democracy?' he once asked me. 'We didn't know. We were just children . . .' He was talking about Mandalay, 1990, when he had marched through the baking streets with thousands of other monks. He recalled his shock when the soldiers opened fire. 'You see, the soldiers knew it was wrong to shoot monks,' he said quietly. 'So instead they aimed at the monks' legs.' Thus immobilised, the monks were thrown into army trucks, a writhing mass of darkening robes, and left to die. Later, when the secret police began raiding the monasteries, Philip fled into the Shan hills to join the Shan resistance. He was nineteen.

A decade later, he was still fighting for the cause: briefing journalists, distributing pamphlets, talking politics – doing anything and everything to grab the attention of a perpetually distracted world. Philip was a highly unusual monk, no doubt about it, but I had come to realise that thousands of people in Burma had similar life stories to tell. I asked him if he felt hopeful about the future.

'Hopeful?' he grinned. 'Always.'

Then he launched into another detailed analysis of Shan military strategy. It was with some effort that I dragged him back to the eternal. I asked him about the Buddhist concept of *anicca*.

'*Anicca*,' he said. 'Nothing lasts. Everything is – what is the English word? – impermanent. We are born, we suffer, we grow old, we die. This is our destiny. Nobody can escape it.'

'Not even Burmese generals?' I asked.

'Of course. Not even them.'

'And do they know this?'

Philip smiled. 'They know,' he said. 'They know.'

AFTERWORD

THE SAFFRON REVOLUTION

The Saffron Revolution

The first and last time I met Jimmy was in a gloomy bar near the National League for Democracy heaquarters in Rangoon. The NLD had arranged the meeting, and Jimmy and I sat together in a booth hemmed in by party elders. Jimmy, whose real name was Kyaw Min Yu, was a softly-spoken Shan with a mop of dark hair and a slow-fading smile. As a physics student at Rangoon University, he had played a leading role in the 1988 democracy uprising. He was arrested in 1989 on charges of 'inciting unrest' and convicted a few months later. He spent the next 15 years in jail.

It was now 2005. Jimmy had been released from Insein Prison only a few days before we met. He was charming but fragile, as if that charm drained the last reserves of his energy. Jimmy had been tortured in Insein and robbed of his youth. He had been badly beaten for taking part in a hunger strike over inmates' rights. Once, he had written a denunciation of prison conditions on his clothes, which were smuggled out and read aloud at a human rights conference in Europe. Afterwards, his sentence had been lengthened.

Jimmy forgave his captors. 'I am not angry,' he told me. 'I have no hatred for anyone. I am . . .' His English was rusty and he sometimes struggled to find the words. He smiled. 'I am a democrat with loving kindness.'

He had been released into a city that was much changed since 1988. Rangoon's population had swollen, as more people fled rural poverty to seek better lives in the city. It had traffic jams, apartment blocks, big hotels. Jimmy was unimpressed. 'Any government can put up tall buildings,' he said. 'Building a democracy is much harder.'

Jimmy was right. Burma's changes were mostly for the worse. In the countryside particularly, people grew poorer, and were stalked by disease and malnutrition. Inflation lurched ever upwards. Schools and hospitals crumbled with neglect. Insurgencies rumbled on along the borders. The brightest Burmese made lives abroad.

The junta remained unchallenged. Over the years, generals had died or been purged, but each time the military closed ranks and stayed intact. Than Shwe had been Burma's absolute ruler since 1992. He was a stout, bespectacled septuagenarian with a fondness for chewing betel nut. He ruled by fear and favour, purging any potential rivals while rewarding his loyalists with military promotions and sweetheart business deals. He despised

Aung San Suu Kyi. In 2003, near Depayin, a town northwest of Mandalay, Than Shwe's thugs attacked a convoy of cars carrying her and her supporters, killing dozens of people. Suu Kyi narrowly escaped with her life.

Than Shwe purged his military intelligence chief Khin Nyunt the following year. Also, like the old Burmese kings, he ordered the construction of a new capital. Naypyitaw ('Abode of Kings') was hacked from parched hills 200 miles north of Rangoon and included a parliament, a zoo, a near-replica of the Shwedagon and – to soothe Than Shwe's apparent paranoia about an Iraq-style U.S. invasion – a secret network of tunnels and bunkers. A few months after I met Jimmy, Naypyitaw officially replaced Rangoon as Burma's capital.

The removal of Khin Nyunt dealt a temporary blow to a once fearsome spy network. With this, and the government's evacuation to Naypyitaw, people in Rangoon seemed to talk a little more freely. Mobile phones and the Internet became increasingly available and, despite being costly and state-controlled, were soon being used by thousands. Student activists jailed after the 1988 protests had been released and were quietly regrouping.

All of this helps to explain what Jimmy did next, and makes me wish that I could recall our meeting in that gloomy bar in more detail. I remember asking him the obvious question: What will you do now? I remember being surprised by his answer – he seemed too frail to risk another spell in jail.

'I will take a rest,' said Jimmy. 'Then I will continue to do my activity for democracy.'

And he did. Two years later, on 15 August 2007, the junta suddenly lifted government subsidies on fuel and natural gas. This caused their prices to soar, which in turn drove up the cost of basic commodities delivered by road, such as rice, eggs and cooking oil. The impact on ordinary Burmese was sudden and catastrophic. Many now struggled to feed their families. Bus fares rose so dramatically that some people couldn't afford to travel to work.

On 19 August, a group calling itself the 88 Generation Students led the first protest against the price hikes. Jimmy was one of them. They had just attended a memorial service for an NLD leader and, rather than pay the inflated bus fares, decided to walk from Kokkine Junction to Tamwe Market. Hundreds of people joined them. It was the biggest demonstration in Rangoon for more than a decade.

The junta responded quickly. Within days, Jimmy was arrested again, along with dozens of other 88 Generation Students. Two

Aung San Suu Kyi, leader of Burma's democracy movement. (Nic Dunlop)

A cartoon in the *New Light of Myanmar* shows Aung San Suu Kyi as a toothless crone backed by scheming foreigners.

weeks later, I read with horror that he had been tortured to death in Insein prison. The report turned out to be untrue, but Jimmy was later sentenced to 65 years in jail. So was his wife, Nilar Thein, another former political prisoner who had joined the protests. Their infant daughter was effectively orphaned by the regime.

Other demonstrations followed, although on a smaller scale. At these, the participants were harassed and beaten by plainclothes thugs from either the USDA – the regime's Rottweilers – or a sinister new paramilitary group called *Swan Arr Shin* ('Masters of Force'). For a while, it seemed as if the protests had been snuffed out. But what Jimmy and his brave friends had done was light the fuse for an even bigger protest. A whole new generation of Burmese was about to get a glimpse of what life might be like without their hated rulers.

A month after Jimmy's arrest, I arrived in Rangoon to witness what still seems like a dream: my first vision of the marching monks.

They poured south from the Shwedagon Pagoda in an unbroken, mile-long column: barefoot, chanting, clutching pictures of Buddha, their robes drenched with the late monsoon rains. They walked briskly – if you stuck to the city's crowded pavements it was almost impossible to keep pace with them – but when they reached Sule Pagoda in central Rangoon they paused to pray. Then they were off again, coursing through the city streets in a stream of red and orange, like blood vessels giving life to an oxygen-starved body.

They chanted a Buddhist mantra whose melody would haunt me for months:

> *Let everyone be free from harm.*
> *Let everyone be free from anger.*
> *Let everyone be free from hardship.*

The effect on Rangoon's residents was electrifying. At first, only a few people applauded. Others clasped their hands together in respectful prayer, or quietly wept. One man, watching the procession without apparent emotion, abruptly folded away his umbrella so that his hands were free to clap, and the falling rain obscured his tears. I asked another onlooker, an elderly teacher, how he felt. Overcome, he pressed a clenched fist to his heart and croaked, 'Happy.'

The monks had been marching for almost a week now. It had begun in Pakkoku, a town on the Irrawaddy River, where on 5

September the monks took up where the 88 Generation Students had left off, and protested against rising prices. They were savagely beaten by soldiers. The violence escalated, and so did the demands of a new group called the All Burma Monks' Alliance. It now wanted not just a government apology and a reduction in prices, but political changes too: the release of Suu Kyi and other jailed dissidents, and a dialogue between the regime and the opposition. When these demands were ignored, monks started marching through cities and towns across the country.

Burma's monkhood and military are roughly the same size – both have between 300,000 and 400,000 men – but the similarities end there. With the monks preaching tolerance and peace, and the military demanding obedience at gunpoint, the protests pitted Burma's most revered institution against its most reviled.

In Rangoon, the protests grew larger with each passing day. By late afternoon, however, the monks vanished and life in the city returned to normal. The tea shops were crowded. Cheroot smoke uncoiled in the humid air. I picked my way along flooded pavements to see Than Sein, a former political prisoner who edited a well-known Burmese-language magazine.

Than Sein was excitedly pacing his cramped office, cigarette in hand. He wore a dark longyi, a crisp white shirt, and a permanent lopsided smile. Most democrats I had met in Burma were gloomy and cautious. Than Sein was the opposite. He was almost nostalgic about his time in the junta's gulag, where he had met activists from across the country. As an editor, his regular battles with the censorship board seemed to invigorate him. He cheerfully – and publicly – referred to Burma's rulers as 'the Thugs'.

Than Sein's office had only one computer, an aging desktop with a slow but reliable internet connection. When he didn't have guests, Than Sein was glued to it. Online news agencies run by Burmese exiles were reporting more protests in Mandalay, Monywa and Bhamo. 'There are 25 reporters following every protest and every one of them has a mobile phone,' he marveled. 'With the internet, nothing can stop the news from spreading.'

Than Sein was already well-informed. He had his own network of reporters across the country, and his tiny office was a magnet for writers, artists, doctors, charity workers and other Burmese determined to challenge the junta's stranglehold on civic life. Than Sein introduced me to young computer scientist called Mimi. The previous day, she had joined several hundred monks who had entered University Avenue and approached the gate to Suu Kyi's lakeside home. To their surprise and joy, Suu Kyi emerged. It was her first public appearance since Than Shwe had put her under house arrest in 2003.

Suu Kyi briefly prayed with the protesters, before tearfully urging them to march on. 'I was crying too,' Mimi told me. 'I just couldn't believe how this cruel government could lock her up for all these years.' She tried to show me a photo she had taken of Suu Kyi, but after marching for hours in the rain her digital camera was so waterlogged that its screen was streaky and malfunctioning. A grainy photograph soon circulated on the internet showing the blurred figure of Suu Kyi behind a phalanx of riot police. The police have their shields raised, as if fearing the monks and their followers will rush the gate.

Mimi couldn't explain why the protesters had been allowed to walk down University Avenue. She couldn't understand why the junta had made no move to stop the protests. And until it did? 'We keep walking,' she said.

The next morning, one of Than Sein's reporters took me to meet some monks at a pagoda in the Shwedagon's shadow, a rallying point for the daily marches. It must have been under government surveillance. So, surely, was the tall figure in a white shirt and dark sarong who greeted me. It was the poet Aung Way, another '88 stalwart, jailed three times for his political views. He pressed a poem into my hand, which I nervously shoved into my pocket and forgot about.

Aung Way introduced me to seven or eight monks of various ages. Some chewed betel-nut, which made their mouths froth alarmingly with blood-red saliva. The oldest monk, who was 49 and from near Mandalay, was holding a Burmese translation of Francis Fukuyama's *The Great Disruption*. He was articulate and resolute.

'We have three demands,' he said. 'Release Aung San Suu Kyi and all other political prisoners. Begin a process of national reconciliation. Lower the prices of daily commodities.' China and Russia must withdraw their support for the junta, he went on, while the United Nations Security Council must discourage it from using violence.

Yet violence was what they expected. 'Next they will use tear-gas and water cannon,' predicted another middle-aged monk. 'Then they will beat and arrest people. We are not afraid.' A third monk, in his early twenties, came from Natmauk, the birthplace of Aung San. 'We mustn't retreat,' he said. 'If we retreat now, we fail.' He continued: 'If the government uses violence, the people and monks will sit down and not react. The most important thing is *metta'* – the Sanskrit word for the Buddhist notion of loving kindness.

The protest was now taking on its own rhythm. The mornings were bright, cool and clear. But by the afternoon the storm-clouds gathered, and so did the monks. They had called for public support of their movement, and among the artists, poets and entertainers who had responded was Zarganar, the comedian who once spent five years in Insein for joking about the junta. He and other 88 Generation activists came to donate food and water to the monks, then returned to homes and hiding places unmolested. It was amazing that democrats such as Zarganar – who was instantly recognizable by his shaven head – were still at large. 'And not just at large,' noted Than Sein, 'but giving telephone interviews to the BBC. This would never have happened under Khin Nyunt.'

Khin Nyunt, the purged spy chief, was the subject of one of many rumours now circulating Rangoon. These rumours, which were impossible to confirm or refute, reflected the rising popular anxiety over how the junta might react to the protests. I had heard that Khin Nyunt had been released from house arrest to orchestrate a crackdown; that hospitals were clearing their wards of non-essential cases to prepare for wounded protesters; that the military, fearing heavy rain would render tear-gas ineffectual, were stockpiling hundreds of canisters of mosquito fumigant to use instead; and that the 77th Light Infantry Division had arrived in town with shoot-to-kill orders. Such rumours seemed incredible one minute, and plausible the next.

The official media provided few clues about what the junta might do next. *The New Light of Myanmar* had published a brief diatribe about 'destructive elements inciting instigation to grab power through short cut', then nothing more. State-run television was no help either. One channel had dedicated five hours to Burma's female football team, which had just beaten Thailand 4-1 on penalties in a Southeast Asian tournament. A senior general was shown presenting tributes to the team in Naypyitaw.

At Than Sein's office, everyone was asking the same question: What were the generals planning? 'I don't think they have a plan,' grinned Khin Maung, one of Than Sein's bravest reporters, who was often joined on the marches by his teenage children. 'They don't know what to do next.'

Than Sein seemed puzzled. 'The Thugs won't give up that easily,' he said quietly.

That evening, Brigadier General Thura Myint Maung, Minister of Religious Affairs, appeared on state television to threaten unspecified 'action' against the monks. Within hours, trucks with loudspeakers were cruising Rangoon's dimly lit streets, announcing a curfew from 9 p.m. to 5 a.m. and threatening to arrest anyone who marched with the monks tomorrow.

The junta was making its first move.

Tuesday. Zarganar and other democracy figures were arrested overnight. The poet Aung Way was now in hiding. Guiltily, I pulled his poem from my pocket and read it for the first time. 'We want freedom,' ran one line. 'We want friendship between our army and our people.' The army wasn't interested. *The New Light of Myanmar* blamed the unrest on 'hot-blooded monks' stirred up by 'internal and external destructionists who are jealous of national development and stability.'

Still they marched. The monks had now been joined by thousands of Burmese, some chanting their own English mantra: 'Democracy! Democracy!' The protest was so large that central Rangoon had a carnival atmosphere. Traffic stopped, shops closed, entire families spilled onto the street. Applause rained down from crowded balconies overlooking the route. NLD members had also joined the march. So had the students, waving red flags bearing their emblem, the fighting peacock – once an anti-colonial emblem, but since 1962 an anti-junta one. At the rear of the column, the chants shifted up a few octaves, and into view came a group of Buddhist nuns in powder-pink robes.

Near Sule Pagoda, where in 1988 soldiers with Bren guns had mown down the crowds, I saw one monk hold an upturned alms bowl over his head. This symbolized his refusal to accept offerings from military families, a potent gesture in a devoutly Buddhist country. Equally striking was the number of people holding up cellphones and cameras to record the monks' protest. Amateur images and footage were now pouring out of Burma via the internet, where they were picked up by major broadcasters and shown to the world. The Saffron Revolution, as many were calling it, was an unprecedented alliance of modern communications and an ancient monkhood.

After years of sneaking around Burma, talking in whispers, always aware of the trouble I might cause the people who dared speak to me, it was liberating to stand amid these euphoric crowds, pen and notebook in hand, openly conducting interviews. The protest was now a major global story. Every day I got emails from colleagues who were desperately trying to get tourist visas to enter Rangoon. They were all at the mercy of whichever Burmese

Embassy was processing their applications. Embassies were still issuing them, possibly because the regime was eager to downplay the unrest and felt that granting tourist visas sent the right business-as-usual message. But it took time.

Journalists covering big foreign events often gravitate to a single hotel. During the Saffron Revolution it was Traders Hotel, an ugly high-rise squatting on the corner of Sule Pagoda and General Aung San roads. The main appeal of Traders was its location: some rooms offered panoramic views of the daily marches. Several UN agencies had offices on the hotel's lower floors, which made us – the journalists posing as tourists – feel more secure. Also, it had a bar. Traders was run by a respected international company, but had been built by a former opium druglord called Lo Hsing Han and his son Steven Law, who were both blacklisted by the U.S. and European governments. Pro-democracy activists still sometimes called it the 'Heroin Hotel.'

The locals seemed to have another name for it. 'Have you noticed,' said Richard, a British friend and colleague who had just flown in, 'that when Burmese people say "Traders" it always sounds like "traitors"?' He was right. Later, when we told a taxi-driver our destination, he looked at Richard and me carefully and replied, 'Ah, traitors!' It was disconcerting, as if he'd fingered us for the 'external destructionists' that *The New Light of Myanmar* routinely excoriated.

Wednesday. The curfew, a ban on public gatherings, threats of unspecified 'action' by the state: the protesters ignored it all and hit the streets again. Many monasteries – especially those famed for their role in the 1988 uprising, such as Ngwe Kyar Yan and Thayet Taw – were now guarded by riot police.

The eastern gate of the Shwedagon was where thousands of monks poured out to begin their march into the city centre. Today, the gate was locked and guarded by soldiers and police. Confronting them were hundreds of monks and students, who sat on the road outside and prayed. As I approached the eastern gate along a backstreet lined with old wooden monasteries, the battle for the Shwedagon erupted.

There were explosions – smoke bombs, meant to shock and disorientate – and the riot police charged, striking the protesters with canes. The monks and students fought back with sticks and rocks, and soon I could hear the unmistakable crackle of live ammunition – the soldiers were shooting above our heads. 'They are not Buddhists,' raged a young man, clutching half a brick, running from the smoke. 'They are not humans. Tell the world. We were praying peacefully and they beat us. They beat the monks, even the old ones.' A geriatric monk stood with him, bleeding from a baton gash on his bald head.

The monks regrouped and surged forward again. Shops along the road were shuttered but people emerged on the balconies to throw bottles of water to the monks and other protesters. Minutes later, a tear-gas canister arced through the air towards the Shwedagon's east gate. The air was full of dense black clouds from a burning car and motorbike.

Running monks retreated through the smoke, many armed with clubs of scavenged wood, one carrying a riot shield he had snatched from the police. They were shaking with rage. 'The United Nations must know about this!' cried one. 'They beat the nuns too,' cried another.

There was another detonation – not a smoke bomb this time, but a great clap of thunder, a sign of cosmic solidarity which the protesters cheered. A monk raised his hands to the heavens and cried, 'The rain is coming! The soldiers will be struck by lightning!' Nearby, a woman retorted, 'Lightning is not enough. They deserve more.' A cheer went up with each subsequent clap of thunder.

The battle stopped. The monks regrouped at a nearby monastery to dress their wounds and prepare for the march downtown. But first came a sobering display of the people's anger, and of the monks' moral authority. A man on a motorcycle rode up. Motorcycles have been banned in Rangoon for years, since – the story goes – a paranoid general feared being shot by assassins riding one of them. Anyone on a motorcycle was therefore assumed to be a spy. The mob pounced. He was pulled off his bike and set upon by students and people armed with wooden sticks. 'Beat him!' they shouted. 'Kill him!'

In 1988, dozens of suspected spies were hanged, decapitated or beaten to death by protesters. Many lynchings were stopped by monks or students; many more were not. Today, this man was lucky. Three monks wrestled him from the crowd and through the gates of a monastery. The mob set upon the man's motorbike with clubs and rocks and smashed it to bits.

Soon, the monks began to march. 'They attacked the monks at the Shwedagon!' shouted protesters through loudspeakers. 'Join us! Let us overthrow the government!' I walked with them. Trucks full of soldiers pursued us, watched from the pavement by now eerily silent crowds. Near Sule Pagoda, trucks were jeered and pelted with rocks, and the soldiers again opened fire over the protesters' heads.

But as dusk approached, the crowds dispersed again. The shops had been shuttered all afternoon, and the pavement tea shops for which Rangoon is famous vanished. Nobody wanted to be out after dark. The curfew would be obeyed. Only dogs and soldiers roamed the streets.

Thursday. *The New Light of Myanmar* described yesterday's events like this: 'On account of unavoidable circumstances, members of the security forces fired some shots, employing the least force to disperse the mob.'

When I read this aloud to Than Sein, he emitted a humourless chuckle. 'Shooting at people is the least force?'

During last night's curfew, troops had surged into monasteries across the city, beating and arresting monks. Richard visited Ngwe Kyar Yan monastery. He found the floors puddled with blood and the thin dormitory walls perforated with what Burmese call 'rubber bullets.' They were actually ball-bearings with a thin rubber coating, shot from a 40mm cartridge. A direct hit at close range can take out eyes, crack skulls, stop hearts.

The raids enraged the people. The lives of Burmese Buddhists are intertwined with the lives of the monks. Monks preside over marriages, chant over the dead; they shelter orphans and care for HIV patients; and they rely upon the people for food, medicine, clothes and shelter. The monks of Ngwe Kyar Yan had helped local high-school children study for their exams.

And so, with soldiers and police still inside Ngwe Kyar Yan, hundreds of local people surrounded it. 'We had no weapons and knew we couldn't compete with the military,' a retired engineer who lived in the area told me later. 'Everyone just wanted to protect the monks.' Eventually, with night approaching, the security forces fought their way out with live rounds, killing two people. Similar violence was reported elsewhere. At Kyaikkasan monastery, I heard, troops had shot dead two people and beat a third so savagely that he died of his injuries.

By 1 p.m., I was wedged among thousands of pro-democracy protesters near the Sule Pagoda. Facing us were hundreds of soldiers and riot police, who looked on edge as they fingered their assault rifles. 'You should get closer,' said a young medical student in the crowd behind me. 'If foreigners are there they won't shoot.' She was terribly wrong.

The protesters, mostly ordinary Burmese clad in sarongs and sandals, appeared undaunted, even jubilant. Defiantly, they chanted that haunting Buddhist mantra –

Let everyone be free from harm.
Let everyone be free from anger.
Let everyone be free from hardship.

– but only a handful of monks had escaped the junta's dragnet to chant it with them. Emotions pass through crowds this dense as if passing through a single body. When more trucks pulled up at the intersection, and the troops inside noisily cocked their rifles, the crowd tensed as one. Seconds later, there were explosions – more smoke bombs – and we were running for our lives.

We ran along the pavements, keeping low, desperately seeking shelter, chased by the sound of gunfire and more explosions. The nearest escape route was 33rd Street, narrow like so many in the downtown area, but it was a seething bottleneck of people. So I ran on and darted up 34th Street. Were they firing over our heads? Not all the time. Not far from where I had been standing lay the body of a Japanese photographer, Kenji Nagai, shot dead by a soldier at point-blank range.

Later, people said the troops used tear gas. They didn't, because I never felt its sting in my eyes. But there were tears nonetheless. I met an old man, a retired engineer, who was choked with emotion. I asked him if he had joined the protests. 'No,' he replied. 'I am too old now to run from bullets.' At that moment, more military trucks raced past; one soldier leant from the back, trained his rifle on the crowds, and scowled.

'Quick, we must go,' said the old man. 'They are going to start shooting us.'

Riot police were marching north up Sule Pagoda Road towards Traders, scores of them, banging their truncheons menacingly against their shields. Even more menacing was what stood behind: hundreds of troops, marching in formation, sealing off downtown Rangoon.

But the people didn't entirely disperse. Between the riot police and the troops were trucks with loudspeakers making announcements to clear the streets. For more than a week – for most of their lifetimes – Burmese had called peacefully for dialogue. This was the closest the junta got to it: screaming at its people through loudspeakers from a truck surrounded by men with guns.

Hundreds, possibly thousands of troops now ruled all the streets of Rangoon. Almost all the streets. All afternoon I heard gunfire, and each time it ended I heard a great cheer go up. Miraculously, despite the bloodshed, people were still protesting, still chanting: *Let everyone be free from danger . . .*

I could still hear gunfire at 5 p.m. – continuous, loud, high-calibre, some of it very close, most of it caroming through the streets from the east. I phoned Khin Maung, one of Than Sein's reporters, who lived in the area. He was holed up in his house with his wife and three children.

'What's happening?' I asked.

He replied, 'They are hunting us.'

The next day, *The New Light of Myanmar* gave its version of the crackdown:

> Groups of demonstrators in [Rangoon] mobbed the security forces, throwing stones and sticks at them, using catapults and swords, and they also tried to grab the arms of the security forces. The security forces had to fire warning shots, as the protesters turned a blind [eye] to their repeated requests. In the clashes 31 security forces were wounded [and] nine unidentified male protesters killed and 10 men and one woman wounded.

The official death toll was nine dead, but everyone believed it was much higher. A United Nations official told me that 40 people had been killed and 3,000 arrested, including 1,000 monks. Another diplomat hazarded 'hundreds' of deaths.

The crackdown had only just begun. The junta's thugs arrested monks, students and protesters, then worked their way through the rest, snatching away anyone who had sheltered the protesters, or taken photographs, or given vantage points to photographers, or witnessed reprisals by soldiers. The curfew had been designed to keep people off the streets, but now it gave the authorities a free hand to raid, abduct and terrorize.

Than Sein heard that Ye Way crematorium in northern Rangoon had been operating through the night, so that the military could destroy all evidence of a massacre. 'We heard the same thing in 1988,' he said. 'Maybe it's just a rumour. Maybe it's true. We just don't know.'

At a briefing for foreign diplomats in Naypyitaw, its distant capital, the junta blamed the violence on two institutions: the U.S. government and the NLD. It was rumoured that Suu Kyi, whose brief appearance had so energized the protests, had been carted off to Insein jail again, but this seemed unlikely. I took a taxi past the entrance to University Avenue. It was blocked by barbed-wire barricades, riot police, and – peeking over a wall of sandbags – a soldier with a heavy machine-gun.

There were no more marches. The protesters' sacred rallying points, the Shwedagon and Sule pagodas, were locked and guarded. Demonstrations still went on, but they were small and sporadic; I watched troops disperse one by firing ball bearings down Anawratha Street. On nearby Pansodan Street, a hundred or so protesters were jeering at soldiers and plainclothed Masters of Force, who were beating people they had arrested. A *thwack!* rang out as a young man, his hands clasped behind his neck, was struck over the head with a cane.

'A schoolboy,' remarked an onlooker angrily. The soldiers pushed the cringing youth into a truck.

The truck had a loudspeaker and a man was making announcements. 'He is saying that gatherings of more than five people are not allowed,' explained another onlooker, a young English student. She had traveled in from her home in the suburbs to see the soldiers for herself. They upset her. 'We can't know what they will do to the people next. The situation is changing from minute to minute.'

But something else upset the student more: me, and the Western nations my presence seemed to represent. When I told her of the world's enormous interest in Burma's plight, she snapped, 'Interest is not enough.' Without more help from the international community, she fumed, 'we can't win. Our hands are empty.'

She had no time to elaborate. There was a muzzle flash at the end of 35th Street – more ball bearings on their way – and everyone scattered. I never saw her again. I didn't ask her name. But I never forgot her sudden, seething anger. She felt betrayed – not by the soldiers, from whom brutality was expected, but from a West that had noisily allied itself with Burma's democrats, then watched helplessly as their efforts were annihilated.

This sense of betrayal deepened in the days that followed. At the Battle of the Shwedagon, I had heard one outraged protester cry, 'The United Nations must hear about this!' The UN did hear, and dispatched its special envoy to Burma, a Nigerian career diplomatic called Ibrahim Gambari.

Gambari's democratic credentials were dreadful. In 1995, as Nigeria's ambassador to the UN, he had defended his government's decision to execute Ogoni activist Ken Saro Wiwa, which had caused global outrage. As a UN envoy, he had visited Burma twice and achieved precisely nothing. His movements were restricted and heavily monitored; the state guesthouse, his gilded cage while in Rangoon, was said to be bugged.

'It is better to send UN troops than Gambari,' said the retired engineer I had interviewed about Ngwe Kyar Yan monastery. 'Better still, send American troops.' It was a measure of their rage and desperation that many Burmese believed that only force could dislodge the junta. During the 1988 uprising, the U.S. Embassy in Rangoon had received messages reading, 'Please invade us.'

On Saturday afternoon, with Gambari about to arrive, the biggest military convoy I had yet seen rolled slowly and menacingly through Rangoon. There were perhaps 25 trucks in all, stuffed with soldiers, riot police and Masters of Force. This was the junta's warning to the city.

The convoy passed Traitors Hotel twice and rattled some of the foreign journalists staying there. Many were already on edge. A few days before, a news agency run by Burmese exiles in Thailand had reported that soldiers had entered the hotel and were going from room to room, searching for journalists to arrest. The report, which was untrue, was repeated on CNN by an excitable representative of Reporters Sans Frontières.

Then the regime shut down Burma's internet. Like most journalists, I didn't have a satellite phone, which meant I now had to connect via a dial-up service in Thailand. This was slow and, for some freelance journalists, prohibitively expensive. (Overseas calls from Burma cost at least $5 a minute.) Adding further anxiety were the power cuts, which grew more frequent. Waiting in the darkness for the hotel's back-up generators to start, it was easy to imagine soldiers stampeding along the corridors and kicking down doors.

That evening, as I was entering the hotel, I bumped into an English colleague who was leaving for the airport and the last flight out to Bangkok.

'Why are you going?' I asked.

'Oh, you know,' he replied.

Moments later, he was joined by an Australian colleague, one of a group of freelance photographers staying at Traitors. They slept in each other's rooms and spent hours in front of their computers, transmitting images to agencies in London, Paris and New York. They were convinced that their rooms were bugged, because the phones sometimes stopped working and hotel staff had to come up to 'fix' them. They spread rumours among themselves until they hardened into facts. They loved scaring each other.

Such jitters seemed laughable in the relative safety of Traitors Hotel. In the past, foreign journalists suspected of secretly reporting in Burma had been detained and swiftly deported by the authorities; that is, they got a free airport transfer followed by a choice of chicken or beef at 33,000 feet. Burmese journalists caught doing the same risk torture and imprisonment, plus the threat of similar treatment for family and friends.

But the killing of Kenji Nagai had suddenly given us a sobering kinship with the Burmese colleagues we admired so much. We had reported the same turbulent protests. We had faced the same trigger-happy troops. For the first time, we understood how dangerous it was to be a reporter in Burma.

Gambari came and went. He met Suu Kyi, twice, and visited Naypyitaw to pose with Senior General Than Shwe for a photograph which later appeared in *The New Light of Myanmar*. The photo was grainy, but one bizarre detail stood out: Gambari and Than Shwe were holding hands.

Gambari's credibility among Burmese flatlined. A statement issued by 88 Generation Students and the All Burma Monks' Alliance, the two groups behind the uprising, accused the Nigerian academic of 'misleading the world with false hopes'.

Just hours after sending Gambari packing, Than Shwe would have settled down to watch Wayne Rooney score the only goal in Manchester United's UEFA Champions League match against AS Roma at Old Trafford. Than Shwe was an avid Man United fan. It was a passion he shared with his teenage grandson who, according to a U.S. diplomatic cable, later urged Than Shwe to buy the club for a billion dollars. That offer never materialized. Still, nobody dared disturb the General while Man United were playing.

'Next time the UN should send Rooney, not Gambari,' I was told by a chain-smoking Burmese scholar I spoke to the next day. When I laughed, the scholar frowned and said, 'I'm not joking.'

The Saffron Revolution was over. Even the monsoon rains – such a feature of these protests, in which the monks sometimes marched shin-deep through flooded streets – petered out. The sun returned and a cheerless rainbow arced across Rangoon's skyline.

Some of the bustle of the old capital returned, along with the old fear. Soldiers lurked at street corners, but shops and street stalls were reopening. This wasn't defiance, it was necessity: people were too poor to protest for long. Beggars reappeared to cruise the traffic-clogged intersections. 'Peace and stability restored, traveling and marketing back to normal,' crowed *The New Light of Myanmar*.

Before leaving Burma, I returned to the Shwedagon. The monasteries around it were either empty or occupied by soldiers; thousands of monks had been ordered back to their hometowns.

The Shwedagon itself was open again, but also heavily guarded. I spent an hour there and spotted only five men in saffron robes. The great pagoda, almost monkless: inconceivable a week before.

Back in Bangkok, I began writing an angry story for a magazine about how the junta's victory over the protesters would prove to be Pyrrhic. Here was the gist:

The assault on the monks had shattered the military's carefully cultivated image as Buddhism's protector and would cause divisions within the ranks. The Burma Army, already hobbled by low recruitment and high desertion rates, wasn't that formidable up close: many troops in Rangoon had carried rusting rifles (and the soldier who killed Kenji Nagai wore sandals). The generals now also faced unpredecented pressure from the international community.

There was one problem with this analysis: I didn't really believe it.

The military had shot monks before – for example, in Mandalay in 1990 – and remained undivided. There was some evidence that desertion rates worried the top brass, but there were still more than enough soldiers and rusting rifles to put down an uprising by unarmed civilians. The generals did seem to understand that they might not survive a bloodbath. During the Saffron Revolution, the troops were issued with live ammunition, but they also had rubber bullets, stun grenades and some rudimentary training in crowd control. Lost in the global outrage over the killings was the fact that, by the bloody standards of 1988, the Burmese military had shown restraint. Depressingly, it had evolved.

And the unprecedented international pressure? Suddenly, it seemed irrelevant. The Saffron Revolution had revealed to Burma's dictators and democrats the limits of what the world was willing or able to do. Ordinary Burmese had less faith than ever that international diplomacy or outrage could overcome the junta or improve their lives.

'There will be change,' Aung San Suu Kyi once said, 'because all the military have are guns.' Maybe that was true in 1988. Today – despite decades of Western censure and sanctions – the generals have much more than guns. They have huge revenues from oil and gas, trade relations with powerful neighbors India and China, and the support of fellow members of the Association of Southeast Asian Nations. They have struck ceasefires with most ethnic rebel armies and set about destroying the rest. Economically, militarily, politically and diplomatically, Burma's generals are much better off than they were 20 years ago.

But the spirit of '88 has not been extinguished. The Saffron Revolution had been efficiently crushed, but not before radicalizing a whole new generation of young Burmese. 'I'm still going strong because of my conscience,' Jimmy had told me, before they locked him up again and threw away the key. But if he was released from jail tomorrow, nobody need ask him what he will do next. We already know. He will take a rest. Then he will continue to do his activity for democracy.

Bibliography

Amnesty International, *Myanmar: Atrocities in the Shan State* (London, 1998 and 1999 update).

Brailey, N. J., 'Sir J. G. Scott and the Fate of Old Siam', published in 'Proceedings of the Fourth International Conference on Thai Studies (4th PICTS)', Kunming, China, 1990, vol. II, pp. 486-96; and related paper on Dora Scott.

Carey, Peter (ed.), *Burma: The Challenge of Change in a Divided Society* (New York, 1997).

Collis, Maurice, *Lords of the Sunset* (London, 1938).

Crosthwaite, Sir Charles, *The Pacification of Burma* (London, 1912).

Dalby, Andrew, 'J. G. Scott (1851-1935): Explorer of Burma's Eastern Borders', in Victor T. King (ed.), *Explorers of South-East Asia* (Kuala Lumpur, 1995).

Davis, Hassoldt, *The Land of the Eye* (New York, 1940).

Desai, W. S., *Deposed King Thibaw of Burma in India, 1885-1916* (Bombay, 1967).

Diran, Richard K., *The Vanishing Tribes of Burma* (London, 1997).

Eliot, Joshua, and Bickersteth, Jane, *Myanmar (Burma) Handbook* (Bath, 1997).

Elliott, Patricia, *The White Umbrella* (Bangkok, 1999).

Ellis, Beth, *An English Girl's First Impressions of Burma* (London, 1899).

Ferrier, A. J., *The Care and Management of Elephants in Burma* (London, 1947).

Government of the Union of Burma's Committee for Propaganda and Agitation to Intensify Patriotism, *Cruel and Vicious Repression of Myanmar Peoples by Imperialists and Fascists and the True Story about the Plunder of the Royal Jewels* (Rangoon, 1991).

Gravers, Mikael, *Nationalism as Political Paranoia in Burma* (Richmond, Surrey, 1999).

Harvey, G. E., *History of Burma* (London, 1967).

———, *1932 Wa Précis: A Précis Made in the Burma Secretariat of All Traceable Records Relating to the Wa States* (Rangoon, 1933).

Houtman, Gustaaf, *Mental Culture in Burmese Crisis Politics* (Tokyo, 1999).

Human Rights Watch, Crackdown: Repression of the 2007 Popular Protests in Burma (New York, 2007).

Jesse, F. Tennyson, *The Story of Burma* (London, 1946).

Lewis, Norman, *Golden Earth* (London, 1952).

Lintner, Bertil, *Burma in Revolt: Opium and Insurgency since 1948* (Chiang Mai, 1999).

———, *Outrage: Burma's Struggle for Democracy* (Hong Kong, 1989).

MacMunn, Sir George, *The Underworld of India* (London, 1933).

Maung Htin Aung, *Folk Elements in Burmese Buddhism* (London, 1962).

Mills, Cyril Bertram, *Bertram Mills Circus: Its Story* (London, 1967).

Milne, Leslie, *Home of an Eastern Clan* (Oxford, 1924).

———, *Shans at Home* (London, 1910).

Mitton, G. E., *A Bachelor Girl in Burma* (London, 1907).

———, *Scott of the Shan Hills* (London, 1936).

Morris, Jan, *Heaven's Command* (1973; reprinted London, 1998).

Pedersen, Morten B., Rudland, Emily, and May R. J. (eds.), *Burma-Myanmar: Strong Regime, Weak State?* (Adelaide, 2000).

Pitchford, V. C., 'The Wild Wa States and Lake Nawngkhio', *Geographical Journal*, no. 90 (1937).

Report of Frontier Areas Committee of Enquiry (Rangoon, 1947).

Rooney, Sarah, 'The Self-Conscious Censor: Censorship in Burma under the British 1900-1939, (dissertation for the School of Oriental and African Studies MA in Asian History, September 1999).

Saimong Mangrai, Sao, *The Shan States and the British Administration* (New York, 1965).

Sargent, Inge, *Twilight over Burma: My Life as a Shan Princess* (Chiang Mai, 1994).

Scott, Sir J. George, *Burma: From the Earliest Times to the Present Day* (London, 1924).

———, *Burma: A Handbook of Practical Information* (London, 1906).

———, *Burma and Beyond* (London, 1932).

———, *The Burman: His Life and Notions* (1882; reprinted New York, 1963).

———, *Gazetteer of Upper Burma and the Shan States* (Rangoon, 5 vols., 1900-1901).

———, *Why Not?* (London, 1929).

Scott, Sir George, and Mitton, G. E., *Under an Eastern Sky* (Allahabad, 1924).

———, *A Frontier Man* (London, 1923).

———, *The Green Moth* (London, 1922).

———, *In the Grip of the Wild Wa* (London, 1913).

Scott's journals, letters, photos and assorted memorabilia are kept at the Oriental and India Office Collections at the British Library, and at Cambridge University Library.

Shan Human Rights Foundation, *Dispossessed: A Report on Forced Relocation and Extrajudicial Killings in Shan State, Burma* (Chiang Mai, 1998).

Singer, Noel, *Old Rangoon* (Gartmore, 1995).

Smith, Martin, *Burma: Insurgency and the Politics of Ethnicity* (London, 1991).

Stewart, A. T. Q., *The Pagoda War* (London, 1972).

Wheeler, Stephen, *History of the Delhi Coronation Durhar* (Delhi, 1991).

White, Sir Herbert Thirkell, *A Civil Servant in Burma* (London, 1913).

Winnington, Alan, *The Slaves of the Cool Mountains* (Berlin, 1962).

Woodman, Dorothy, *The Making of Burma* (London, 1962).

Yawnghwe, Chao Tzang, *The Shan of Burma: Memoirs of a Shan Exile* (Singapore, 1987).

Acknowledgements

I was detained and deported from Burma in 2008 for secretly reporting on the aftermath of Cyclone Nargis, which killed at least 140,000 people. It was three years until I was able to return. In December 2011, with Aung San Suu Kyi now free and Burma embarking on historic reforms, the government invited me to openly report on the arrival of Hillary Clinton, the first U.S. Secretary of State to visit the country for half a century.

At the presidential palace in Naypyitaw, I saw Clinton shake hands with Thein Sein, the bookish-looking former general handpicked by former dictator Than Shwe as his new head of state. Back in Rangoon, flanked by Secret Service agents, I watched from the well-trimmed lawn of a famous house on University Avenue as Clinton and Aung San Suu Kyi embraced.

Jimmy, Nilar Thein and scores of other political prisoners were released the following month. In April 2012, after a campaign that brought ecstatic crowds onto streets across Burma, the NLD won 43 seats in a by-election landslide, and Aung San Suu Kyi became a member of parliament.

These events, which a year before would have been almost inconceivable, were thrilling to witness. But many people, most notably Aung San Suu Kyi, remained cautious. The reform process had barely begun; it could easily stall or even slip into reverse. The civil war continued, with Burmese troops still committing what human rights groups called war crimes.

Than Shwe retired into the shadows. The new political landscape had been carefully engineered to protect the military and ensure that it prospered. The regime's own Union Solidarity and Development Party had won the 2010 election by a landslide. A quarter of the seats in the new parliament were reserved for the military's appointees. The constitution gave it the right to run its own affairs with no civilian interference. The military was unreformed, unrepentant, untouchable.

The chances of Than Shwe or his fellow officers facing justice for their well-documented atrocities seemed remote. On a recent trip to Taunggyi, I drove past that billboard which read 'NEVER HESITATING ALWAYS READY TO SACRIFICE BLOOD AND SWEAT IS THE TATMADAW'. It had been repainted.

So, a decade after this book was first published, I still feel I cannot safely name the many people – Burman, Karen, Palaung,

Kayan, Pa-O, Shan, Wa – who helped me during my travels in Burma, often at some risk to themselves and their families. I owe them an enormous debt of gratitude.

I would also like to thank: Nel Adams a.k.a. Sao Nang Noan Oo ('Princess Soft Dignity'), Aung Zaw and the staff of *The Irrawaddy*, Philip Ba Than, Nigel Brailey, Andrew Campbell, Peter Carey, Pippa Curwen, Andrew Dalby, Tony Davis, Dennis a.k.a. Moon Aung, Richard Diran, Thierry Falise, Dominic Faulder, Magnus Fiskesjö, Cushla Geary, Gustaaf Houtman, John Jackson, Prue Jeffreys, Jeanne Hallacy, Gwen Hamilton, Jerry Harmer, Patricia Herbert, Tim Hulse, Hseng Noung Lintner, Kheun-sai Jaiyen, Khun Leng at TTO Travel, Inge Sargent, Pacharin Sinlawan, Paula Martin, Min Zin, Camilla Mitchell, John Okell, Dawn and James Rooney, Sarah Rooney, Gordon Samuels, Eric Sayettat, Siu-lan Law, Sudaduang Puengrung, Daphne Taylor, Thein Htike Oo, Justin Watkins, Greg Williams and Zhang Lijia.

Special thanks to Philip Blenkinsop, Nic Dunlop, Abigail Haworth, David Joannes, Bertil Lintner, Richard Lloyd Parry and Pascal Rüegg.

I am very grateful to past and present editors at TIME magazine and TIME.com (where some material in the afterword first appeared) who have supported my reporting in Burma and many other countries: Zoher Abdoolcarim, Howard Chua-Eoan, Michael Elliott, Liam Fitzpatrick and Karl Taro Greenfeld. Many thanks also to Narisa Chakrabongse, Paisarn Piemmattawat, Stephen Murphy and the staff of the charismatic Bangkok publishing house River Books for doing it once more with feeling.

As ever, I was sustained by the love, encouragement and occasional raised eyebrow of my own tribes: Marshall, Simpson, Taylor and Straessle.

"Sugar-cane is always sweet," runs a Burmese saying, "but men only sometimes." That goes double for newsmen, with their abrupt departures to faraway places, although my wife Natalie is far too sweet to admit it. Her love, support and understanding made it all possible and make it all worthwhile.

Index